PERSPECTIVES ON THE HISTORY
OF ECONOMIC THOUGHT,
VOLUME III

CLASSICALS, MARXIANS
AND NEO-CLASSICALS

# Perspectives on the History of Economic Thought Volume III

## Classicals, Marxians and Neo-Classicals

Selected Papers from the
History of Economics Society Conference,
1988

Edited by
D. E. Moggridge

Published for the
History of Economics Society
by Edward Elgar

Published by
Edward Elgar Publishing Limited
Gower House
Croft Road
Aldershot
Hants GU11 3HR
England

Edward Elgar Publishing Company
Old Post Road
Brookfield
Vermont 05036
USA

**British Library Cataloguing in Publication Data**

History of Economics Society *Conference* (1988: Toronto, Canada)
Classical, Marxians and neo-classicals: selected papers from the History of Economic Society Conference, 1988.
(Perspectives on the history of economic thought; v. 3)
1. Economics. Theory, history
I. Title II. Moggridge, D. E. (Donald Edward) *1943-* III. Series
330.1

ISBN 1 85278 293 5

Phototypeset by Input Typesetting Ltd, London

ISBN 978 1 85278 293 1

Printed and bound by CPI Group (UK) Ltd, Croydon, CR0 4YY

# Contents

# Introduction
## D. E. Moggridge

This volume and its companion (volume IV) contain a selection of the over 135 papers presented at the conference of the History of Economics Society in Toronto in June 1988. Afterwards, those presenting papers were asked to submit either the version circulated at the conference or a revised version to the editor by the end of the summer of 1988. From those thus available, some 60, the editor and Professor Mark Blaug made a final selection which, less a few unanticipated dropouts, appears here.

The volume opens with Gianni Vaggi's re-examination of the concept of profit in the eighteenth century, with special reference to the origins of Adam Smith's views, in order to throw some new light on the classical notion of competition and on the associated notion of a uniform rate of profit. There then follows one of the results of the Society's fruitful experiment of providing a forum for a series of papers organized by the Bentham Society, Marco Guidi's exercise in attempting to elucidate the scientific part of Bentham's political economy in terms not of modern theory but of the other parts of his own system and contemporary discourse and to integrate the revisionist restatement of the core of Bentham's thought with the two related but independent realms of discourse in it.

There follow two papers concerned with the interrelation between post-Ricardian economics and other developments. Timothy Alborn's paper on Thomas Chalmers on Poor Law reform and epistemology clearly shows the complexity and close interrelationships involved in debates on natural theology, political economy and practical legislation, as well as the process by which they were slowly disentangling themselves. Margaret Schabas takes another example of possible interpenetration, the relationship between classical political economy and the notion of the economy of nature used by Darwin and Lyell. She suggests that in the case of Darwin, although there was the acknowledged influence of the influence of Malthus's demographic model, there was little influence from Ricardo and that in the case of Lyell, even though acknowledgements are not present, there is a greater probability of influence.

Marx and his influence form the major theme of the next four papers. In the first, Shalom Groll and Ze'ev Orzech attempt to sort through the roles that the three notions of the composition of capital play in Marx's theory and the confusions that result in the Marxian literature from a failure to distinguish clearly between them and their implications. Ian Steedman then examines P. H. Wicksteed's October 1884 critique of Marx's value theory in *Today*, 'The Monthly Magazine of Scientific Socialism', which proved so influential in English socialist circles. As well as setting out Wicksteed's critique of the theory set out in volume I, he clearly develops its Jevonian roots and then discusses Marx's more general theory in the context of Wicksteed's views. In the subsequent paper, M. C. Howard and J. E. King turn their attention to Russian revisionism, in particular the work of Tugan-Baranovsky who, rather than Peter Struve, they argue was the main theoretical force within both subsequent Russian and 'western' Marxism. Finally, Noel Thompson examines the movement in the thought of John Strachey from the 'liberal market socialism' of *Revolution by Reason* (1925) through the 'Comintern communism' of his publications of the mid–1930s to the liberal Keynesian socialism of *A Programme for Progress* (1940), tracing the intellectual and other influences involved at each step.

The next three papers shift the focus from Marxism to continental economic theory. In the first Robert B. Ekelund Jr and Robert F. Hébert emphasize the advances over the theories of Cantillon and Say in the theory of entrepreneurship put forward by Jules Dupuit, advances which they argue were squeezed out of economic theory after the marginal revolution and which have not been fully recovered even in recent neo-Austrian theorizing. In the second, Claude Mouchot and Pierre-Henri Goutte outline the editorial problems involved in producing a synthetic edition of Leon Walras's *Eléments d'économie politique pure*, volume VIII of the *Oeuvres économiques complètes d'Auguste et de Léon Walras*. Then Richard Gonce argues that the doctrine of 'consumer sovereignty' is the over-arching identifying doctrine in the version of substantive Austrian economic theory developed by Ludwig von Mises. In his contribution he examines Mises's use of the notion and arrives at an assessment of his resulting contribution.

Contributions from American economists are the subject of the next three papers. Toshihiro Tanaka is concerned with the causes of the change in John Bates Clark's thought from an early repudiation of the competitive system and support of the cooperative system as the ideal to a sophisticated justification and defence of competitive capitalism. He argues that this was not a change in emphasis but radical conversion of view and attempts to identify some of the factors involved. Patrick Raines sets forth Frank Knight's contributions to social economics and John T. Harvey examines a recent attempt to test the predictions of the Stolper-Samuelson theorem and Cairnes's theory of non-competing groups that could have done with a greater understanding of the history of economics.

The volume concludes with two papers on aspects of the history of one of the subdisciplines of economics, economic history, particularly the form it has taken in the United States. Originally there were to be three, but the third, Samuel Williamson's paper on cliometrics, will appear in a *Festschrift* to our contributor, Jonathan Hughes. Hughes's concern is with the relatively neglected influence of European scholars and traditions on the distinctive development of the subject in the United States. Louis Cain concludes the volume with a discussion of how business history in the United States became separated from mainstream economic history in the United States and how, despite their having come increasingly to share a common body of economic theory, it has been difficult to bring the two fields together.

# Contributors

Timothy L. Alborn, Department of History of Science, Harvard University, Cambridge, Massachusetts, USA.

Louis P. Cain, Departments of Economics, Loyola University, Chicago and Northwestern University, Evanston, Illinois, USA.

Robert B. Ekelund, Jr, Department of Economics, Auburn University, Auburn, Alabama, USA.

R. A. Gonce, Department of Economics, Grand Valley State University, Allendale, Michigan, USA.

Pierre-Henri Goutte, Centre Auguste et Léon Walras, Faculté de Sciences Économiques et de Gestion, Université Lyon, France.

Shalom Groll, Department of Economics, University of Haifa, Haifa, Israel.

Marco E. L. Guidi, Facolta di Scienze Politiche, Instituto di Studi Economici e Statistici, Universita 'G.D'Annunzio', Teramo, Italy.

John T. Harvey, Department of Economics, Texas Christian University, Fort Worth, Texas, USA.

Robert F. Hébert, Department of Economics, Auburn University, Auburn, Alabama, USA.

M. C. Howard, Department of Economics, University of Waterloo, Waterloo, Ontario, Canada.

Jonathan Hughes, Department of Economics, Northwestern University, Evanston, Illinois, USA.

J. E. King, Department of Economics, La Trobe University, Bundoora, Victoria, Australia.

D. E. Moggridge, Department of Economics, University of Toronto, Toronto, Ontario, Canada.

Claude Mouchot, Centre Auguste et Léon Walras, Faculté de Sciences économiques et de Gestion, Université Lyon, Lyon, France.

Ze'ev B. Orzech, Department of Economics, Oregon State University, Corvallis, Oregon, USA.

J. Patrick Raines, Department of Economics, University of Richmond, Richmond, Virginia, USA.

Margaret Schabas, Department of History of Science, University of Wisconsin, Madison, Wisconsin, USA.

Ian Steedman, Faculty of Economic and Social Studies, University of Manchester, Manchester, UK.

Toshihiro Tanaka, Department of Economics, Kwansei Gakuin University, Nishinomiya, Japan.

Noel Thompson, Department of History, University College, Swansea, UK.

Gianni Vaggi, Department of Economics, University of Pavia, Pavia, Italy.

# 1 The classical concept of profit revisited

## Gianni Vaggi

This paper investigates the modifications undergone by the concept of profit in the eighteenth century, and in particular the origin of Adam Smith's notion of a rate of profit on the capital invested. However, philology is not the main aim of the work, which provides an evaluation of the role of the notion of profit in the analytical framework of classical political economy and of Adam Smith's theory of wealth in particular. This exercise should throw some fresh light on the classical notion of competition and on the associated idea of a uniform rate of profit. Thus the paper provides new elements to discuss these categories and to examine the debates and the misunderstandings around classical political economy, which despite having abundantly flourished in recent years, do not seem to have 'gravitated' towards a single view. I then provide a personal assessment of the major analytical features of the theories of surplus.

Section I presents the state of distribution theory before 1776, with particular attention to physiocratic thought. Section II examines Adam Smith's main contributions and the way in which they became part of the analytical framework of classical political economy. The above framework and the discussions about it are the subject of section III.

## I

In the second half of the seventeenth century Sir William Petty put forward the idea that economic systems were made up of different social classes, characterized by different roles in the process of production and circulation of commodities. This is the concept of social division of labour which was to play a crucial place in economics for the following two centuries. Petty linked the existence of different classes to the concept of social surplus: the part of the social product exceeding the consumption of agricultural workers (Petty, 1662, pp. 30–31, 88–90). As far as the theory of distribution was concerned, Petty's view was quite simple: the surplus was appropriated by the landlords as rent (ibid., p 43; Aspromourgos, 1986, pp. 31–2).

Following a lead by Petty, Cantillon said that landowners maintained all social classes by means of the expenses out of their revenue, that

*1*

is to say rent (Cantillon, 1755, p. 43). Notwithstanding the emphasis on landlords' expenditures, Cantillon believed that the farmers played an essential role in the organization of the productive process of agriculture. This new class of farmers seemed to share many of the features of capitalist entrepreneurs. The farmer received two-thirds of the product of cultivation, which were used to pay the wages of the peasants and as compensation for his own activity (ibid., pp. 43–5). The other third accrued to landlords; this is the theory of the 'three rents'. But even if he underlined the positive role of the farmers, Cantillon did not include profits in the net product of the economy.

Petty and Cantillon provided interesting analyses of the value of commodities. Sir William believed that 'all things should be valued by two natural Denominations, which is Land and Labour' (Petty, 1662, p. 44). Cantillon worked out the implications of this statement by finding the 'Par, or Equation between Land and Labour' (Cantillon, 1755, p. 43), which should allow the expression of the value of every commodity in terms of an equivalent amount of land. This 'land theory of value' is a way of expressing the idea that the relative prices of commodities depend on the physical costs which have been incurred in their production. Roughly speaking, wages and raw materials – evaluated in land equivalents – determine the intrinsic value of a product (ibid., p. 41). Thus, under the influences of Petty and Cantillon, at the middle of the eighteenth century there was a widespread view that the value of commodities was determined mainly by the sum of all the material expenses required in their production (Meek, 1962, pp. 334, 352).

Cantillon and, through him, Petty exerted a major influence on physiocracy. However, Quesnay's analysis of the capital employed in cultivation was much more detailed than those of Petty and Cantillon, in particular physiocracy ascribed an important role to all the items which make up the fixed capital, the well-known *avances primitives* of the farmers. The amount and the quality of the fixed capital determined the productivity of the agricultural sector. Following Cantillon, Quesnay completed the identification of the farmer with the capitalist entrepreneur. He alone was responsible for the process of production, therefore he controlled the accumulation of capital and the introduction of new techniques of cultivation. Rich farmers could build up large capital stocks which make possible the introduction of methods of cultivation more and more productive, thus raising the *produit net* of agriculture (Quesnay, 1756, pp. 427–9). The Physiocrats regarded agricultural output as the main element of national wealth, which could be increased by means of capital accumulation. The richer the farmers, the wealthier the whole country.

The importance ascribed to the farmers and the emphasis on the accumulation of capital as the road to welfare and prosperity cause expectations to arise about Quesnay's analysis of profits and income distribution. After all, farmers' profits should be the source of investment and technical progress. Quesnay regarded farmers' profits as elements of the country's net product, as was clear from the articles he wrote for the *Encyclopédie* immediately before the *Tableau* (Quesnay, 1757a, p. 463). Profits emerged from Quesnay's analysis of the value of agricultural commodities, a rather forgotten part of physiocracy. The fundamental price of the products of cultivation was the sum of all the technical costs incurred in production – wages, raw materials and capital amortization – plus the rent which had to be paid to the landlords (Quesnay, 1757b, pp. 532–3). This was the minimum price the farmers could accept; below it they would make a loss. Profits were the difference between the price at which the products were actually sold and the fundamental one. However Quesnay did not give a satisfactory explanation of the reasons why the actual selling price was higher than the fundamental one, thus leaving a profit to the farmers. He said that competition among those willing to buy food-stuffs was always very high, but failed to explain why agricultural output did not increase up to the point of closing the gap with demand, as happened for manufactured goods (Vaggi, 1987, pp. 116–20).

Quesnay had the great merit of defining farmers' profits as part of the social surplus, and not as a salary of superintendence. However, profits were still outside the fundamental value of commodities, their size depended mostly upon the state of the market and bore no precise relation to the value of the capital invested in production. (For a different opinion, see Groenewegen, 1983, p. 16.) The physiocratic concept of profits still retained important features of the mercantilist notion of profit upon alienation, that is to say, the difference between the selling and the purchasing price of a good. Of course, there is a remarkable difference between the two concepts. The fundamental price, the threshold above which there are positive profits, depends upon the methods of cultivation and upon the relative strength of two social classes – farmers and landlords – in the distribution of surplus. This implies that profits increase not only when the actual selling price rises, thanks to the ability of the farmers as dealers in exchange, but also when they manage to reduce the costs of production and when class relationships become more favourable. Nevertheless, the size and the existence of farmers' profits were volatile and it was hard to see how this fragile part of the surplus could become the source of accumulation and prosperity.

Sir James Steuart's theory of value and profits deserves to be mentioned. First of all, his analysis was not confined to agricultural products. Moreover Steuart believed that the profits of the entrepreneurs became consolidated in the intrinsic value of the products, that is to say, in their cost of production (Steuart, 1767, vol 1, p. 193). Thus profits became a permanent and stable element of the price of commodities, however they still originated out of market competition, and their size depended upon the state of trade. Therefore, in Steuart, as in Quesnay, we find a slightly modified version of the mercantilist notion of a profit upon alienation (ibid., pp. 177–8, 193–5). No clear relationship existed between entrepreneurial profits and the amount of capital invested.

## II

I shall examine Smith's theory of distribution from three points of view. First, profits were no longer outside the natural, or fundamental, value of commodities. Second, profits were now defined as a rate on the capital invested. Third, he distinguished the mechanisms determining rent from those affecting profits. Of course, these three aspects of Smith's theory of profit were related to one another: I separate them only for convenience of exposition. I must also point out that Turgot shared with Smith the merit of having introduced the notion of a rate of profit on the capital invested, and of having clearly included profits in the value of commodities. The similarities and the differences between the two authors will become clear in the rest of this section.

The introduction of the profits of the entrepreneurs inside the concept of natural price had important consequences in classical political economy, because it provided the analytical link between the theories of value, of distribution and of growth of national wealth. This link was still missing in physiocracy, where the role of profits as an element of social surplus was still overshaded by that of rent. Smith gave profits the same dignity and stability as the other shares of the social product. The exchange value of commodities must include that part of social surplus which is the source of accumulation, and thus the springboard of economic development.

Turgot too regarded profits as part of the fundamental value of commodities, which was made up of workers' wages, of the raw materials which have been used in production and of an interest on the capital invested. This interest was a true entrepreneurial profit and must not be confused with either capital depreciation or with a salary of superintendence (Meek, 1973, p. 17; Groenewegen, 1971, pp. 327–40).

A second important contribution from Turgot and Smith was the fact that profits were no longer defined as a difference between two prices. Both authors abandoned the mercantilist notion of profit upon alienation and regarded entrepreneurs' profits as a percentage rate on the capital invested in production. Therefore, the origin and the size of profits no longer depended upon the state of the market, but derived from the technical conditions of production. Of course, profits accrued to the entrepreneurs through the exchange value at which they sold the products, but their right to have a profit did not depend upon market circumstances. Moreover, the size of profits was now related to the amount of capital invested. The economic functions of the capitalist entrepreneur were clearly distinguished from those of the merchant and of the landowner. The different functions of these three social classes implied different ways of appropriation of the social surplus. Smith clearly spelt out that there were new rules in the distribution of income with respect to those prevailing in feudal societies.

Coming to the third point – the separation of profit from rent – I must point out some differences in the approaches of Turgot and of Smith. In the eighteenth century a widespread view prevailed that there were several possible ways of employing a given amount of monetary capital. Turgot highlighted five different possibilities facing a financial investor:

1.  to buy a piece of land and become a proprietor,
2.  to lend money at interest,
3.  to become an industrial entrepreneur,
4.  to rent land and become a farmer,
5.  to buy commodities and resell them as a merchant (Turgot, 1766, pp. 150–55).

Turgot believed that, thanks to competition, all these different employments should have yielded similar rates of return on the money invested. Thanks to the existence of competition on investment markets, different rates of return would induce people to transfer their monetary capital in search of the highest possible remuneration. This did not mean that the rates of return should be uniform in all types of investments, because each way of employing capital had a different risk, which justified the existence of different degrees of profitability.

But rate differentials among different investments tended to be fixed (ibid., pp. 171–3). Therefore entrepreneurs' profits were a share of the net product, but for Turgot, as for Petty, Cantillon, Quesnay and Steuart, landlords' rents were still the most important part of the social surplus. Profits were no longer upon alienation, but the economic mechanisms determining the size of the rate of return on the investment of capital were not yet clearly separated from those affecting rent. These forces were generally identified with those of competition, which brought about uniform rates of return on all type of investments and hence across all social classes – except for salaried workers.

It is well known that in the *Wealth of Nations* the economic forces which tended to equalize the profit rates in all sectors of the economy were different from those which determined landlords' rent and the rate of interest on money loans. Rates of return were uniform, or similar, for each type of investment, but were different for different social classes. Smith's notion of competition was not new, but certainly the use he made of this concept and the way in which he adapted it were highly innovative. Competition among capitalist-entrepreneurs was defined as free circulation of capital and its result was the tendency towards uniform profit rates. On commodity markets competition produced the tendency of market prices to gravitate towards natural prices (Smith, 1776, p. 75). Thus, the notions of natural price and of uniform rate of profit for all capitalist entrepreneurs 'reconciled' the working of competition in the circulation of commodities and in the circulation of capital.

The separation of rent from profits reflected the evolution of the English economy during the eighteenth century, but it also fulfilled an important analytical role in classical political economy. It is only with Smith that the economic mechanisms that determine profits were clearly identified. Since profits were the source and the motive of economic change, we can now appreciate the forces that influenced the evolution of economic societies. No doubt Smith's improvement over Turgot was due to the different notion of capital he adopted. Capital was no longer regarded mainly as an amount of money, but it included also several types of physical magnitudes, including machines and workers' provisions (ibid., pp. 280–83, 332, 343). This fact justified the existence of competitive mechanisms among the capitalist entrepreneurs which were different from those prevailing either among landlords, or among moneylenders and, of course, among the workers. The very same index of Book I of the *Wealth of Nations* – from chapter VI to XI – was a proof of the way in which Smith distinguished social classes and their output shares. (On the difficulty of interpreting Smith's theory of rent, see Erreygers, 1987, pp. 22–39.)

## III

In recent years, and in particular after the publication of Garegnani's article on the different concepts of equilibrium (Garegnani, 1976, pp. 26–9), there have been many debates about whether or not market prices gravitate towards natural ones. Most commentators refer to Smith's Book I and in particular to chapter VII, 'Of the natural and market price of commodities'.

Thanks to the analysis of the previous sections we can now distinguish the analytical role played by prices and profits in Smith's theory from the historically contingent way he adopted to present them. We have seen that the notions of natural price and of rate of profit on the capital invested gave unity to the theories of value, of distribution and of economic growth. The source of accumulation was now a permanent element of the exchange value of commodities. To put it in another way, the prices of commodities depended upon the rules according to which the net product must be distributed. The existence of positive profit rates was a necessary condition for the reproduction of the social division of labour which was typical of a capitalist society.

Let us now examine the way in which Smith presented the above notions and their relationships. Turgot already believed that competition would bring about uniform rates of return on all kinds of investments. It should be no surprise to see that Smith resorted to the idea of a uniform profit rate in all sectors of the economy. Uniform rates looked much more anti-mercantilist than the existence of many rate differentials; the natural price was opposed to the monopoly price (ibid., pp. 78–9) and the natural conditions of the employment of capital were opposed to state intervention (ibid., pp. 132, 135ff.). Moreover Smith himself pointed out that there were many situations in which rates for profits and for wages were different in different employments. This was clear from chapter X of Book I, which immediately followed the chapters dealing with the analysis of prices and distribution.

The ideas of gravitation towards natural prices and of uniformity of profit rates appeared as a convenient way of expressing the opinion that in the natural order of society there was a relationship between the different employments of capital. It may be that Smith himself believed that gravitation would have actually followed, provided that all the requirements of perfect liberty existed. He certainly believed in the power of market forces. But the major analytical role of the concept of natural price was the fact that it showed that profits were a permanent element of the value of commodities even if there were no monopolies, corporations and other exclusive privileges.

The core of value and distribution theory in classical political economy was the idea that the value of commodities depended upon the techniques of production and upon the rules according to which the net product was distributed. This view was expressed by Smith in Book I of the *Wealth of Nations*, and it represented the conclusion of a century-long investigation on the problems of profits and prices in a surplus economy. If this is the idea that somebody does not like, then it would be better to attack it directly instead of dealing with gravitation. In my opinion, gravitation was the historically contingent form adopted by Smith to express his views about the role of profits in an economy characterized by social division of labour and by the existence of surplus.

Of course, given the appropriate hypothesis market prices should become equal to the natural ones, but there does not seem to be conclusive mathematical evidence either in favour or against this result (Duménil & Lévy, 1987, pp. 141–3, 148–53). In any case, if we find the idea of mechanical gravitation disturbing for twentieth-century men we can substitute it with a more vague view that in the long run there must be some relationship between the profitability rates in different investments. Neither the idea of socioeconomic classes, nor the concept of social surplus, nor the fact that relative prices have the role of reproducing capital and of distributing the net product will be undermined. All the fundamental elements of classical political economy and of the surplus theories of value and distribution would still be there.

## References

Aspromourgos, T. 1986, 'Political economy and the social division of labour: the economics of Sir William Petty', *Scottish Journal of Political Economy* 33.

Cantillon, R. 1755, *Essai sur la nature du commerce en général*, ed. H. Higgs, Frank Cass, London, 1959.

Duménil, G. & Lévy, D. 1987, 'The dynamics of competition: a restoration of the classical analysis', *Cambridge Journal of Economics* 11 (2).

Erreygers, G. 1987, 'La théorie classique de la rente foncière et sa critique par Marx dans les Theorien über der Mehrwert', mémoire, Université de Paris X, Nanterre, October.

Garegnani, P. 1976, 'On a change in the notion of equilibrium in recent work on value and distribution: a comment on Samuelson', in *Essays in Modern Capital Theory*, eds. M. Brown, K. Sato and P. Zarembka, North-Holland, Amsterdam.

Groenewegen, P. D. 1971, 'A reinterpretation of Turgot's theory of capital and interest', *The Economic Journal* 81, June.

Meek, R. L. 1962, *The Economics of Physiocracy*, Allen & Unwin, London.
— — 1973, *Turgot on Progress, Sociology and Economics*, Cambridge University Press, Cambridge.
Petty, W. 1662, *A Treatise of Taxes and Contributions*, in *The Economic Writings of Sir William Petty*, ed. C. H. Hull, vol. 1, Cambridge University Press, Cambridge 1899.
Quesnay, F. 1756, 'Fermiers', in *François Quesnay et la Physiocratie*, Institut Nationale d'Etudes Démographiques, Presses Universitaires de France, Paris, 1958.
— — 1757a, 'Grains', in *François Quesnay et la Physiocratie*.
— — 1757b, 'Hommes', in *François Quesnay et la Physiocratie*.
Smith, A. 1776, *An Inquiry into the Nature and Causes of the Wealth of Nations*, vol. 1, Oxford University Press, Oxford, 1976.
Steuart, J. 1767, *An Inquiry into the Principles of Political Oeconomy*, vol. 1, Oliver & Boyd, Edinburgh, 1966.
Turgot, A. R. J. 1766, 'Réflexions sur la formation et la distribution des richesses', in *Oeuvres de Turgot et Documents le Concernent*, ed. G. Schelle, vol. 2, Libraire Felix Alcan, Paris, 1912–23.
Vaggi, G. 1987, *The Economics of François Quesnay*, Macmillan, London.

## 2 'Shall the blind lead those who can see?' Bentham's theory of political economy

*Marco E. L. Guidi*

Bentham's concern with political economy can be dated back to the end of the 1770s, when he still considered this discipline as a separate branch of legislation, to which those laws and regulations which tend to promote the growth of wealth and population belong (UCL, LXXXVII, pp. 2–4; XCVI, p. 104; CLX, p. 18). Pursuing his inquiry into the nature and subdivision of legislation during the 1780s, when he was working on a *Projet d'un corps de loi complet à l'usage d'un pays quelconque*, he arrived at the conclusion that there is no distinct 'economic legislation' and that political economy should rather be defined as a branch of the science of legislation, sharing with all other branches its starting point: the analysis of the general end of political society, collective utility and of a series of 'subordinate' purposes – subsistence, abundance, security and equality (UCL, XXXIII, p. 88; XXIX, p. 23; XCIX, p. 149; Bentham, 1793–5, p. 226; 1801–1804, pp. 307–308). This point of departure, in its turn, clearly reveals Bentham's intention to present his theory as a radical utilitarian reformulation of the *Staatszwecke* doctrine, which was the current normative foundation of the German and Continental political thought of his times (Raeff, 1975; Tribe, 1984).

According to Bentham, the chances to fulfil the ends of government depend on the quantity of available material resources: the object of political economy is therefore the inquiry into the conditions which render the production of a maximum of wealth and of a maximum of population possible (Bentham 1801–1804, p. 318).

To analyze Bentham's political economy from this viewpoint has led a growing number of scholars (for example, Long, 1977; Steintrager, 1977; Hume, 1981; Boralevi, 1984; Dinwiddy, 1989) to improve our understanding of the meaning of Bentham's writings on this subject, and also to criticize Halévy's commonly shared interpretation (1901–4), according to which Bentham's economics was basically a theory of the 'natural identification of individual interests', a point that Bentham never wished to prove.

Such attempts to challenge this and other non-Benthamite interpret-

*10*

ations of Bentham is clearly related to recent *revisionism* in Adam Smith and classical political economy studies (Winch, 1978; Haakonssen, 1981; Hont and Ignatieff, 1983; Collini, Winch and Burrow, 1983). Both criticize the abstract method by which these thinkers have been connected to an equally abstract liberal tradition, and suggest a 'Copernican revolution' against Marxist and liberal interpretations of classical economists and political philosophers: from the perspective of political economy as the science of civil society, of natural harmonization, they move to the perspective of the science of a legislator. From surplus value or market equilibrium, they shift the emphasis to the rules of justice and to their jurisprudential or utilitarian foundations.

Now, revisionism, although not explicitly, also challenges the history of analysis approach, in a Schumpeterian sense: the Kuhnian methodology more or less adopted by revisionist interpreters negates the possibility of extracting from the 'vision' of all economic theorists of the past a common analytical core, constantly evolving from rough intuitions to more sophisticated formalizations, and always intelligible in modern economic language (see, for example, Hollander, 1987). But non-evolutionist histories of economic analysis can also be criticized from this viewpoint, in as much as they reduce the different epochs in the history of economic thought to their supposed correspondence or non-correspondence to more modern paradigms (the Marxian, the Sraffian, the Keynesian ones, for example), often misunderstanding the sense and the function given to their 'economic' arguments by the past thinkers they study.

Although I share the main methodological achievements of revisionism, I wish to discuss a problem it poses: is what we now call history of analysis a total nonsense? Is it impossible to isolate a core of theoretical propositions concerning the understanding of economic facts, apart from considerations about the nature and purposes of political economy within the whole philosophical system of an author? The answer to this question reveals itself more problematic than we can expect.

The fact is that, starting at least from the reception of Smith's *Wealth of Nations* (Teichgraeber III, 1987), and with the growing institutionalization of political economy in universities (Le Van Lemesle (ed.), 1986; Augello et al. (eds), 1988; Barber (ed.), 1988; Tribe (ed.), 1989), in associations and clubs (Coats, 1961) and in the press (Fetter, 1953, 1962), some authors begin to discuss a set of theoretical explanations concerning social and economic events, to a certain extent *independently* from the philosophical framework of their works. They also accept or criticize other economists' theories on 'positive' economics, although their political opinions radically diverge from each other, or they have different views about the nature, methods and purposes of the economic discourse. Thus Ricardo in England, Say in France and, e.g., Storch in Russia discuss Smith's theory of value and relate it in different but communicating ways to the problem of distribution and growth, although they have very different conceptions of the scope of political economy and of its relationships with the other parts of the social and political sciences. A language of descriptive economic theory is born and it runs parallel to various languages of political economy as a branch of the science of legislation. Of course, like every language, it is subjected to evolution and to different uses in each individual *parole*. Moreover, like every specialized language, it interacts with other languages.

In this sense, Bentham's peculiar contribution seems to consist in his clear distinction between political economy as an art, and political economy as a science, a distinction already suggested, although less clearly, by James Steuart (Hutchison, 1964), and which Bentham derives from his 'encyclopedical' classification of sciences, especially of those related to moral and political subjects (Bentham, 1983a). Whereas art deals with normative (or 'critical', in Bentham's words) matters related to legislation, science includes the descriptive and analytical part of the reasoning (Bentham, 1793–5, p. 224). It is in this sector that Smith's and other economists' analytical theorems are discussed.

In the following paragraphs, I shall concentrate on the 'scientific' part of Bentham's political economy, *in the sense in which he himself isolates and defines it*. In other words, I shall not try to read and evaluate Bentham's statements in terms of modern economic theories, but to understand the signification he gives to descriptive economic theories, the languages he employs to formulate them, the tradition of theories and concepts to which this part of his discourse refers, and the relationships between economic science and the other branches of his system. My aim is to integrate the revisionist restatement of the logical 'centre' of Bentham's political economy with the suggestion that there are at least two related, but in the last resort independent universes of discourse within it:

1.   what Bentham refers to as 'the art', including critical references to *Staatswissenschaften*, to the natural law tradition and also to the languages of the English political debate, and

2. 'the science', in which a discussion of Smith's, Condillac's and other economists' analytical theorems is actively pursued.

To interpret these as distinct parts of Bentham's philosophy helps us to improve our understanding of it as a whole.

The problem is: are there any relevant interactions between the 'scientific' part of Bentham's economics and his general conception of political economy? If the answer is at least in some cases positive, as I believe, we shall reach the proof that both function as separate streams of his discourse.

I shall try to test the validity of this approach by concentrating my inquiry on a peculiar character of Jeremy Bentham's economic theory, i.e. its emphasis on the psychological factors – especially 'motives' – which influence individual actions. The purpose of this paper is to elucidate some theoretical and methodological components of this attitude, and to show how many relevant results of Bentham's economics – the analysis of the conditions of investment, or the analysis of the relationship between credit and production – are related to it. By that, I do not want to affirm that the whole of Bentham's economic science can be reduced to the analysis of motives. It is certain that, as Donald Jackson has suggested (Jackson, 1973), moving from Bentham's notion of labour as the source of wealth, other important aspects can be elucidated. Rather, I shall try to show how Bentham's theory of labour (not to forget land) and aggregate wealth is connected with his analysis of motives: the latter defines the qualitative causal factors from which the growth of wealth depends, whereas the former analyses the material resources on which growth is based and by which it is limited (Bentham, 1793–5 pp. 225, 228–33). Both are necessary conditions of growth; but without the existence of adequate motivations, growth is only a material potentiality.

# I

The utilitarian approach, considered as a method of describing and analysing practical choices and their social consequences, began to be looked at, during the eighteenth century, as a means of explaining the market price of goods. Among others Galiani and Condillac, but also to a lesser extent Cantillon and Turgot, found in the utility of commodities, compared with their relative scarcity, the basis of exchange value.

Conversely, Bentham's political economy rarely refers to the problem of value. However, he does not miss the importance that other economists attach to this problem: in his notes on Smith, for example, he discusses the labour theory of value, but discards it, as others had done, for not giving enough consideration to the contribution of land (UCL, XCIX, p. 183). It is true that some obscure allusions to wages as a component part of prices may suggest Bentham's subscription of the (Smithian?) adding-up cost theory of value (Hollander, 1979), but these allusions are never developed into a complete theory. Lastly, it would be an error to read in Bentham's theory of labour as the only source of wealth a formulation of the theory of value.

The utilitarian approach to value was also well known by Bentham. And if from the mid–1780s we can find direct quotations from Condillac's *Du commerce*, he probably already knew the essential elements of this theory one decade before. In a manuscript of this period (reported in Baumgardt, 1952), Bentham employs some concepts apparently derived from the utility approach to value in order to formulate a method of calculating pleasure and pain in every field of human existence. These concepts are: the idea of a qualitative uniformity between pleasant and painful sensations – so that, in modern terms, we can consider them as a *continuum* of intensive magnitudes, with positive or negative values, and with the zero-value corresponding to a state of indifference (Bentham, 1983b, p. 342) – or the problem of what we now call diminishing marginal utility (see Bentham's manuscript reported in Halévy, 1901–1904, vol. I, p. 428), already suggested, more or less explicitly, by other thinkers. Furthermore, in discussing this subject, Bentham frequently recurs to the utility of money, which he considers as the best available measure of the utility of every object, but also a highly imperfect instrument for this purpose, being itself submitted to diminishing marginal returns.

But when he writes *An Introduction to the Principles of Morals and Legislation* (*IPML*, printed in 1780), Bentham seems to give less emphasis to the 'psychometric' project of only some years before. General statements on the universal applicability of the felicific calculus and on the necessity of understanding its mechanisms are indeed not absent: what is lacking is their full development. The place previously taken by the analysis of calculation is now covered by an attempt to establish an exhaustive classification of the motives which compel men to act and of the circumstances which influence their actions (Bentham, 1970, chs. 6–7 and 10). Some sheets of the manuscripts *Projet Matière*, (*c.* 1782–7), dedicated to what Bentham now calls 'Axioms of mental pathology', clearly show his scepticism about the possibility of a full quantitative interpersonal comparison (UCL, XXXII, p. 5; XCIX, p. 55. See also James, 1986). To this scepticism is also related Bentham's attention to the variety of motives: reading

Hume and Smith, Bentham had had many occasions to meditate on the difference between interest and benevolence, both of them typical of human relations, though not in an equal proportion. At this stage of the research, considering the difficulties involved in the comparative calculation of pleasures and pains related to interested and benevolent actions, Bentham seems to consider the felicific calculus as a *hypothesis*, in the negative sense attributed to this term by Newton, i.e. as a 'gratuitous proposition', not inferred from a rigorous inductive or empirical procedure.

The preliminary task of 'descriptive' ethical theory, then, is to explain human action. In chapters 3–12 of *IPML*, Bentham does that by means of two complementary approaches:

1. a causal explanation, which relates action to its motivational or psychological components (like expectations, intentions, etc.), then to the external environment, i.e. on those 'circumstances' (Helvétius) which influence the course of action, and finally to its social and practical consequences;
2. a systematic classification, applied to each of the links of that causal chain, but especially to motives and intentions, in order to reach a perfect understanding of volitional ideas.

Each of them is explained as a mode of the general 'fictitious entity' motive, i.e. the expectation of future pleasures and exemptions from pain, which brings man to act (according to Bentham's language, pleasure and pain are the only 'real entities').

Bentham's interest in political economy begins just when he is elaborating this part of his ethical theory. Therefore, it is not surprising that Bentham's political economy as a science is strictly connected with 'descriptive' ethics. From this viewpoint, in fact, political economy might be considered as a first test, or an essential stage, of the 'causal' and 'taxonomic' theory of human action elaborated by Bentham. Is it not true that just in production and exchange we can observe a sharp heterogeneity of behaviour and individual ends? Surely, the attitudes of a banker or an entrepreneur (BPU, L, pp. 230, 260), adopting a rational way of life, pondering and choosing the most appropriate means to attain maximum profit (or interest), sharply differ from those of an idle rentier or an aristocratic landlord, defined by Bentham as *'purement consommateur'* (Bentham, 1811, pp. 307–8), or from those of the hungry and improvident poor (labourer), who prefers a meagre enjoyment today to a greater tomorrow (Bentham,

1838a p. 367), and whose behaviour reveals a strong tendency to anomie.

Therefore, the first task of political economy consists in the analysis and classification of human action, in as much as it is connected with economic ('pecuniary') motives, and with the problem of the growth of wealth and population. This priority, and the logical position of economics within descriptive ethics, can help us to explain why Bentham's 'analysis' is less interested in the problem of value than other contemporary and subsequent theories. It simply aims to explain other relationships: the relationship of pecuniary motives to accumulation; the relationship of labour to growth.

The absence of a direct link between a hedonistic theory of action and the problem of value looks strange to us, because we are prepared to expect it both by the developments of marginal economics and by the presence of a 'subjective' approach to value within classical and pre-classical political economy. But some major objections impeded Bentham from elaborating a theory of value strictly connected with his analysis of human choices. He was, in fact, sceptical about the possibility of translating market value in terms of subjective utility, of pure lots of pleasure and pain, because the problem of how individuals attribute differing degrees of enjoyment to different goods, whether they share the same capacity for reason, what and how much they are disposed to sacrifice to attain their purposes, etc., was still to be analysed. To compare exchange value according to subjective utility was possible in theory, but only under a series of restrictive hypotheses, that Bentham had discarded, such as the universality of the egoistic motive and of a means-ends rationality.

## II

We could restate what I have enunciated by saying that Bentham is perhaps less interested in the *measurement* of growth, than he is in the explanation of the *possibility* of economic development in terms of individual decisions. At the basis of Bentham's explanation there are individuals, all of them characterized by the same fundamental structure, i.e. the tendency to seek pleasure and to remove pain. Only their concrete motives are different. For example, both an entrepreneur and a rentier act to augment their total happiness, but whereas happiness is for the former, above all, maximum profit, for the latter it is enough rent to maintain a high level of consumption.

The explanation of aggregate economic events starts from individual choices, or from classes of choices, and studies the ways in which they relate – either by combining their effects or by clashing together

– and generate particular collective situations. Collective events are therefore considered as the unintentional result of many individual choices, formally based on the search for happiness, and motivated by concrete, empirically recognizable ends. This method undoubtedly shifts Bentham's attention towards the analysis of all significant and recurrent microeconomic events. In fact, this analysis is always carried within what we now call a (classical) macroeconomic framework, based on social surplus value, the alternative between consumption and investment, and the relationship between aggregate savings, credit economy and growth, etc. This framework is used to predict in which cases individual choices are compatible with one another, and conversely in which cases their collective consequences are socially negative, or even destructive. But what Bentham is more interested in is how the individual acts and reacts to different social circumstances, under these macroeconomic constraints. Collective events are simultaneously a result of individual choices, and a constraint upon an individual when making these choices.

This attitude brings Bentham to emphasize also within the economic discourse the role played by 'mental pathology'. First, his attention to motives is accompanied by a study of expectations and their function in orienting individual decisions. Expectations can be either optimistic or pessimistic; they can also vary in intensity, being moderate or transforming themselves into states of either euphoria or panic. Individual choices rely on expectations because future events – originating from other individuals' choices and other external phenomena – are uncertain and cannot be controlled by the single individual. Bentham's economic analysis often stresses the importance of expectations in determining collective states.

Secondly, as I have already remarked, Bentham is convinced that to different motives are related radically different models of behaviour. To the motive of profit is connected a maximizing and rational way of life, whereas the motive of subsistence is often related to a very inconsistent and improvident behaviour. This fact has some important consequences on collective events: not all kinds of behaviour are *a priori* compatible with one another.

Lastly, motives and expectations may vary as a consequence both of variations in external factors, and of the results of the social composition of previous decisions. New, unforeseen circumstances are continually generated by the actions of individuals, and new motives spring from these circumstances. Expectations may or may not be confirmed by facts, generating very different attitudes in both cases. Therefore, the emphasis Bentham gives to choices and to the psychological factors which accompany them, leads him to the conclusion that economic development has no predetermined and single path; on the contrary, as choices may combine in a variety of ways, a large variety of paths are equally possible. Only by studying the individual level of reaction to aggregate changes can we enhance the capability of economic theory to predict the actual path that is prevailing at any given moment. Moreover, among the changes affecting motives and expectations, Bentham also contemplates the vanishing of socially beneficial motives, to the advantage of negative ones. Alternatively, some motives, the results of which are advantageous to general welfare within certain limits, by trespassing upon these limits, may produce negative effects. Bentham's economic world is therefore a highly unstable one: a consistent growth is a likely result in a commercial and industrial society, but a general crisis is also equally possible. The admission of the non-uniqueness of the path of growth and of the possibility of crisis are two of the more original features of Bentham's economic theory.

## III

This method is at the basis of some of Bentham's major contributions on the subject of political economy. The first of them can be found in the manuscripts headed *Projet. Economie* (*c.* 1786–7) – most of them missing (but see UCL, XCIX, pp. 149, 190–91), but used by E. Dumont for the fourth book of *Théorie des récompenses* (chs. XI and XIII) – and in *Manual of Political Economy* (pp. 226–31). Bentham's macroeconomic framework is formulated here for the first time. Bentham assumes that the annual income of a nation can be disposed of in various ways, among which the most important are: '1. subsistence: 2. enjoyment: 3. security: 4. encrease'. But if this income is employed only in the first three uses, it will be entirely consumed. To have at the end of a period a quantity of wealth at least equal to that at the beginning, we have to invest a portion of it in the shape of productive capital, and the surplus (Bentham's 'encrease') deriving from this investment is to be at least equal to consumption. Let us define $Y_t$ the total income at the beginning of the period, and $Y_t - \triangle - \star \triangle +_1$ the income produced at the end of the period, K the capital (we assume that it is composed only by circulating capital, including salaries) and C the total consumption; we can write

$$Y_t = K + C \qquad (1)$$

and

$$Y_t+_1 = K(1 +a) \tag{2}$$

where a = average efficiency of capital. It follows that $Y_t+_1 \geqslant Y_t$ only if $Ka \geqslant C$.

Every increase of total output depends only on two variables: the quantity of capital and the 'advantageousness of the direction' of capital itself. Now, especially in analysing the latter variable, Bentham attributes to *motives* and individual decisions the role of primary factors of growth. The efficiency of capital is in fact the result of two subjective elements: '1. the choice of the trade itself: 2. the choice of the mode of carrying it'. At the root of every change in efficiency lies therefore a double choice – between different allocations of capital, and between different available techniques. Moreover, this choice is a maximizing one ('the best choice'), and its chances of success are '1. in proportion to the degree of *interest* which he, by whom the choice is made, has in making the *best possible*: 2. in proportion to the *chance* he has of possessing the *faculties of knowledge* and *judgement* in relation to the business *in the highest degree possible*' (Bentham, 1793–5, p. 229; emphasis added). The opportunity to possess the right knowledge largely depends, in its turn, on interest.

A third condition is represented by 'power'. Power can be distinguished into *legal* (the protection of government, but equally the privileges conceded by it), *physical* (money and other goods), and *intellectual* (knowledge itself, considered as a resource) (Bentham, 1793–5, p. 232; 1801–1804, p. 323). The consideration of power introduces the role of government to the analysis. A central authority can modify the spontaneous allocation of income by acting on these three kinds of 'power'. But it is virtually certain that the reallocation thus obtained will be less efficient than what is determined by market forces: the unsubstitutable link between private interest and specific knowledge, the casual distribution of understanding and information, the non-additive and non-reversible nature of time and attention, all such factors imply that it is impossible to concentrate in any single person the decision concerning the direction that the economic system is to take. Government – the purpose of which is to maximize social utility – ought to leave the distribution of scarce resources to the spontaneous interactions between individuals, limiting its intervention to two major tasks: the protection of people and their property (security) and a general circulation of information (*transparence*) (see Robbins, 1952, pp. 12–13).

**IV**

In *Defence of Usury* (1787), Bentham emphasizes the role played by psychological factors in stimulating the increase of capital and capital efficiency. Here, two new elements are added: savings and the role of entrepreneurs ('projectors'). Total income can be divided into two parts, 'wealth employed in the shape of capital' and '[wealth] employed in the shape of unproductive consumption and expenditure'. Only the first of these parts represents the savings of a nation, as 'whoever saves money, as the phrase is, adds proportionably to the general mass of capital' (Bentham, 1787, p. 196).

Let us define S the savings; it is clear that S = K, and the (1) can be rewritten

$$Y_t = S + C \tag{3}$$

Nevertheless, the identity between savings and investments should be considered as a mere 'phrase': savings are, in fact, available for capital investment, but some mechanisms can intervene, the result of which is to shift a part of them towards unproductive consumption. Moreover, according to (2), the future increase of income depends on the quantity of capital and its efficiency. However, the efficiency of capital is greatly increased by 'projectors' (Bentham, 1787, pp. 168, 170, 177), who introduce both new methods of production and new raw materials, as well as contributing to general welfare in other ways – by enlarging the market, introducing new commodities or improving those that are already in existence. The purpose of the entrepreneur is to produce an extra-profit by the innovation he has introduced; this extra-profit will tend to vanish as soon as this innovation is imitated by other people. Moreover, the entrepreneur is endowed with an understanding and a propensity to take risks which exceed common standards. It is true that an innovation implies a high degree of uncertainty, and this was the reason why Smith had condemned *projectors* as imprudent men (see Pesciarelli, 1989), dangerous to the well-being of society. Nevertheless, to innovate is not to act irrationally: those who invest formulate accurate expectations concerning future on the basis of past experience, and the improvement of the ability to anticipate events is assured by personal interest, as well as by an historical process of learning by (indeed dramatic) trials and errors. As Bentham says, 'The career of art, the great road which receives the footsteps of projectors, may be considered as a vast, and perhaps unbounded, plain, bestrewed with gulphs, such as Curtius was swallowed up in. Each requires an human victim to fall into it ere it can close, but when it once closes, it closes to open no more, and so much of the path is safe to those who follow' (Bentham, 1787, p. 180).

The security of innovations is also assured by a further element: the interaction between entrepreneur and moneylender. When an entrepreneur needs money to make an investment, he is obliged to submit his 'project' to the examination of the proprietor of funds, 'whose prejudices are certainly not likely to be on the favourable side' (LVI, p. 181). Therefore, those who possess money have the power to select innovations. Bentham is especially interested in the problem of how the supply of money for investments and the rate of interest influence the distribution of savings among different groups of claimants. Capital can be increased (within a closed economy) only by an increase of savings, and savers are confronted with an alternative: either to invest their capital, or to lend it. The proportion between these two parts depends on their comparative profitability. Available credit is therefore equivalent to total savings minus the share of them that is directly invested by savers. This mass of money is then distributed among three competing groups: unproductive consumers ('dissipating borrowers'), 'innovators' and *routiniers* (the last two being productive consumers or 'accumulating borrowers'). Moreover, Bentham supposes that the rate of interest is free to float in both directions. Monetary capitalists agree to finance projectors under two conditions: a careful examination of the chances the 'adventure' has to be successful, and a rate of interest sufficiently high to compensate the risk of innovation. The entrepreneur, for his part, expects to be able to refund his creditor at such a rate, since he expects high extra-profits. Therefore, *well-grounded* innovations tend to appropriate all the quantity of available savings they need. Only what remains will be allocated between the two other groups. The quantity of savings allotted to the two groups of investors is transformed into capital: but as the flux of innovations is not homogeneous and continuous, and bankers can also lend their money to unproductive consumers, the capital fund varies from time to time. Therefore, savings are not automatically equal to investments. The simple hypothesis of a separation between the function of saving and that of investing, though with a credit of pure intermediation, brings Bentham to attribute to banks the power to shift resources from *routine* investment to innovations, from consumption to investments, and vice versa.

## V

The central role of motives and individual actions emerges also from a third set of manuscripts (1801), of which only Dumont's French version, *Sur les prix*, survives (BPU, L, 30 *et seq.*, partially published and translated in Stark (ed.), 1952, vol. III, pp. 61–216). Before this work, Bentham's economic theory runs on two parallel and non-interacting paths. On one side, the role of banks is only to transfer money from savings to investments. On the other side, Bentham elaborates a theory which relates prices and quantities to the mass of money and its velocity of circulation, and identifies in the increase of money the origin of such phenomena as inflation and forced saving (Stark (ed.), 1952, vol. I, pp. 269–71; Bentham, 1801–4, pp. 342–9; Hayek, 1932).

Nevertheless, a more accurate inquiry into the operations of the English banks of his time – particularly the London banks and the country banks – leads Bentham to believe that his description of a credit economy is not realistic. From this standpoint, *Sur les prix* is an attempt to transpose his theory of money to the case of the relationship between credit and investments. Additional hypotheses are now introduced. First, the amount of bank financing is no longer limited to existing savings. Instead, a credit multiplier is introduced: banks open credits – in the shape of paper money – above the limits set by the amount of money which they have. Since no legal restraints are supposed to be introduced, credit supply to entrepreneurs is only limited by the wisdom of the banker and by his expectations about the profitability of investments (BPU, L, pp. 98, 111, 201). These subjective variables explain the fluctuations in the total amount of credit supply.

With the money thus obtained, entrepreneurs buy additional raw materials and instrumental goods, and employ an additional number of labourers, thus exerting a pressure on the demand of these factors. If the latter are fully employed, the additional demand produces inflation and reallocation of resources to the benefit of those entrepreneurs: therefore, they draw resources both from consumers (forced saving), and from other capitalists, as the additional money and the expectation of high profits allows the entrepreneurs to pay higher prices for raw materials, instrumental goods and labour. A limited growth of total output is the result of this allocation, but its unacceptable human and social price is a high rate of inflation (Bentham, 1801–4, p. 343). On the other hand, if factor supply is elastic, the additional money allows those who receive it to employ labour and resources which were lying unemployed: the result is an increase in total income. In this case indeed, the only cause of inflation is to be found in the demand of necessities by the additional labour force, or in the additional demand for some of the other resources, which may happen to be fully employed: but this is only a sectoral inflation, which will tend to diminish as soon as the new goods arrive at the market, and capital is reallocated among its various branches. Thus 'L'effet de ce torrent de capital sera d'avancer la production de la richesse réelle aussi longtemps qu'il restera une capacité de travail à mettre en oeuvre et aussi rapidement que cette capacité peut être mise en action' (BPU, L, p. 51; see also LVI, pp. 102, 134; and, on inflation, LVI, p. 142).

The hypothesis of unemployment of resources tends to modify Bentham's analytical framework. If we assume that the employment of labour can increase only when capital goods increase, we can omit reference to variations in the employed labour force (Bentham, 1801–4, pp. 310, 332–3). We also assume that no flux of savings goes to 'dissipating borrowers'; in this case, *Defence of Usury* concluded that savings were equal to investments. But in *Sur les prix* Bentham argues that a share of aggregate income is neither consumed nor invested: it lies idle within the system. If we still call S only the share that is actually transformed into productive capital, we are obliged to separate it from a quantity H of 'hoarded' resources. Equation (3) is therefore modified thus:

$$Y_t = S + C + H \tag{4}$$

As $S = K$, without creation of money, at the end of the period we would have

$$Y_t+_1 = K(1 + a) + H$$

The new credit transforms H into productive capital. Let us call $K'$ the capital equal to H. If we suppose for the sake of simplicity that the efficiency of the new capital is equal to that of the former, we have

$$Y'_t+_1 = K(1 + a) + K' (1 + a)$$

therefore $Y'_t+_1 \geqslant Y_t+_1$ of a quantity equal to $K'a$.

Therefore, bank financing puts in motion a set of idle resources, *by transferring them into the hands of entrepreneurs*. This produces an increase in aggregate income.

In fact, a general growth is no more than one of the formally possible events. The same interaction between bankers and entrepreneurs can also be at the origin of the opposed phenomenon of instability. Bentham's explanation of crises relies on two elements: 1. the fact that financing decisions are taken only on the basis of *expectations* of future profitability of the investments; and 2. the concrete choices of entrepreneurs, especially in choosing from different technologies. On this choice depends the rate of efficiency of capital, thence the amount of surplus to divide between profit and interest. But he who receives money can make the wrong choice and make an unprofitable investment. Because of his failure, he is unable to refund his creditor. If the latter depends on the debtor's refund for current payments, he will encounter serious difficulties in pursuing his operations, or refunding the debts contracted with other banks (BPU, L, p. 132). The risk is, of course, greater when the proportion between created deposits and reserves is greater. But long before these problems emerge, a psychological mechanism can anticipate and accelerate the bankruptcy: panic (*alarme*) pushes savers to run to the bank and withdraw their deposits. As a consequence, the bank goes bankrupt and, in a chain reaction, those banks which were linked to it also go bankrupt. A general bankruptcy – and, along with it, a general economic crisis – can be the final result of this chain of events (BPU, L, pp. 201, 298, 302).

These conclusions entail, of course, Bentham's (at least implicit) self-criticism on a fundamental point: the knowledge that bankers and entrepreneurs possess can lead them to the wrong choice. It is true that this simple possibility was already contemplated in *Defence of Usury*, but not only was Bentham more optimistic about the future; he also thought that the consequences of errors were less serious, as failure concerned only a few individuals: the improvident lender and the borrower, as well as the labourers employed by the latter. Once he has admitted the existence of created money, however, he thinks that the errors of a few men may entail a long chain of negative events, and also a general crisis. More importantly, the causes of these events are a series of psychological factors, negative motives and pessimistic expectations. Bentham is interested in the way in which these factors emerge as a consequence of bad information, and propagate their effect to the whole economic system.

## VI

What I have stated about Bentham's economic analysis suggests at least three conclusions. First, Bentham treats what in modern terms we call economic analysis as a separate and definite part of his economic discourse. But the distinction between science and art does not originate from within political economy. Instead, it derives from the fundamental partition of ethics into a descriptive and a 'critical' part. Thus, both the method and the content of economic science are related in many ways to descriptive ethics.

Second, Bentham's analysis of economic events in terms of motives and actions tends to suggest that potential disequilibria are structurally present in society, and also in those relationships by which the production of the means of subsistence and enjoyment is assured. This conclusion is strictly related to Bentham's radical break with the language of Natural Law, on which his science of legislation is built. The Natural Law foundations of political economy had encouraged in Smith the search for systematic aspects of society. And although Smith was conscious of social conflicts and potential disequilibria (Smith, 1976, pp. 83–5), he firmly believed that a natural tendency to order was a characteristic of market mechanisms (pp. 606, 687).

According to Bentham, the notion of 'natural law' is a fiction which cannot be related in a unique and unambiguous way to the only 'real entities' on which rigorous and scientific reasoning should rely – 'human feelings', i.e. pleasure and pain (Harrison, 1983, pp. 173–4). This notion always reflects the subjective opinions of the speaker about what he thinks is (or ought to be) natural (Bentham, 1970, pp. 21–9). According to Bentham, the employment of such 'fictitious entities' as action, decision, (social) relation, is legitimate only in so far as these logical fictions can be explained in terms of individual expectations of pleasure and pain (Bentham, 1838b, pp. 210–11). Therefore, social order depends entirely on individual actions. Bentham is indeed convinced that, generally speaking, men tend to calculate their choices in a rational way. But nothing guarantees that collective results are always positive and satisfying for individuals. On the contrary, variations in socially prevailing motives and expectations are likely to produce very bad results.

These remarks lead us to our third conclusion: 'Scientific' reasoning, although rigorously separated from normative economics, interacts with art, modifying in the course of years Bentham's opinions about the scope of government intervention in the economic field. In *Defence of Usury*, Bentham puts this question to his readers:

> Shall the blind lead the blind? is a question that has been put of old to indicate the height of folly: but what then shall we say of him who, being necessarily blind, insists on leading, in paths he never trod in, those who can see? (p. 178)

The question was, of course, largely rhetorical. Government *was* blind, because it did not have the same degree of interest and knowledge as private individuals had. Only the latter were able to make the kinds of choice which were more advantageous to society. Once he has admitted that the same positive motives can have very bad consequences for social welfare, or even that they can change themselves into negative and pessimistic motives, Bentham is compelled to enlarge the sphere of government intervention in the economic field. But government cannot replace private interactions efficiently. Therefore, such measures as restrictions on credit and central control on bank activities are justified only in so far as they limit the bad tendencies of the system and, in the last resort, protect the *security of expectations* (BPU, L, pp. 200–8). Government is still blind, according to Bentham: it cannot replace private decisions with efficient centralized choices, at least in the field of investment and innovation. Economic growth still relies on individual motives and expectations.

## Acknowledgement

I wish to express my thanks to P. F. Asso and E. Santarelli for discussing a previous version of this paper. Don Jackson's comments on my Toronto paper helped me to elucidate the limits of my research, which cannot be considered as a comprehensive reconstruction of Bentham's economic theory. I also owe a great deal to David Crosier for his careful editing of the text. The mistakes are my own.

## References

### Unpublished sources

University College, London, *Bentham Manuscripts* (referred to in the text as UCL).
Bibliothèque Publique et Universitaire, Geneva, *Manuscrits Dumont* (referred to in the text as BPU).

### Published sources

Augello, M. M. et al. (eds), 1988, *Le cattedre di economia politica in Italia. La diffusione di una disciplina 'sospetta' (1754–1900)*, F. Angeli, Milano.
Barber, W. (ed.) 1988, *Breaking the Mould. The Development of Academic Economics in XIXth-century America*, Wesleyan University Press, Middletown, CT.
Baumgardt, D. 1952, *Bentham and the Ethics of Today*, Princeton University Press, Princeton, N.J.
Bentham, J. 1787, *Defence of Usury*, in *Jeremy Bentham's Economic Writings*, W. Stark (ed.), vol. I.
—1793–5, *Manual of Political Economy*, ivi.
—1801–1804, *Institute of Political Economy*, ivi, vol. III.
—1811, *Théorie des peines et des récompenses*, E. Dumont (ed.), de l'Imprimerie de Vogel et Schultze, Londres, T.II.
—1838a, *Tracts on Poor Laws and Pauper Management*, in *The Works of Jeremy Bentham*, J. Bowring (ed.), vol. VIII, Tait, Edinburgh.
—1838b, *Fragment on Ontology*, ivi.
—1970, *An Introduction to the Principles of Morals and Legislation*, Athlone Press, London.
—1983a, *Essay on Nomenclature and Classification*, in *Chrestomathia*, M. J. Smith and W. H. Burston (eds), Clarendon Press, Oxford, pp. 139–276.
—1983b, *Deontology, together with A Table of the Springs of Action and The Article on Utilitarianism*, A. Goldworth (ed.), Clarendon Press, Oxford.
Boralevi, L. 1984, *Bentham and the Oppressed*, W. de Gruyter, Berlin and New York.

Coats, A. W. 1961, 'The Political Economy Club: a neglected episode in American economic thought', *American Economic Review* September, pp. 624–37.

Collini, S., Winch, D. and Burrow, J. 1983, *That Noble Science of Politics. A Study in Nineteenth-Century Intellectual History*, Cambridge University Press, Cambridge.

Condillac 1946–51, *Le Commerce et le gouvernement considérés relativement l'un à l'autre* (1776), in *Oeuvres Philosophiques de Condillac*, G. Le Roy (ed.), vol. II, Presses Universitaires de France, Paris.

Dinwiddy, J. R. 1989, *Bentham*, Oxford University Press, Oxford.

Fetter, F. W. 1953, 'The authorship of economic articles in the *Edinburgh Review*, 1802–47', *Journal of Political Economy* 61, pp. 232–59.

—1962, 'Economic articles in the *Westminster Review*, and their authors, 1824–51', *Journal of Political Economy* 70, pp. 570–96.

Galiani, F. 1963, *Della moneta* (1751), in *Della moneta e scritti inediti*, A. Caracciolo (ed.), Feltrinelli, Milano.

Haakonssen, K. 1981, *The Science of a Legislator. The Natural Jurisprudence of David Hume and Adam Smith*, Cambridge University Press, Cambridge.

Halévy, E. 1901–4, *La Formation du radicalisme philosophique*, 3 vols, Alcan, Paris (*The Growth of Philosophical Radicalism*, J. Plamenatz (ed.), Faber, London 1972. (A. M. Kelley, Clifton, N.J.)

Harrison, R. 1983, *Bentham*, Routledge & Kegan Paul, London.

Hayek, F. A. 1932, 'A note on the development of the doctrine of "forced saving" ', in *Quarterly Journal of Economics* 47, pp. 123–33.

Helvétius, C.-A. 1983, *De l'esprit* (1758), Marabout, Verviers, Belgium.

Hollander, S. 1979, 'The role of Bentham in early development of Ricardian theory', *The Bentham Newsletter*, no. 3, pp. 2–17.

—1987, *Classical Economics*, Basil Blackwell, Oxford.

Hont, I. and Ignatieff, M. 1983, *Wealth and Virtue. The Shaping of Political Economy in the Scottish Enlightenment*, Cambridge University Press, Cambridge.

Hume, L. J. 1981, *Bentham and Bureaucracy*, Cambridge University Press, Cambridge.

Hutchison, T. W. 1964, *'Positive' Economics and Policy Objectives*, Alen & Unwin, London.

Jackson, D. 1973, *Bentham's Democratic Transformation of Lockean Liberalism*, unpublished paper presented at the LSE and UCL, London.

James, M. 1986, 'Bentham's democratic theory at the time of the French Revolution', *The Bentham Newsletter* 10, pp. 5–16.

Le Van Lemesle, L. (ed.) 1986, *Les Problèmes de l'institutionnalisation de l'économie politique en France au XIXe siècle*, special issue of *Oeconomia* 6.

Long, D. 1977, *Bentham on Liberty*, University of Toronto Press, Toronto.

Pesciarelli, E. 1989, 'Smith, Bentham and the early making of two contrasting theories of entrepreneurship', in *History of Political Economy*, forthcoming.

Raeff, M. 1975, 'The Well-ordered police state and the development of modernity in seventeenth- and eighteenth century Europe: an attempt at a comparative approach', *American Historical Review* 80, pp. 1221–43.

Robbins, L. 1952, *The Theory of Economic Policy in English Classical Political Economy*, Macmillan, London.

Smith, A. 1976, *An Inquiry into the Nature and Causes of the Wealth of Nations*, R. H. Campbell, A. S. Skinner and W. B. Todd (eds), Clarendon Press, Oxford.

Stark, W. (ed.) 1952, *Jeremy Bentham's Economic Writings*, Allen & Unwin, London.

Steintrager, J. 1977, *Bentham*, Cornell University Press, Ithaca, N.Y.

Teichgraeber III, R. F. 1987, ' "Less abused than I had reasons to expect": the reception of "The Wealth of Nations" in Britain, 1776–90', *The Historical Journal* 30, pp. 337–66.

Tribe, K. 1984, 'Cameralism and the science of government', *Journal of Modern History* 56, pp. 263–84.

Tribe, K. (ed.) 1989, *Trade, Politics and Letters. The Art of Political Economy and*

*British University Culture 1755–1905*, Cambridge University Press, Cambridge (forthcoming).

Winch, D. 1978, *Adam Smith's Politics. An Essay in Historiographic Revision*, Cambridge University Press, Cambridge.

# 3 Thomas Chalmers's theology of economics

*Timothy L. Alborn*

During the decades following Ricardo, despite attempts at secularization and political neutrality, British economic debates continued to feel the influence of contemporary theological and political controversies. What appeared to be comfortable alliances in economics were often disrupted by differences over politics, theology or epistemology – differences capable of breaking down the initial terms of agreement. The Scottish moralist Thomas Chalmers offers an example of the ambivalence with which heterodox opinions were received by the classical economists of his day. In both the political realm of Poor Law reform and in the epistemological realm of natural theology and scientific method, Chalmers initially found powerful support for his views from orthodox economists such as William Nassau Senior. He eventually parted ways with classical political economists, however, when they came to realize that he was either unwilling or unable to reconcile his Scottish Evangelical views on pauperism and science with those views of his early allies.

This paper outlines Chalmers's initial acceptance among economists and the eventual loss of his acceptance, with regard first to Poor Law reform and second to epistemology. In both cases, the factors surrounding his selection to write the Bridgewater Treatise on 'the moral and intellectual constitution of man' – essentially a natural theological discourse on political economy – will be the centrepiece of my discussion. The fact that economists in the 1830s were still interested in lending their professional support to natural theology reflects the lingering existence of the invisible hand amid the largely secular ambitions of Ricardo, Senior and George Poulett Scrope. The fact that Chalmers was chosen as the representative to lend such support led to tensions, resulting from the retention of theology in a discipline still far from reaching a consensus about its proper scope and method. The rise and fall of Chalmers's popularity paralleled the shifting positions many contemporary economists took regarding Adam Smith's eighteenth-century view of the economic order. Although Chalmers's theology of economics ultimately rendered him an outsider in the British economic community, therefore, the story of how he achieved that status is well worth telling.

The Bridgewater Treatises owed their origin to a bequest of £8000 left in 1830 by Francis Henry Edgerton, the eighth Earl of Bridgewater, for the Royal Society to publish 'a work on the Power, Wisdom, and Goodness of God, as manifested in the Creation'.[1] Charles Blomfield, Bishop of London and William Howley, Archbishop of Canterbury agreed to help select the authors of the proposed treatises, who included such scientific luminaries as William Whewell, Charles Bell and William Buckland, representing the whole range of the natural sciences from astronomy to entomology. One of the treatises, as stipulated in Edgerton's will, turned from the physical constitution of nature to the moral constitution of man. Given the popularity and political importance of economics in 1830, as well as its undisputed historical ties with moral philosophy, it was only natural that Blomfield and Howley in this case appealed to the field of political economy. The two clerics selected Chalmers to represent that field for a variety of practical reasons. Although Howley knew Chalmers only by reputation, Blomfield's association with the Scot dated back to the early 1820s, when Chalmers had experimented with new forms of poor relief as a parish priest in Glasgow. His published account of those experiments, *Christian and Civic Economy of Large Towns* (1821–3) had earned him a reputation as a thoughtful and maverick economic reformer. Blomfield, who faced similar problems of poor relief in London, was impressed both by Chalmers's practical experience fighting pauperism and by his wide popularity as a public speaker.[2]

Significantly, Blomfield's closest contact in economic circles – through their common cause of Poor Law reform – was Nassau Senior, Professor of Political Economy at Oxford and later head of the 1832 Poor Law Commission with Edwin Chadwick. Senior also had good reasons for supporting Blomfield's choice for the Bridgewater Treatise on the moral and intellectual constitution of man. In 1830 Chalmers had reported to Parliament on Irish poor relief, repeating his opposition to the old Poor Laws as too generous and not sufficiently connected to the Church. Senior appended sections of that report to his 'Letter to Lord Howick on a Legal Provision for the Irish Poor', published the following year, declaring that Chalmers had 'admirably summed up' the argument against compulsory poor relief.[3] Chalmers shared more than his strong opposition to the old Poor Laws with Senior's Oxford/London circle of Anglicans, which included Richard Whately and Richard Jones as well as Blomfield. He also traced a common (though complex) intellectual lineage to Scottish common-sense philosophy and a willingness to support natural theology, which was unusual for an Evangelical Presbyterian. Several other factors, however, combined to make an alliance between Chalmers and the Anglicans precarious and eventually untenable. These ranged from his aversion to the new Poor Laws and his insistence on conjoining morality with political economy, to his uncomfortable stance regarding the proper place of economics in natural theology. Many of these differences can be attributed to Chalmers's theological views. All of them played a role in the lukewarm critical reception accorded to his Bridgewater Treatise, to which I shall first turn. At a deeper level, they affected his grudging and discreet failure to acknowledge political economy as an independent science which could be pursued separately from religion. This decision came at a time when other economists, and Senior in particular, were vigorously defending epistemological autonomy in their field. This situation will be discussed in the second and concluding part of the paper.

**Politics**
The two main factors behind Thomas Chalmers's selection as a Bridgewater author were the opposition which he shared with Blomfield and Senior against the old Poor Laws, and his support of natural theology from the unlikely camp of Evangelicism. Any potential alliance between Chalmers and his Bridgewater selectors, however, rested more on practical convenience than on any truly shared beliefs. Senior's approach to Poor Law reform, which included a political partnership with the utilitarian Edwin Chadwick, permanently separated him from Chalmers on economic questions. Similarly, Chalmers's position on natural theology in his Bridgewater Treatise made it clear that Blomfield's choice may have been premature. Although I shall focus on Chalmers's relation to his selectors on the Poor Law question in this section, his stance on natural theology suffered a similar fate. Initially selected as one of the few leading Evangelical spokesmen willing to support natural theologians such as Adam Sedgwick, Chalmers's final position on the argument from design as stated in his Bridgewater Treatise was to insist that any such argument must be kept subordinate to God's revealed moral law.[4]

The initial agreement between Chalmers and the classical economists on the Poor Laws was largely based on his practical experience with pauperism in Glasgow. Like many other Evangelicals, Chalmers's reading of Malthus convinced him that compulsory poor relief was counterproductive, since it went against the 'natural law' of positive checks which punished those who did not help themselves.[5] In 1817 and 1818 Chalmers submitted articles for the *Edinburgh Review* entitled 'Causes and Cures of Pauperism', in which he pressed for increased voluntary aid and for education programmes which would teach the wisdom of self-help and thrift. When Chalmers moved to Glasgow in 1819, the city council gave him an opportunity to put his plan into operation in the local St John's parish. At St John's, Chalmers implemented traditional parochial means of poor relief in an urban setting with surprisingly efficient results. By dividing supervision of the poor among the laity of the established Church, he was able to keep the Church in control of relief without sacrificing close administration. He gave high priority to education by encouraging existing Sunday schools and creating new 'day' schools to operate during the week.[6]

When the Poor Law Commission was formed in 1832 to address pauperism in England, an aide to Senior reported that 'St John's still flourished', but doubted its applicability on a nationwide scale.[7] The chief dividing line between Chalmers and the Commission was his emphasis on religious education and parochial administration. At the heart of this parting of ways was Chalmers's evangelical interpretation of Malthus, which differed dramatically from Senior's and Edwin Chadwick's incorporation of Malthusian economic doctrines into utilitarian social thought. This difference was also the point at which Chalmers's ideological agreement with Whig reformers such as Senior and Blomfield began to weaken. The winds of change were detectable upon the publication of his lectures on *Political Economy* in 1832 and even clearer the following year when his Bridgewater Treatise appeared. These treatises, both of which significantly were not published until *after* his selection by Blomfield, represented Chalmers's most complete theoretical statement on economics. In less than five years, Chalmers had gone from being the orthodox political economists' chosen emissary to being an outcast in the eyes of many.

Chalmers proclaimed in the preface to his *Political Economy* that he intended to demonstrate, through a survey of Smith's theory of wealth and Malthus's principle of population, 'the intimate alliance which obtains between the economical and the moral; in so much, that the best objects of the science cannot, by any possibility, be realized, but by dint of prudence and virtue among the common people'.[8] The book was based on lectures which Chalmers had recently delivered from the chair of Theology at the University of Edinburgh, where he preached on the vital need for future parish priests to be well versed in the laws of political economy. Chalmers's professional insistence on parochial authority angered his critics, who faulted his pessimistic Malthusian critique of classical economics and his contention that religious establishments were the only social institutions capable of resting national prosperity. Above all, however, critics univocally opposed Chalmers's strict application of Malthus's arguments against free trade. Chalmers had defended protectionist legislation on the grounds that the higher food prices which they produced were an effective check against overpopulation. Both George Poulett Scrope in the *Quarterly Review* and John McCulloch in the *Edinburgh* disputed this equation as inhuman. The only reviewer giving any credence to his Malthusian principles was Thomas Thompson of the *Westminster*, and even he argued that the population principle did not necessarily preclude anti-protectionist laws. Following the logic of many optimistic British and French economists in the 1830s, Thompson pointed out that Chalmers had fallen prey to the Malthusian fallacy of confusing the possibility of population surpassing means of subsistence with the necessity that it would do so. Against Chalmers's pessimism, Thompson stressed the potential for British economic growth: 'though one expedient and one dinner may be ineffectual to permanent good, a succession may form a chain, of which very different things may be predicted'.[9]

The heated reaction to Chalmers's *Political Economy* in 1832, paired with its close similarity in subject matter with his Bridgewater Treatise, led to the latter being largely ignored in the reviews when it appeared the following year. The *Quarterly* dismissed it in two pages in the middle of a glowing review of the other three Bridgewater Treatises published that year, professing disappointment that Chalmers had emerged from 'the closet of the political economist' to produce a work bogged down by 'complicated and endless mazes of language'. The *Edinburgh* and *Westminster Reviews* ignored Chalmers's new book, leaving the *Athenaeum* alone in qualified praise.[10] Although Senior and Blomfield did not publicize their views of Chalmers's lectures and his Bridgewater Treatise, they probably would not have differed greatly from Thompson's opinion in the *Westminster Review*. Indeed, Senior virtually repeated Thompson's argument in his own published lectures on economics, although he did not specifically direct it against Chalmers: 'Because additional population *may* bring poverty, [certain thinkers] suppose that it necessarily *will* do so. . . . It furnishes an easy escape from the trouble or expense implied by every project or improvement'.[11] This kind of response supports the conclusion, reached by historians such as Robert Young and Boyd Hilton, that Chalmers's use of Malthus was consistent with utilitarian reform only up to a point. His emphasis on prudence and self-help, which had been the basis of his alliance with Senior against existing relief methods, similarly guided the 'less-eligibility' principle upon which the new Poor Law was patterned. It was his 'Evangelical twist', whereby he opposed all forms of compulsory relief, that Senior refused to follow.[12]

**Epistemology**

The chief methodological precept professed by most British economists in the 1830s was that their discipline be kept separate from ethics and legislation. As Nassau Senior critically observed, this precept was broken by nearly all who pledged it. Senior and his teachers at Oriel College in Oxford were more consistent than most of their contemporaries to his claim that 'The business of a Political Economist is neither to recommend nor to dissuade, but to state general principles, which it is fatal to neglect, but neither advisable, nor perhaps practicable, to use as the sole, or even the principle, guides in the actual conduct of affairs.' In his lectures published in 1836, Senior was careful to distinguish between the 'science of Political Economy' and the 'art of government', which was 'more important, but far less definite', and when John Stuart Mill wrote 'On the definition of political economy' the same year he made exactly the same distinction. In principle, Chalmers agreed with Senior and Mill. He commenced his Bridgewater Treatise with a similar distinction between ethics and the 'physiology of the mind', which was 'collected, like all other experimental truth, by a diligent observation of facts and phenomena'.[13]

For many economists in the 1830s, the distinction between the general principles of political economy and the 'art' of ethics or legislation was rooted in a long tradition of Scottish philosophy. Senior and his Oxford colleagues were particularly indebted to Dugald Stewart's *Philosophy of the Human Mind*, which proposed that it was hypothetically possible to construct theories in political or moral science along the same deductive lines used in mechanics or geometry. Stewart had intended his demonstration to detract from the truth-value assumed to exist in axiomatic sciences. The Oxford economists turned that demonstration to their own use: the deductive 'science' of political economy, which for Stewart could only be hypothetical, was transformed into a doctrine possessing all the mathematical power and predictability of physics.[14] Although Chalmers attended Stewart's lectures in Edinburgh at the turn of the nineteenth century, he was actually more influenced by the earllier Scottish philosopher James Beattie. In his *Essay on Truth* (1770), Beattie (unlike Stewart) had been content to trust that certain self-evident principles were capable of achieving the status of truth through our common-sense perception of them. Far from doubting the truth of geometrical principles of nature, Beattie firmly held that self-evident truths such as these were 'fixed, unchangeable, and eternal'. This conception of truth, which originally had appealed to Chalmers for its power in opposing religious scepticism, later came to be his main tool in formulating an epistemology of moral science.[15] Beattie's wider definition of truth undoubtedly affected Chalmers's tendency to extend his 'physiology of the mind' into realms Senior was careful to avoid. It did not, however, lead to any practical difference between the two regarding the certainty of the laws of political economy. Senior's reinterpretation of Stewart effectively transformed the principles of wealth accumulation and population into truths just as self-evident as Chalmers's propositions.

Unlike Senior, however, Chalmers was much more interested in the religious status of morality than in the epistemological status of political economy. Similarly, the methodological advantages that Senior found in narrowing the scope of political economy to questions concerning wealth and exchange were far from Chalmers's mind. A narrower scope of inquiry, which Senior and his predecessor Richard Whately had established in order to keep economic and religious controversies in separate spheres, would have cut off the field exactly where he was concerned to extend it. He therefore applied the scientific certainty, which both he and Senior had granted to the laws of wealth, to other areas of human conduct, including compassion, education and conscience. This connected the relatively self-contained laws of exchange, or 'catallactics', as Whately called them, back to the more general system of natural morality which he had learned from eighteenth-century Scottish philosophy. Chalmers's dramatic turn accomplished, at an epistemological level, the same sort of split which he had created politically when he extended Malthusianism beyond the narrow realm of self-help.

In his Bridgewater Treatise, Chalmers distinguished between laws describing man's moral constitution and laws relating that constitution with society. In the latter camp belonged the law of 'possessory affection', which dictated man's natural sense of property. As evidence for this law he appealed to pre-societal possessive feelings which he observed in children and to the natural feeling of ownership attaching itself to craftsmanship, concluding that the 'feeling of property' was 'anterior to the sanctions or the application of law'. He agreed with other classical economists that since such feelings about the attainment and possession of wealth were natural to mankind, they should take precedence over what he called the 'hurtful schemes of artificial charity which so teem throughout the cities and provinces of our land'.[16] But Chalmers, significantly, did not stop with the 'law of property'. To refute compulsory poor relief, it was additionally necessary to rely on 'another of our special affections – our compassion for the distress, including . . . the destitution of others'. This involved recognizing the laws mentioned above describing man's moral constitution, which taught prudence on the part of the poor and charity on the part of the rich. He continued that these laws, 'if not tampered with and undermined in their force and efficacy by the law of pauperism . . . would have prevented the vast majority of those cases which fill the work-houses, and swarm around the vestries of England'.[17] His appeal to the natural force of prudence and charity rendered his version of *laissez-faire* much more radical than that of Senior, who was willing to allow state intervention in all areas other than the strict accumulation of wealth.

Chalmers based his laws of property and compassion, which described social relations, on more basic laws describing the 'moral constitution of the human mind'. Chief among these laws was the supremacy of conscience, which he described as the 'great psychological fact in human nature'. This psychological basis of social laws blurred the common split between economics and ethics proposed by writers such as Senior and Mill. Indeed, Chalmers intentionally flirted with a naturalized ethics by defining the crucial distinction as one between objective virtue (the province of moral philosophy) and 'the mental process by which man takes cognizance of virtue' (the province of social science).[18] Senior and Mill, in contrast, by specifically limiting political economy to the study of wealth, consciously avoided grounds normally reserved for moral philosophy. The epistemological schism between Chalmers and Senior on the question of economics and ethics had definite religious underpinnings. As D. F. Rice has observed, Chalmers's claim that the recognition of moral laws was a natural phenomenon provided him with a powerful apologetic for the Evangelical emphasis on revealed religion and personal responsibility. His reworking of Scottish philosophy grounded human responsibility on a non-Biblical foundation, producing what Rice aptly terms 'the touchstone for an anthropology of accountability'.[19] According to this view of morality, human actions may remain separate from ideal virtue, but their relation to the ideal changes. What had been formerly a strictly Biblical decree became, for Chalmers, a natural pattern of recognition which was benevolently provided by God. In this way moral law truly became the supreme arbitrator within Chalmers's theology.

In the course of Chalmers's overriding effort to describe a natural basis for moral responsibility, the epistemological status of political economy was bound to be relegated to secondary importance. Another side-effect of Chalmers's 'anthropology of accountability' was his refusal to consider the claims of political systems which did not fit into his logic of natural laws, the result of which has already been described in the context of Chalmers's Malthusian economics. In contrast to Chalmers, Senior's epistemology conveniently allowed him to keep questions of economics and legislation completely separate, letting him view the utilitarian legislative parts of the new Poor Law as distinct from his economic contributions to its passage. This is not to imply, of course, that Senior denied moral or political responsibility for those parts, since he explicitly approved of the proposed remedies. Of key importance for our discussion, however, is that Senior's methodology of political economy left him logically free to agree or disagree with the new Poor Law, and Chalmers's did not. For Chalmers, utilitarianism drew 'all its materials from the realm of conjecture', precisely because the greatest happiness principle threatened to replace his own principle of the supremacy of conscience.[20] In summary, we may describe Senior's approach as an epistemology of concession, which allowed him to side with thinkers either to his right or left when he deemed it politically desirable (witness his simultaneous alliance with both Chalmers and Edwin Chadwick), and Chalmers's approach as an epistemology of entrenchment.

Thomas Chalmers's Bridgewater Treatise, and the events leading up to its publication, reveal the complexity which was involved in debates on natural theology, political economy, and practical legislation in Great Britain during the 1830s. Such complexity was partly the result of the close interrelation among the fields, and partly the result of personal alliances which were close enough to offer grounds for initial agreement but which often fell short of complete unanimity. Chalmers was faced with a political situation which encouraged him to seek allies such as Nassau Senior against the old poor laws, and with an intellectual situation which made that alliance seem philosophically justified. But because Chalmers was as much an Evangelical theologian as an economist, that alliance was doomed to break down. Its breakdown manifested itself in the political sphere when Chalmers split with the Whigs over the passage of the new Poor Law. It manifested itself in the sphere of natural theology and economics when he refused, in his Bridgewater Treatise and other writings, to separate the laws of nature from the natural morality of man.

**Notes**

1. Cf. W. H. Brock 1966, 'The selection of the authors of the Bridgewater Treatises', *Notes and Records of the Royal Society of London*, **21**, p. 164. Chalmers 1833, *On the Power, Wisdom, and Goodness of God, as Manifested in the Adaptation of External Nature to the Moral and Intellectual Constitution of Man*, New York, 1834, p. i.

2. Blomfield cited Chalmers in his diocesan charge in 1830, and again referred to Chalmers in support of the bastardy clause which he was trying to append to the new Poor Act in 1831; cf. R. A. Soloway 1969, *Prelates and People; Ecclesiastical Social Thought in England 1783–1852*, University of Toronto Press, Toronto, p. 175. On Chalmers's early work on pauperism, see J. McCaffrey 1985, 'The life of Thomas Chalmers', in A. C. Cheyne (ed.), *The Practical and the Pious: Essays on Thomas Chalmers (1780–1847)*, St Andrews Press, Edinburgh, p. 51.

3. Senior 1831, *A Letter to Lord Howick on a Legal Provision for the Irish Poor*, London, pp. 85–104, 54.

4. For Chalmers's early support of Sedgwick, see his *Evidences and Authority of the Christian Revelation*, Edinburgh, 1815, pp. 183–4. For an extended discussion of Chalmers and natural theology, see D. F. Rice 1971, 'Natural theology and the Scottish philosophy in the thought of Thomas Chalmers', *Scottish Journal of Theology* **14**, pp. 23–46.

5. The best treatment of Evangelical political economy is in B. Hilton 1987, *The Age of Atonement*, Oxford University Press, Oxford.

6. There is much overlapping secondary information about the St. John's experiment, including R. A. Cage 1981, *The Scottish Poor Law 1745–1845*, Scottish Academic Press, Edinburgh, pp. 90–110; Cage and E. O. Checkland 1976, 'Thomas Chalmers and urban poverty: the St. John's parish experiment in Glasgow, 1819–1837', *Philosophical Journal* 13, pp. 37–56; Cheyne 1983, *The Transforming of the Kirk*, St Andrew Press, Edinburgh, pp. 22–8; and S. J. Brown 1982, *Thomas Chalmers and the Godly Commonwealth in Scotland*, Oxford University Press, Oxford, pp. 122–31.

7. Brown, op. cit., p. 204.

8. Chalmers 1832, *On Political Economy in Connexion with the Moral State and Moral Prospects of Society*, New York, p. iv.

9. (Scrope 1832), 'Chalmers on political economy', *Quarterly Review* **48**, pp. 39–69, 53; (McCulloch 1832), 'Dr Chalmers on political economy', *Edinburgh Review* **56**, pp. 52–72, 68; (Thompson 1832), 'Dr. Chalmers on political economy', *Westminster Review* 17, pp. 32–3.

10. *Quarterly Review* **50** (1834), p. 4; (W. Cooke Taylor), *Athenaeum* (1833), pp. 396–7.

11. Senior 1836, *Political Economy*, 2nd edn London, 1850, p. 50.

12. Hilton, 'Chalmers as political economist' in Cheyne, op. cit., pp. 144–5; and Hilton, op. cit. A. M. C. Waterman 1983, in his article 'The ideological alliance of political economy and christian theology, 1798–1833', *Journal of Ecclesiastical History* 34, pp. 231–44, makes a similar observation about the variant interpretations of Malthus by Chalmers and the Oxford Anglicans (in this case Whately), but since his main aim is to stress continuity among Christian economists he does not emphasise the point. Hilton, it may be added, does not pursue the implications which Chalmers's 'Evangelical twist' had on his equally distinct methodological and natural theological views. R. Young 1969, in 'Malthus and the Evolutionists', reprinted 1985 in *Darwin's Metaphor: Nature's Place in Victorian Culture*, Cambridge University Press, Cambridge, pp. 32–8, discusses Scrope's criticism of Chalmers and the *Quarterly Review*'s reaction to Chalmers's Bridgewater Treatise; M. Blaug 1958, in *Ricardian Economics*, New Haven, Conn.: Yale University Press, pp. 114–15, mentions the response of McCulloch and Scrope to Chalmers's *Political Economy*.

13. Senior, op. cit., pp. 2–3; Mill 1836, 'On the definition of political economy', in E. Nagel (ed.) 1950, *John Stuart Mill's Philosophy of Scientific Method*, Hafner, New York, pp. 407–40; Chalmers, *On the Power*, op. cit., p. 13.
14. P. Corsi, 'The heritage of Dugald Stewart: Oxford philosophy and the method of political economy', forthcoming in I. B. Cohen (ed.), *The Natural Sciences and the Social Sciences*.
15. Beattie, *Essay on Truth* (1770); quoted in Rice op. cit., p. 29.
16. Chalmers, *On the Power*, pp. 183, 143–4, 136.
17. Ibid., pp. 173–4.
18. Ibid., pp. 43–4.
19. Rice, op. cit., pp. 40–1.
20. Chalmers, *On the Power*, pp. 161, 177–8.

# 4 Ricardo naturalized: Lyell and Darwin on the economy of nature

*Margaret Schabas*

Ricardo conquered England as completely as the Holy Inquisition conquered Spain.

> John Maynard Keynes,
> *The General Theory of Employment, Interest and Money*
> (Macmillan, London, 1936, p. 32)

Time and again, appraisals of Charles Darwin's theory of evolution have noted the many striking similarities to economics. Marx, for example, marvelled at 'how Darwin recognized among beasts and plants his English society with its division of labour, competition, opening up of new markets, invention and the Malthusian "struggle for existence" '. More recently, Garrett Hardin deemed Darwin's theory 'just a vast generalization of Ricardian economics'.[1] Two historians of science, Silvan S. Schweber and Robert M. Young, have argued that Darwin, either wittingly or unwittingly, borrowed extensively from the political economy of his day.[2] The most compelling piece of evidence is Darwin's debt to Malthus for the notion of intraspecific competition. We also know that Darwin had read Bernard Mandeville's *Fable of the Bees* and Adam Smith's *Wealth of Nations*, and had possibly discussed the subject with Simonde de Sismondi, who was related by marriage. Still, the case is not conclusive, at least with respect to the point that Darwin was cognizant of the specific details of Ricardo's text or wished to incorporate them in his *Origin of Species* (1859).

Two other aspects of Darwin's work that might suggest these links are his enthusiasm for Herbert Spencer's evolutionary sociology and his frequent use of the concept of an economy (or polity) of nature. But it does not follow that his readiness to subscribe to the Spencerian term 'survival of the fittest', or general acceptance of Victorian conservativism were rooted in a detailed understanding of the science of political economy. A far more plausible case can be made for the many economic analogies in the *Origin*, whether it be the division of labour, competition or the set of commercial activities he used to characterize the complex web of relations among organisms. But the concept of an economy of nature did not originate with Darwin. Charles Lyell had used it extensively in his discussion of the 'species question', drawing upon ideas articulated in Carl Linnaeus' treatise, *Oeconomy of Nature* (1749; English translation 1759). And one can readily trace the metaphor back to the Aristotelean notion that nature does nothing in vain. Darwin's notion of an economy of nature was superseded in 1866 by Ernst Haeckel's science of oecologie. For almost a century, this served to eclipse many of the conceptual parallels between biology and economics. But with the development of game theory and mathematical ecology, intellectual trade between the two disciplines has once again resumed.[3]

According to some historians, the Linnaean concept of the economy of nature remained more or less intact in Lyell and Darwin.[4] Others, however, have argued that one of the important turning points in Darwin's conceptual genesis was his breach with the Linnaean economy, stimulated by his reading of Malthus and Henri Milne-Edwards.[5] But in my estimation, Lyell was as or more pivotal. His concept of the economy of nature is rich with equilibrating mechanisms that set it apart from eighteenth-century theorists.

There is also some evidence to suggest that Lyell was more susceptible to incorporating economic analogies, particularly of the Ricardian persuasion, than Darwin. It would have been possible for Darwin, immersed as he was in Lyell (and also not one to read extensively in other fields), to have worked out his distinctive economy without the direct influence of Ricardian economics. This does not preclude the possibility that Darwin absorbed economic notions on his own, as many a Victorian gentleman was wont to do. But when it comes to the specific mechanisms of his economy of nature, there is nothing that is distinctly Ricardian. This is somewhat surprising if one accepts the view that Ricardo's ideas dominated the very period during which Darwin worked out his own theory (1830s and 1840s).[6] I shall suggest here that, *if* a debt can be drawn to Ricardian economics (and it is by no means clear that there was one), it was contracted by Lyell rather than by Darwin. Furthermore, given Darwin's strong appreciation for Lyell's works – as he once remarked, 'I always feel as if my books came half out of Lyell's brain' – it seems reasonable to suppose that Darwin absorbed his economics not from Ricardo directly, but in a roundabout fashion from Lyell. Somewhat ironically, Darwin's specific developments of the concept of the economy of nature have strong Smithian overtones, suggesting a peculiar reversion in the history of ideas.

At the time of Linnaeus, the word 'oeconomie' still held to the Aristotelean notion of good or efficient household management. But it had also, during the course of the seventeenth century, come to connote the flow of commerce. Linnaeus read both meanings into nature. God's great household evinced his unbounded wisdom in arranging things with such efficiency, orderliness and frugality. Each species reproduced in just the right numbers to provide nourishment to others and to sustain themselves intact as a species. This was manifest both in the number of offspring per species and the average lifespan of each. There was, in short, no waste. All that was produced was consumed. Even the seemingly random distribution of seeds, via the digestive tract of animals and winged devices, evinced perfect efficiency:

> By the Oeconomy of Nature, we understand the all-wise disposition of the Creator in relation to natural things, by which they are fitted to produce general ends, and reciprocal uses. . . . Whoever duly turns his attention to the things on this our terraqueous globe, must necessarily confess, that they are so connected, so chained together, that they all aim at the same end, and to this end a vast number of intermediate ends are subservient.[7]

Linnaeus showed no hesitation in drawing analogies between the social and natural realms, comparing, for example, our human economy to the more 'excellent oeconomy of nature' (p. 126). In a later treatise on the *Polity of Nature* (1760), he maintained that the mosses, grasses, herbs and trees fulfilled the roles of the peasants, yeoman, gentry and nobility: 'Thus we see Nature resemble a well regulated state in which every individual has his proper employment and subsistence, and a proper gradation of offices and officers is appointed to correct and restrain every detrimental excess.'[8] Insects, for example, were delegated to keep law and order; they were, quite literally, the 'police of nature'.

Since every species was created either as a single pair or individual hermaphrodite, it followed that the quantity of life had once grown considerably. But in so far as species have a geometric rate of increase, it would not take long, Linnaeus maintained, to populate the globe. As a result, the land is everywhere teeming with life. 'The great Author and Parent of all things decreed, that the whole earth should be covered with plants, and that no place should be void' (Linnaeus, *Tracts*, p. 67). He considered the possibility of the globe's inhabitants doubling or tripling, and concluded that they would all perish, since 'the surface of the earth can support only a certain number of inhabitants'.[9]

Linnaeus had, in effect, a stationary economy. Although he believed that the surface of land, through deposition, was growing, it did not occur to him that, given the many intricate relationships between life-forms, this might disrupt the preordained balance. Nor did he follow out possible changes that might ensue from agriculture and growth in human population. Man 'increases the number of vegetables immensely, and does that by art, which nature, left to herself, could scarcely effect' (ibid., p. 124). For Linnaeus, all of this was part and parcel of the ratios consummately calculated by the supreme being.

Lyell read Linnaeus carefully, but having followed both the Enlightenment and the religious backlash to the Enlightenment, he took pains to disassociate geology from theology. Armed with theories of extinction and the immensity of the geological scale, Lyell began to break with the traditional notion of design and to undercut teleological explanations. The second volume of Lyell's *Principles of Geology* (1833) is noted for its attack on the evolutionary theory of Jean Baptiste Lamarck. Although species have a propensity to migrate, and thus adapt somewhat, they are not, Lyell argued, capable of indefinite transmutation. Paradoxically, whereas Lamarck rejected the possibility of extinction, Lyell embraced it as a commonplace event. Since habitats change, extinction is a frequent occurrence: 'Stations comprehend all the circumstances, whether relating to the animate or inanimate world, which determine whether a given plant or animal can exist in a given locality, so that if it be shown that stations can become essentially modified by the influence of known causes, it will follow that species, as well as individuals, are mortal.'[10]

Because of his emphasis on the uniformity and gradualism of geological action, Lyell sought these 'known causes' in the 'powers of migration and diffusion conferred on animals and plants'.

> When any region is stocked with as great a variety of animals and plants as the productive powers of that region will enable it to support, the addition of any new species, or the permanent numerical increase of one previously established, must always be attended either by the local extermination or the numerical decrease of some other species. (ibid., p. 142)

In order to explain the existence of great organic diversity and the seeming absence of natural monopolies, Lyell postulated the creation of new species to fill the gaps caused by extinction: 'We could imagine the successive creation of species to constitute, like their gradual extinction, a regular part of the economy of nature' (ibid., p. 179). What produces new species he did not say. This was in short that 'mystery of mysteries' that Darwin set out to solve.

Lyell explained the relative stability of life forms by postulating a quantitative balance in nature:

> We must imagine the relative resources of man and of species, friendly or inimical to him, to have been prospectively calculated and adjusted. To withhold assent to this supposition would be to refuse what we must grant in respect to the economy of Nature in every other part of the organic creation; for the various species of contemporary plants and animals have obviously their relative forces nicely balanced, and their respective tastes, passions, and instincts, so contrived, that they are all in perfect harmony with each other. In no other manner could it happen, that each species surrounded as it is by countless dangers should be enabled to maintain its ground for periods of considerable duration (ibid., p. 42).

For Lyell, then, not only did the supply of food equal the demand, but there were forces to restore this balance in the case of disruptions. In effect, he envisaged a dynamic equilibrium in which the reproductive rates and lifespans of individuals, as well as the rates of extinction and creation of new species, tend to balance out.

Lyell postulated different rates of stabilization, depending on the type of disturbance. In the case of a temporary climatic change, instability was short-lived: 'there may undoubtedly be considerable fluctuations from year to year, and the equilibrium may be again restored without any permanent alteration' (ibid., p. 142). But in the case of the arrival of a new plant or animal, 'it must require ages before such a new adjustment of the relative forces of so many conflicting agents can be definitively settled' (ibid., p. 145). Extend these processes far enough back in time, say one million years, and it followed that the constant action of these forces 'must work an entire change in the state of organic creation' (ibid., pp. 156–7).

To make clear the difficulties involved in restoring equilibrium, Lyell considered the imaginary situation in which the western hemisphere was rendered devoid of life. Species in the eastern hemisphere, which would be fully stocked, are gradually transported to the west. But, as Lyell pointed out, unless certain grasses or plants are allowed to spread sufficiently to insure survival prior to the arrival of sheep or goats, neither group would be able to survive. One saving grace, however, was the ability of most species to substitute one source of nourishment for another in times of scarcity. An English buzzard, for example, which is content to eat rabbits, mice, birds, frogs and even insects will, in the case of an excess supply, help to restore equilibrium: 'the profusion of any one of these . . . [creatures] may cause all such general feeders to subsist more exclusively upon the species thus in excess, and the balance may thus be restored' (ibid., pp. 138–9).

Insects, because their supply is so elastic, also render a great service in restoring a balance.[11]

In Lyell's schema, there is no room for additional life. True, new species are created, but only to fill the gaps brought on by extinction. He considered the possibility of man having increased the total yield of a given region. As we cultivate land, it is difficult to suppose 'that we have not empowered it to support a larger quantity of organic life' (ibid., p. 147). But, he insists, human population has grown only at the expense of other life forms. Men, 'considered merely as consumers of a certain quantity of organic matter' (ibid., p. 146) are no different from any other species in this respect. They are simply more effective, or destructive, depending on one's point of view.

Drawing on recent discoveries in chemistry, Lyell also discussed the process by which the principal elements of life – hydrogen, carbon and oxygen – are recycled from the atmosphere to the plants and animals. Throughout, he invokes the principle of the conservation of matter to show that a balance exists between the organic and inorganic realms:

> If we supposed the quantity of food consumed by terrestrial animals, together with the matter absorbed by them in breathing, and the elements imbibed by roots and leaves of plants, to be derived entirely from that supply of hydrogen, carbon, oxygen, azote, and other elements, given out into the atmosphere . . . then we might imagine that the vegetable mould would, after a series of years neither gain nor lose a single particle by the action of organic beings. (ibid., p. 189)

Clearly, his belief that the entire earth and its atmosphere were in a state of constant fluctuation about a fixed quantity of matter and life was an analytic device of central importance.

Darwin took several important steps away from Lyell. Although he certainly granted the efficacy of migration and geological change, ongoing reproductive variation was enough to alter the economy of nature. Moreover, for Darwin the set of relations between the species and their physical habitat can always be improved upon. 'No country can be named in which all the native inhabitants are now so perfectly adapted to each other and to the physical conditions under which they live, that none of them could anyhow be improved.'[12] Hence, in contrast to Lyell, no species literally replaces another. Darwin's economy has so little stability that the slightest change will set off a chain reaction which might result in an entirely new set of relationships and places.

Darwin sets down 'the principle that the greatest amount of life can be supported by great diversification of structure' (ibid., p. 114). He cites an experiment in which he weighed grasses grown on two identical plots of land, one sown with just one type of grass, the other with several distinct genera of grasses. The second plot yielded a far greater 'biomass' than the first. This implied that divergence enables the quantity of life in a given region to increase: 'in the general economy of any land, the more widely and perfectly the animals and plants are diversified for different habits of life, so will a greater number of individuals be capable of there supporting themselves' (ibid., p. 115).

Since 'natural selection will not produce absolute perfection', 'probably no region is as yet fully stocked'. Greater diversification leads to the formation of more protected places, that is, places which are less susceptible to interspecific competition. At any given point in time, however, there is a set quantity of life over which the species, particularly those most closely allied, compete. This competition, concomitant with the production of slight variations in reproduction, generates new species who then attempt to seize upon new places in the economy. This may in turn yield a greater amount of life. Since 'natural selection is daily and hourly scrutinising', (ibid., p. 84) however, there is no balance in nature. If there is an apparent equilibrium at a given point in time, it is an unstable one which, at the slightest disturbance, is upset and never regained. Hence, Darwin does not adopt the Lyellian model of a fixed quantity of life oscillating in various forms about an equilibrium point. The economy of nature, for Darwin, is ever expanding (or contracting).

It should by now be apparent that the concept of the economy of nature itself evolved in the hands of Linnaeus, Lyell and Darwin. In the case of Linnaeus, the conceptual apparatus is at best Aristotelian. It is a common-sense, static economy, with elements of competition and implicit ratios of exchange, but none of the mechanisms later associated with classical political economy. But in the case of both Lyell and Darwin, we find numerous insights that have analogues in classical political economy. The most striking one, between Darwin and Smith, is the link between diversification and quantity of life or the Smithian insight that the size of the market is a function of the division of labour.

A significant modification of the concept of the economy of nature came with Lyell's recognition of time-consuming equilibrating processes. This seems to resemble Ricardo's theory of production and distribution far more than Smith's. For the latter, due to the steady influx of precious metals, the money wage was frequently shifting, such that the natural wage was rarely attained. A similar degree of instability, we saw, was captured in the Darwinian scheme. But Ricardo transcends money wages, treating them as more sensitive to population changes than the quantity of gold and silver at hand. As a result, much more emphasis is placed on the return to an equilibrium, due to the action of a self-restoring mechanism. But it is less than instantaneous. An increase in wages will engender a differential profit rate, due to different amounts of capital in different industries. Firms gradually move their resources into the more profitable areas and, due to an increase in supply, lower the market price of that good. This will persist until the profit rate in the capital-intensive industries equals, once again, the profit rate in the labour-intensive industries.[13] In Lyell, we find a similar equilibrating process which hinges upon a difference in 'factors of production', or food and physical conditions required by different life-forms.

Ricardo was also more concerned with the problem of distribution between economic classes, and sceptical about the benefits of innovation (new machinery) in the work place. Lyell, more than Darwin, took species rather than individuals as the unit of analysis. Although Ricardo did not skirt questions of economic growth, in contrast to Smith, the prospect of a steady-state economy loomed on the horizon. Likewise, Lyell, we saw, put much stock in the notion of a fixed quantity of life, which man may usurp from other species but can never increase overall. Darwin, on the other hand, had the remarkable insight that this quantity could grow by a more diverse use of the physical resources at hand.

These analogies are all quite tentative. I simply wish to suggest that, while Darwin has little of Ricardo in him, Lyell seems to bear some resemblance to Ricardo. But did either naturalist cull any of these insights directly from political economy, or were they able to arrive at these concepts using Linnaeus and evidence from natural history alone? Others at the time, George Poulett Scrope most notably, considered links between natural history and economics.[14] At a meeting celebrating the thirtieth anniversary of the Geological Society (to which Ricardo had once belonged), both Lyell and Darwin heard Richard Jones speak on the similarities between political economy and geology. But this failed to inspire Darwin to read further on the subject. To the best of my knowledge, there is no evidence to suggest that he took the trouble to study Ricardo or Mill. Lyell's correspondence, on the other hand, points to a keener interest in the subject. He was also close friends with both Scrope and Nassau Senior and took the trouble to attend J. R. McCulloch's lectures on political economy for an entire year.[15] Martin Rudwick has argued that, more than his contemporaries, Lyell 'saw his geology as a much more open-ended enterprise. . . . [with] little sense of cognitive compartments and boundaries. . . . Lyell was able to quarry creative analogies from a wide range of extra-geological sources.'[16]

One major problem with this thesis is that, to the best of my knowledge, neither Darwin nor Lyell acknowledge Smith or Ricardo in their texts. Professor Schweber has suggested, in the case of Darwin, that this was due to the political overtones surrounding the discipline of economics.[17] But Darwin showed no hesitation in pointing to Malthus as a source of inspiration. Even if one separates Malthus's demographic model from economics (something not in keeping with the period), it was as controversial as any other tenet in Ricardo. Unless further evidence comes to light, it seems we ought to resist imputing to Darwin a witting assimilation of Ricardian economics in his study of the natural world.

## Notes

1. Garret Hardin 1960, 'The competitive exclusion principle', *Science* 131, p. 1295.
2. For their most recent arguments see S. S. Schweber 1985, 'The wider British context in Darwin's theorizing', and Robert M. Young, 'Darwinism *is* social', in David Kohn (ed.) *The Darwinian Heritage* (Princeton University Press, Princeton, N. J.).
3. See, for example, Jack Hirschleifer 1977, 'Economics from a biological viewpoint', *Journal of Law and Economics* 20 pp. 1–52.
4. Robert Stauffer 1960, 'Ecology in the long manuscript version of Darwin's *Origin of Species* and Linnaeus' *Oeconomy of Nature*', *Proceedings of the American Philosophical Society* 104, p. 241; Frank Egerton 1973, 'Changing concepts of the balance of nature', *Quarterly Review of Biology* 48, pp. 341–2; Donald Worster 1977, *Nature's Economy: The Roots of Ecology*, Sierra Club Books, San Francisco, p. 142.
5. See Camille Limoges 1970, *La Selection naturelle: etude sur la première constitution d'un concept*, Presses Universitaires de France, Paris. Henri Milne-Edwards provided Darwin with the notion of the physiological division of labour, which he had extracted from the texts of Jean-Baptiste Say.
6. Also see Neil de Marchi 1970, 'The empirical content and longevity of Ricardian economics', *Economica* 37, pp. 257–76.
7. Carl Linnaeus 1791, *Miscellaneous Tracts Relating to Natural History, Husbandry, and Physick*, trans. Benjamin Stillingfleet. J. Dodsley, London, pp. 39–40. It is interesting to note that Adam Smith had a long-standing interest in Linnaean botany, though to the best of my knowledge, no one has pursued this further.
8. Quoted in Stauffer, op. cit., p. 240.
9. Linnaeus, *Tracts*, p. 119. Others, e.g. William Derham and Lyell engaged in the same thought experiment and reached the same conclusion.
10. Charles Lyell 1830–3, *Principles of Geology*, 2 vols John Murray, London, p. 130 (all quotes are from volume 2).
11. Lyell draws an analogy between insect reproduction and the efficiency of a steam engine; 'no sooner has the destroying commission been executed, than the gigantic power becomes dormant' (ibid., p. 134).
12. Charles Darwin 1859, *The Origin of Species by Means of Natural Selection or the*

*Preservation of Favoured Races in the Struggle for Life*, John Murray, London, p. 82.

13. See Samuel Hollander 1979, *The Economics of David Ricardo*, University of Toronto Press, Toronto, p. 303.

14. See M. J. S. Rudwick 1974, 'Poulett Scrope on the volcanoes of Auvergne: Lyellian time and political economy', *British Journal for the History of Science* 7, pp. 205–42.

15. See Salim Rashid 1981, 'Political economy and geology in the early nineteenth century: similarities and contrasts', *History of Political Economy* 13, p. 729.

16. Martin J. S. Rudwick 1979, 'Transposed concepts from the human species in the early work of Charles Lyell', in L. S. Jordanova and Roy S. Porter (eds) *Images of the Earth: Essays in the History of the Environmental Sciences*, British Society for the History of Science, Chalfont St Giles, Buckinghamshire, p. 79.

17. Silvan S. Schweber 1977, 'Darwin and the political economists: divergence of character', *Journal of the History of Biology* 10, pp. 195–289, especially p. 213.

# 5 Marx's composition of capital: a critical re-examination of some of the theories
## Shalom Groll and Ze'ev B. Orzech

'The question is,' said Alice, 'whether you *can* make words mean so many different things.'

Lewis Carroll, *Alice Through the Looking Glass*

## Introduction

Any general model of the economy must provide clear-cut definitions of the factors of production and specify the mutual relations between them. This is so because there cannot be a general economic theory without rules of production, and because the mutual relations between the factors of production determine different, continually changing socioeconomic situations. This is particularly true of Marx's economic theory which emphasizes the fundamental importance of these relations for society and for historical and economic development, or for what he calls the 'economic base'. Marx refers to the relations between the factors of production as the 'composition of capital'.

The composition of capital is best known in connection with Marx's theory of the falling rate of profit. However, the concept serves a much broader purpose and is used by Marx in the analysis of problems such as the introduction of machines, the level of productivity, value magnitudes, input-output relations, unemployment, the accumulation of capital, economic reproduction and others. The composition of capital plays a crucial role in all these diverse economic processes.

Unfortunately, the very nature of this important Marxian concept is replete with ambiguities and therefore the subject of much controversy. This paper addresses the confusion surrounding the composition of capital.

## Marx's definitions of the composition of capital

Marx explicitly introduces multiple notions of the composition of capital and assigns to each a different meaning. Unfortunately, these different meanings have not always been respected or even considered by Marx's commentators and students. With few exceptions, interpreters do not differentiate among all the compositions of capital and refer to only one or two of them. It is mainly in the last 15–20 years that we have witnessed more analytical attempts to grasp the meanings of the different expressions of this concept and their importance for the Marxian model.

Marx defines the composition of capital in *Capital* I (p. 612). Similar definitions are given in *Capital* III (pp. 144–5), and in volumes II (pp. 275–89, 379–84) and III of *Theories of Surplus Value* (pp. 382–96). The definitions in *Capital* I must be regarded as the most authoritative, for this is the only volume that Marx published himself. Although he introduced changes in many places in the second German edition (1873) of this volume, the changes pertaining to the composition of capital are mainly of a stylistic nature. The later French edition (1875) contains the final version of Marx's compositions of capital. He writes:

> The composition of capital is to be understood in a two-fold sense. On the side of value, it is determined by the proportion in which it is divided into constant capital or value of the means of production, and variable capital or value of labour-power, the sum total of wages. On the side of material, as it functions in the process of production, all capital is divided into means of production and living labour-power. This latter composition is determined by the relation between the mass of the means of production employed, on the one hand, and the mass of labour necessary for their employment on the other. I call the former the *value-composition*, the latter the *technical composition* of capital. Between the two there is a strict correlation. To express this, I call the value-composition of capital, insofar as it is determined by its technical composition and mirrors the changes of the latter, the *organic composition* of capital. (*Capital* I, p. 612).

There is no question that Marx could have defined the composition of capital in a clearer, more accurate language. Still, although we may decry the confusing language of the definitions, his critics deserve no less to be criticized for their misreading and often more confusing interpretations thereof. For, despite their imprecise language, the definitions are sufficiently clear to enable us to decipher Marx's intentions. In the following section we present our interpretation of them.

## Interpretation

### The definitions

We contend that Marx, as he explicitly states in his definitions, employs a tripartite division of the composition of capital into technical (TCC), value (VCC) and organic (OCC) compositions. Each of these concepts stands for a unique relationship, and although the latter two may coincide under certain circumstances, they must yet be viewed as separate entities.

TCC expresses the techno-productive relations between the inputs of the various means of production; it is the ratio of the products of past labour and the input of actual, living labour. TCC thus measures physical quantities (though, as we shall see, these may be expressed in some common unit): the definite quantity of the means of production, K, and the definite amount of the entire (both paid and unpaid), living labour, L, technologically required to operate them. Therefore, for Marx, every TCC represents a specific process or method of production and defines a specific level of productivity: 'the degree of productivity of labour, in a given society, is expressed in the relative extent of the means of production that one labourer, during a given time, with the same tension of labour-power, turns into products . . . the growing extent of the means of production, as compared with the labour-power incorporated with them, is an expression of the growing productiveness of labour' (*Capital*, I, p. 622).[1]

Diagrammatically, in a set of coordinates where the axes measure L and K, TCC is represented by a ray from the origin. It defines a specific point on a given iso-product curve (*Capital*, I, pp. 314–15).[2]

VCC expresses a *cost ratio*,[3] the relation between the sum invested in means-of-production inputs, and the sum expended on hired, living labour-power (i.e. the sum paid as wages and salaries: a part of and not the entire labour-force). Diagrammatically, it is equivalent to the iso-cost line expressed as $P_K K + wL$, where $P_K$ and w are the evaluations of capital and labour. The slope of the line is given by $w/P_K$. (*Capital*, III, p. 51).[4]

The third composition, OCC, is also a cost ratio, but a very particular kind of cost ratio. It is a cost expression derived solely from and imposed by the technical factors and prevailing production conditions. It is, therefore, independent of all other economic factors. Since TCC expresses productivity levels and OCC results from the impact of these levels on values, OCC expresses the ratio of the cost relations in value terms (*Capital*, I, pp. 612, 631).[5] It is useful to restate and underline the differences between the three concepts. TCC differs from VCC and OCC in that:

1.  TCC is a technical expression whereas the other two are cost expressions.
2.  TCC, being a technical expression, cannot be measured directly in its physical units by a common index. It may be viewed, indirectly, as measuring the number of units of living labour needed to produce a given amount of output by the given means

of production. To avoid the aggregation problem, Marx expresses the different physical capitals in value units.

3. TCC, being a techno-productive expression, must refer to the entire amount of labour employed (i.e. the whole workday). It is, thus, relevant for any mode of production and reflects Marx's sociological concept of 'forces of production' (*Capital*, I, pp. 183–4).

We proceed to a discussion of the relations and differences between VCC and OCC. Keeping Marx's definitions in mind, several basic questions must be asked: If OCC is VCC 'in so far as it is determined by . . . [TCC]', what is VCC *when it is not determined* by TCC? What are the factors which determine VCC independently from TCC? And, in case VCC is independently determined, what are the relations between VCC and OCC? We believe that Marx uses the clause 'in so far as' in his definitions not just for stylistic reasons, but to differentiate between economic situations that are expressed in value terms and those that are determined by techno-productive conditions and therefore diverge from values. He is explicit about the possibility of such a divergence of the two measures of the composition of capital. After a detailed discussion of the changing components of the composition of capital, he concludes: 'In other words, capitals of equal organic composition may be of different value-composition, and capitals with identical percentages of value-composition may show varying degrees of organic composition and thus express different stages in the development of social productivity of labour' (*Capital*, III, p. 766; see also pp. 263–5). OCC is directly determined by the prevailing productivity level whereas VCC diverges from OCC because of the influence of economic forces which raise or lower the evaluations from those given by OCC. These new evaluations are market prices.

Our interpretation of Marx's definitions leads us to the following conclusions:

1. Both VCC and OCC are cost relations for a given level of output.
2. So long as the cost relations which specify VCC are determined by production conditions (i.e. TCC) and are therefore equal to the labour-value of the cost components in the production process, VCC and OCC are identical expressions of the (technically generated) costs. In Marx this represents an equilibrium situation.
3. This identity is not maintained, however, if there are other economic forces capable of imposing pressures on the components of

the cost relations. If such forces come into play, they are capable of 'liberating' VCC from being determined by the technical conditions. In this case, VCC departs from OCC.

4. Such a situation is feasible when the exchange ratio between the cost components in the market ceases to be equal to the exchange ratio as determined by the production process. In this case, market forces (e.g. supply and demand) impose evaluations on the relevant commodities that differ from those given by the production conditions.

5. OCC signifies the technically necessary conditions, whereas VCC shows economically possible conditions. OCC represents the cost relations expressed in value terms whereas VCC, 'liberated' from its dependence on OCC, represents the deviation of costs from values. Marx expresses this as the deviation of prices from values and in particular as the deviation of market prices from market values. Prices, therefore, are defined by factors other than production conditions.

6. Marx is concerned with the interaction between techno-productive conditions and the market. Changes in the former represent changes in the mode of production associated with changes in productivity that, in turn, bring about changes in values and cost relations. These changes are of a long-run character. Market forces, on the other hand, are incapable of changing levels of productivity and values. They represent, therefore, temporary, short-run changes as do all market fluctuations. Marx puts it as follows:

> The organic changes and those brought about by changes of value can have a similar effect on the rate of profit in certain circumstances. They differ however in the following way. If the latter are not due simply to fluctuations of market prices and are therefore not temporary, they are invariably caused by an organic change in the spheres that provide the elements of constant or of variable capital. (*Theories*, III, p. 386)

7. There exists an explicit link between the rate of surplus value and the composition of capital. In OCC, the denominator represents the value of the labour power as determined by the labour theory of value. That magnitude changes only with changes in the values of the relevant wage goods. These changes, in turn, are brought about by changes in the productivities in the wage-goods industries. Given the length of the working day, changes

in the value of the labour-power thus determine the size and the rate of surplus-value.

When VCC deviates from OCC and is determined by market conditions rather than by technically-imposed conditions, wages differ from labour values and both the magnitude and the rate of surplus value differ from the ones imbedded in OCC. It should be noted though that labour income – as it appears in the rate of surplus value and in the composition of capital – remains the same in either case.

8. Since productivity changes are transmitted directly from TCC to OCC, a change in OCC represents qualitative changes and is associated with new values, while a change in VCC represents quantitative or market changes.

9. The divergence of the market cost evaluation from the techno-productive evaluation represents the lack of adaptability of Marx's 'production relations' to his 'production forces'. Taken as a cumulative process, this lack of adaptability in the long-run takes the shape of Marx's 'basic contradiction', while in the short run it creates the need for the so-called 'transformation problem'.

10. The divergence process is not affected by the terms in which prices are expressed: market prices or prices of production. We digress briefly from our line of exposition to discuss the difference between these two.

*A digression on prices*
'Market prices' are determined by the interaction of market forces, i.e. supply and demand. Marx's 'prices of production', on the other hand, are calculated by adding to production costs the average profit rate applied to these costs. Production costs vary from industry to industry and the average rate of profit is generated by competition among industries and migration of capital from one industry to the other. The 'price of production' is therefore a relative (general equilibrium) price and not an absolute price. This price distributes the various factors of production among the industries in the economy. Products, on the other hand, are sold at absolute (i.e. market) prices. Products, though, do not have two prices (production and market) attached to them. Only those market prices that clear all markets and enable industries to attain the average profit rate, are included in the price of production. Thus, every price of production is a market price, though not every market price is a price of production.

Both components of the price of production, i.e. costs of production and the average profit rate, can be expressed either in value terms (as in OCC) or in price terms (as VCC). When VCC diverges from OCC, prices of production diverge from their value content. This is the essential nature of the 'transformation problem'. Marx's equalities between the *sum* of values and the *sum* of prices, and between the *sum* of profits and the *sum* of surplus value are not affected by the divergence of VCC from OCC. Since both the costs of production and the average profit rate are evaluated in the same terms (for each of the compositions) when the deviation occurs, the two equalities will be maintained.

*The divergence of VCC from OCC*
Before we proceed to other interpretations of the composition of capital, let us see how Marx explains the divergence of VCC from OCC. The separation of the two measures is rooted in the economic process. The mechanism by which VCC becomes an independent entity is given by the fluctuations of market prices around market values. Since VCC and OCC are singularly specified cost relations, it is necessary to explain how they are determined in a heterogeneous industrial structure.

The heterogeneity stems from the different levels of productivity present in each industry, expressed by their individual TCCs. Marx analyses this in *Theories*, II, and in *Capital*, III, ch. 10. To simplify, he classifies the different levels of productivity into low, average and high (*Theories* II, p. 204).[6] Although the individual values of the products produced in each of the three groups differ depending on the particular level of productivity at which each is produced, the value of the product for the industry as a whole is determined by the 'normal production conditions' of the socially necessary labour, and not by the individual values. Normal conditions of the socially necessary labour are determined by the relative shares of high, average and low productivity components in the total output mix (*Theories*, II, pp. 204–5).[7] This, then, determines *market value* (*Capital*, III, pp. 182–5).[8]

*Market price*, however, can and does deviate from market value. Marx discusses three cases: Case 1, in which market price equals market value; Case 2, in which market price exceeds market value; and Case 3, in which market value exceeds market price (*Capital*, III, pp. 185–7).[9] The condition for Case 1 is the equality of what Marx calls 'total social need' and total output. In essence, this amounts to an equality of effective demand and effective supply. In this case, it is immaterial which level of productivity defines the 'normal conditions' of production: market price equals market value.

In Case 2, total social need exceeds total output. Market price, in this case, equals the market value that would have prevailed had the normal conditions been determined by the least productive category of the industry. This holds true even though most of the output is produced under more favourable techno-productive conditions. In this case, market price exceeds market value.

In Case 3, total output exceeds total social need. Market price, in this case, equals the market value that would have prevailed had the normal conditions been determined by the most productive category of the industry. This holds true even though most of the output is produced under less favourable techno-productive conditions. In this case, market value exceeds market price.

It is because of these 'oscillations of market price around market value' that VCC diverges from OCC. For, as we have shown above, VCC reflects the market price, and OCC the normal techno-productive conditions of the socially necessary labour. Only under the conditions of Case 1 are VCC and OCC equal to one another. In Cases 2 and 3, VCC deviates from OCC and the prevailing cost relations are not defined according to the socially necessary labour. (For a more extensive analysis of normal conditions, market values and prices, see Groll, 1980, pp. 354–70.)

**Variant interpretations**

*A sample of partial definitions*
We believe that the tripartite division of the composition of capital presented above corresponds to Marx's intentions and thus helps to clarify his model. It can also serve to dispel the confusion which so permeates the Marxian literature. That such confusion exists can be deduced from the large number of definitions extant. In general, writers agree as to the distinction between TCC on the one hand, and OCC and VCC on the other. The confusion arises mainly in discussions of the mutual relations between OCC and VCC, with some writers ignoring differences between the two, and others explicitly defining them away. To illustrate this point, we limit ourselves to a few examples from the literature of the post-war period.

Starting with Paul M. Sweezy (1946, p. 66), we find confusion between value and technical measures. He writes: 'Let us designate [the organic composition] by the letter q. Then we have $c/(c+v)=q$. In non-technical language the organic composition of capital is a measure of the extent to which labour is furnished with materials, instruments and machinery in the productive process.' Sweezy speaks of 'labour', i.e. total labour rather than of paid labour; his definition therefore corresponds to TCC and not OCC. Moreover, since he denotes q as c/(c+v), he should have defined his measure (OCC) as the ratio (in value terms) of costs of materials, instruments and machinery in the productive process, to the total sum of costs.

In discussing Marx in her book on models of economic growth, Irma Adelman manages to define OCC in three distinct and contradictory ways (1961, p. 71): 'Marx uses the ratio of constant to variable capital C/V, which he called the "organic composition of capital". This ratio measures the capital and raw materials used per worker employed or "the mass of means of production, as compared with the mass of labour-power that vivifies them".' We see three distinctly separate definitions used interchangeably. Although she discusses OCC (Marx's 'ratio of constant to variable labour C/V'), she defines it first as measuring 'the capital and raw materials used per worker employed' which surely corresponds to TCC and not OCC. She then confuses the issue further by adding, 'or "the mass of means of production, as compared with the mass of labour-power that vivifies them"', which refers to the physical amount of the means of production divided by the physical amount of labour-power. The problem here lies in the confusion between labour-power and the labour of an entire labour day. The former implies a value measure, whereas the latter refers to TCC.

Mark Blaug (1968, p. 229) fails to find any definition of OCC in Marx and therefore imposes two of his own: 'Marx himself never explicitly defined the so-called "organic composition of capital". What he had in mind, however, is clearly the ratio of embodied labour to current labour or of machine costs to labour costs.' We believe that Marx did define OCC although he was not very clear in his definitions. Blaug's substitutions, though, do not fill the bill. For, if the word 'current' in the first part of his definition has any meaning at all, it must refer to TCC and not OCC. The ratio of machine costs to labour costs cannot be considered as OCC, either, so long as its connection to the technical factors is not specified. If the technical conditions are not specified the measure refers to VCC rather than to OCC.

In contrast to the above writers, David S. Yaffe (1973, p. 194) identifies TCC with VCC. He writes: 'Increases in productivity involving increases in the *technical composition of capital* are represented under capitalist production by changes in the *value composition of capital*, i.e. the ratio of constant capital, or value of means of production, and variable capital or value of labour power.' Although Yaffe quoted Marx's definition: 'in so far as it is determined', he, too, does not address the question what VCC represents when it is not determined by TCC.

Philippe Van Parijs (1980, p. 3) also proposes two definitions for OCC (his mnemonic is OCK):

> The OCK can be understood in at least two ways. On the one hand, it can be understood as identical to the *value composition of capital* (VCK), defined as the ratio of the stock of constant capital to the stock of variable capital: VCK = C/V. On the other hand, it can be understood as identical to the *ratio of dead to living labour* (RDL), defined as the ratio of the stock of constant capital to the flow (or stock) of labour-power.

Van Parijs's first definition clearly identifies OCC as VCC. His second definition, however, muddies the water: the first part of it ('ratio of dead to living labour') is in physical terms as used by TCC, whereas the second part is in value terms. It is the more confusing because while using value terms he speaks of 'labour-power', i.e. the entire L.

In contradistinction to Van Parijs who identifies OCC with VCC, Donald J. Harris (1983, p. 313, note 3) equates it with TCC. He recognizes the confusion that exists with respect to the various definitions:

> There is disagreement in the literature about the appropriate measure of the organic composition of capital, that is, whether it should be q or q/v. In using q we follow a now common practice which distinguishes q/v as the 'value composition of capital' from q as the organic composition of capital. The latter is the ratio of labour embodied in means of production (dead labour) to currently employed (living) labour and, as such, may be taken to represent changes in production conditions independently of distributional changes. Both measures give the same result if v is constant. When output is measured in terms of currently employed labour, the organic composition in this sense is equivalent to the familiar concept of 'capital-output ratio' if capital is defined to include only constant capital.

Harris, in identifying OCC as 'the ratio of labour embodied in means of production (dead labour) to currently employed (living) labour', equates it with TCC. In this he contravenes Marx who explicitly distinguishes between them. On the other hand, he correctly distinguishes between the two value measures OCC and VCC. He says that OCC 'may be taken to represent changes in production conditions independently of distributional changes'. Unfortunately he explains neither the reason why, nor the process by which, OCC remains free of these changes.

*Wolff's conception*

Yet another approach to the different concepts of compositions of capital is used by R. P. Wolff. In his attempt to reconstruct Marx, Wolff deviates from him in two important respects: (1) he differentiates between the technical and the physical compositions of capital, and (2) he expresses the latter in value terms.

As to point (1): Wolff criticizes Marx for not being specific in his definition of TCC. He defines it as the vector of all inputs – non-labour technical coefficients plus labour time – necessary to produce one unit of output. His definition is, thus – as is Marx's – in physical terms. On the other hand, he defines the physical composition of capital as the ratio of dead to living labour (Wolff, 1984, p. 216).

Marx, though, does not differentiate between the technical and the physical compositions of capital and uses the concepts interchangeably. He refers to the relationship as 'the amount of raw material and means of labour, that is, the amount of constant capital – in terms of its *material elements* – which corresponds to a definite *quantity of living labour* (paid or unpaid), that is, to the *material elements of variable capital*' (*Theories*, III, p. 382).[10]

Secondly, Wolff deviates from Marx in expressing his 'physical' composition of capital in value terms. He is compelled to do so since he is dealing with an n-sector economy and has to find a common denominator to add up the various inputs.

What is lost by using Wolff's definitions? By defining the compositions of capital his way, Wolff loses the important connection between TCC and the level of productivity. Productivity is basic to the Marxian system because it determines the value of the output. Wolff criticizes Marx's definitions unjustly for omitting the connection between units of input and output (1984, p. 207). Yet, in fact, besides the above-quoted definition of productivity (couched in terms of input-relations), Marx provides a second definition of productivity which is tied to the level of output: 'By increasing the productiveness of labour, we mean, generally, an alteration in the labour-process, of such a kind as to shorten the labour-time socially necessary for the production of a commodity, and to endow a given quantity of labour with the power of producing a greater quantity of use-value' (*Capital*, I, p. 314).[11]

Whereas the first definition emphasizes the decrease of labour relative to capital in the input relations, the second focuses on the decrease of labour relative to output. There is no contradiction between the two definitions. For Marx, technological progress is a capital deepening process, and is represented by an increasing ratio of dead to living labour. Both definitions are completely consonant with the neoclassical definitions of productivity.

Can the important relationship between productivity and the above mentioned ratio be arrived at by using the Wolffian formulations? Wolff reproduces the Marxian concept of the physical composition of capital by writing:

$$\frac{C_i}{V_i+S_i} = \frac{\lambda X_i}{L_i}$$

where, for each industry i (i=1 . . . n), C, V and S stand for the usual Marxian concepts of constant capital, variable capital and surplus value, respectively; $X_1$ is an n-dimensional row vector of non-labour inputs per unit output of i; $\lambda$ is an n-dimensional column vector of labour values of non-labour inputs for the system as a whole; and $L_i$ is the direct labour input per unit output. An increase in productivity affects both the numerator and denominator of the ratio. The numerator is the product of a matrix multiplication. Though one cannot say of a vector that it 'decreases', in Wolff's terms we would expect most of the constituent elements of $X_i$ to decrease with an increase in productivity. The elements in $\lambda$, too, decrease for, according to Marx, the increase in productivity decreases the value per unit of the commodity produced. The numerator therefore decreases. The denominator decreases as well, since it represents a larger output per living labour. The direction in which the ratio changes remains, however, unspecified since Wolff's formulation does not contain any hints as to the relative rates of decrease of the numerator and the denominator. Consequently, the important connection between changes in productivity and changes in the technical composition of capital is missing.

In contrast, in his definition, Marx clearly determines the increase in TCC brought about by an increase in productivity. He says: 'The increase in labour productivity consists precisely in that the share of living labour is reduced while that of past labour is increased, but in such a way that the total quantity of labour incorporated in that commodity declines; in such a way, therefore, that living labour decreases more than past labour increases' (*Capital*, III, pp. 260–61).

Finally, although Wolff is aware of Marx's distinction between the organic and value compositions, he does not incorporate it into his reconstruction.

### Conclusion

Our interpretation of Marx's concept of the composition of capital is exegetical in nature. We base ourselves on Marx's definitions, and draw on the various elements of his theory which connect the contents of the definitions to the operational mechanism of the 'movement of capital as a whole'. We believe that the interpretation we propose brings out the inner logic of the Marxian system and preserves its cohesiveness. It is impossible to understand Marx's economic theory ( as well as his sociological and philosophical ideas) without a thorough understanding of the composition of capital and the role it plays in his *Weltanschauung*.

## Notes

1.  Cf. also, *Capital*, I, pp. 210–11, 314–15, 519–20, 622, 604, 644; *Capital*, III, pp. 60, 102, 108, 145, 163, 205, 212, 216, 222, 226–7, 247, 249, 260–1, 758–9; *Theories*, II, pp. 109, 415–16, 596; *Theories*, III, pp. 227–8, 310–11, 365, 385.
2.  Cf. also *Capital*, I, pp. 612, 622, 645; *Capital*, III, pp. 46, 60, 145, 163, 212, 216–17, 765; *Theories*, II, pp. 276, 277, 278, 279, 282, 283, 288, 455; *Theories*, III, pp. 310–11, 382–3, 365.
3.  'Costs' here refer to capitalists' costs and not 'social' costs as used by Marx.
4.  Cf. also *Capital*, III, pp. 60, 145; *Theories*, II, pp. 276, 278, 280, 283; *Theories*, III, pp. 383, 385(b), 386(c), 387.
5.  Cf. also *Capital*, III, pp. 145–6, 212, 215, 216, 217, 249, 758–9; *Theories*, II, pp. 212, 216, 276–7, 279, 380–1, 382–3; *Theories*, III, pp. 310–11, 383, 386.
6.  Cf. also *Capital*, III, pp. 182–5.
7.  Cf. also *Capital*, III, p. 179.
8.  Cf. also p. 190; *Theories*, II, pp. 204–5, 270–72.
9.  Cf. also *Capital*, III, pp. 198–9; *Theories*, II, pp. 203–10, 254–75, 507–10.
10. Or again, speaking of the technical composition of capital: 'A definite number of labourers corresponds to a definite quantity of means of production, and hence a definite quantity of living labour to a definite quantity of labour materialized in means of production' (*Capital*, III, p. 145). See also *Capital*, I, pp. 210–11, 612, 628; *Capital*, III, pp. 46, 145, 148, 212, 765; *Theories*, II, pp. 276–9, 282, 288; *Theories*, III, pp. 310–11, 382.
11. See also, ibid., pp. 519–20; *Theories*, II, pp. 263, 266.

## References

Adelman, Irma 1961, *Theories of Economic Growth and Development*, Stanford University Press, Stanford, CA.

Blaug, Mark 1968, 'Technical change and Marxian economics', in David Horowitz (ed.) *Marx and Modern Economics*, Monthly Review Press, New York.

Groll, S. 1980, 'The active role of "use value" in Marx's economic analysis', *History of Political Economy* **12** (3).

Harris, Donald J. 1983, 'Accumulation of capital and the rate of profit in Marxian theory', *Cambridge Journal of Economics* **7**.

Marx, Karl 1967, *Capital* I and III, International Publishers, New York.

—1971, *Theories of Surplus Value* II, Progress Publishers, Moscow 1968; Vol. III, Progress Publishers Moscow 1971.

Sweezy Paul, 1946, *The Theory of Capitalist Development: Principles of Marxian Political Economy*, Dobson, New York.

Van Parijs, Philippe 1980, 'The falling rate of profit theory of crisis: a rational reconstruction by way of obituary', *Review of Radical Political Economics* **12** (1) (Spring).
Wolff, R. P. 1984, *Understanding Marx, A Reconstruction and Critique of Capital*, Princeton University Press, Princeton, N.J.
Yaffe, David S. 1973, 'The Marxian theory of crisis, capital and the state', *Economy and Society*, **II** (2).

# 6 P. H. Wicksteed on *Das Kapital*, Volume I

## Ian Steedman

Few critiques of Marx have been more effective than Philip Wicksteed's '*Das Kapital* – a criticism' which appeared in the socialist
*To-Day* in October 1884. (E. J. Hobsbawm, 1979, p. 247)

## I

When Philip Henry Wicksteed (1844–1927) published his critique of
Marx's value theory in 1884, he had been the Unitarian minister of
Little Portland Street chapel, just to the east of London's Regent
Street, for some ten years. Both in London and earlier in the industrial
town of Dukinfield, where he had been minister from 1870–4, Wicksteed was fully alive to the 'social question'. It was thus not surprising
that he became an informed and sympathetic observer of and commen-
tator on – although not an active participant in – the socialist revival
of the 1880s. Collini has written of 'October 1883, the month which
more than any other marked the beginning of that great stirring of
the national conscience over "the social question" which dominated
the rest of the decade' (1979, p. 54), while Wolfe, with a somewhat
different emphasis, has claimed that the 'interest created by the Socialist revival was at its peak [in] the fall of 1883' (1975, p. 162). E. P.
Thompson, in similar vein, has suggested that 'it is possible to date
the effective birth of modern Socialism in Britain from 1883' (1977,
p. 298), there having been no socialist propaganda in Britain during
the period 1860–80 (ibid., p. 276). The first Fabian Tract was published
in April 1884 and in August of that year Hyndman's Democratic
Federation became the Socialist Democratic Federation; by the end
of 1884, William Morris's Socialist League had already split off from
the SDF (ibid., pp. 301, 344). Even these few brief reminders will
perhaps suffice to indicate that Wicksteed's article of October 1884
was, at the very least, topical.

Many of the British socialists of the 1880s – and even later – appear
to have been significantly influenced by the ideas of Henry George.
Wicksteed too came under George's spell. According to R. F. Rattray,
writing in the Unitarian newspaper *The Inquirer* (9 March 1946, pp.

66–7), Wicksteed read *Poverty and Progress* on a Glasgow to London train and 'felt that, if the book was true, there would be a revolution in England; if the book was not true, it must be answered. On his return to London, he as soon as possible gave himself up to the study of economics.' Certainly, Wicksteed wrote to George in 1882 and 1883 and defended Georgeist ideas in three articles in *The Inquirer* during April-May 1883 and in three further *Inquirer* pieces in February 1884. He was also a co-founder, in 1883, with Miss Helen Taylor, Stewart Headlam and J. L. Joynes, of the Land Reform Union and helped in raising money to support George's lecture tour of England and Scotland in 1883–5.

By the end of 1882 or early in 1883, however, Wicksteed had started to study – and be impressed by – Jevons's *Theory of Political Economy* (see his letter of 23 June 1883 to *The Inquirer*) and he was soon expounding Jevonian theory to others. According to R. F. Rattray (cited above), 'The "Economic Circle" was founded by some students at MNC [Manchester New College, Gordon Square, London] among them E. I. Fripp, but the meetings were conducted by Wicksteed. They began in 1884. Presently a Mr. Beeton began to attend and the meetings were transferred to his house [in Belsize Square]. The circle began to be known among economics. H. S. Foxwell, F. Y. Edgeworth and Webb frequently attended and took part. Graham Wallas, Marshall and Cunningham also attended.' (See also, Herford, 1931, pp. 204–11.) Wicksteed and Edgeworth were also involved, according to Wolfe (1975, pp. 178–9) in a Hampstead 'reading circle' for the study of *Capital* I, started in the winter of 1884–5 by a number of Fabians, including George Bernard Shaw and Charlotte Wilson. (See also the reference to 'Mrs. Wilson's economic tea parties'!, op. cit., p. 206: Charlotte Wilson edited Kropotkin's anarchist newspaper *Freedom* from October 1886.) Again according to Rattray (op. cit.), 'The Fabians, who were then Marxist, challenged him [Wicksteed] to write a criticism of Marx for the Socialist monthly, *To-Day*.' We need pursue here neither the question to what extent the Fabians were Marxists, nor the issue whether the challenge arose within the context of the 'economic tea parties' but we should, before turning to Wicksteed's critique of Marx's theory, consider briefly its Jevonian background, in section II. After a brief historical note on the journal *To-Day* in section III, Wicksteed's critique will be presented in section IV. Section V provides a more general discussion of Marx's theory and its relation to Wicksteed's arguments.

## II

As Collison Black points out in his editorial introduction to a recent edition of Jevons's *The Theory of Political Economy*, Jevons 'shifted the focal point of value theory from long-run "normal" values determined by cost of production to short-run exchange-ratios determined by the psychology of the parties making the exchange' (1970, p. 11; note that this edition follows the fourth edition prepared by Jevons's son, H. S. Jevons, in 1911, while Wicksteed in 1884 would have been familiar with the first edition, of 1871, and/or the second, of 1879). Yet while Jevons indeed shifted the *focus* of value theory to the short run, he by no means ignored long-run value theory (and nor does Collison Black imply otherwise). Jevons's chapter IV, 'Theory of Exchange', concludes with a section on 'The Origin of Value', in which Jevons suggests that his value theory 'will, for the most part, harmonize with previous views upon the subject. Ricardo has stated, like most other economists, that utility is absolutely essential to value' (p. 184). Jevons claims that his theory is *both* consistent with the classical theory, when the latter is correct, *and* goes beyond it, in being able to explain the value of rare statues, paintings, costly but redundant products of labour, etc.; his theory is presented as more general (pp. 185–6). Jevons nevertheless gives explicit recognition to the role of labour as a 'determining circumstance' of value (p. 186). Since labour can, in many cases, change the quantities of commodities, it can influence marginal utilities and *hence* values – but marginal utilities are always the immediate regulators of value (pp. 186–7). Although Jevons does not refer here to any long-run/short-run distinction, it might be thought that, had he done so, his notorious 'catena' might not have been seen as merely ridiculous. Even while acknowledging the role of labour as a regulator of value, however, Jevons at once insists both that labour is extremely heterogeneous – which is hardly controversial – and that wage rates must be determined by the values of products and not vice versa; this second claim is not consistent with Ricardo's treatment of relative wages as exogenous, to which Jevons refers here.

The sixth, seventh and eighth sections of Jevons's chapter V, 'Theory of Labour', also bear very directly on Wicksteed's critique. In the sixth section, 'Distribution of Labour', Jevons explains clearly how a man who is free to allocate his time between leisure, 1, and amounts of labour $h_x$ and $h_y$ in the production of two desirable outputs, x and y, will so allocate it that

$$\frac{\partial u}{\partial x} \frac{\partial x}{\partial h_x} = \frac{\partial u}{\partial y} \frac{\partial y}{\partial h_y} = \frac{\partial u}{\partial l}$$

(pp. 199–200, our notation). It follows at once, of course, that

$$\frac{\partial u / \partial x}{\partial u / \partial y} = \frac{\partial h_x / \partial x}{\partial h_y / \partial y}$$

so that the ratio of the marginal utilities of the two outputs is equal to the corresponding ratio of the marginal labour costs of those outputs. Indeed, Jevons opens his seventh section, 'Relation of the Theories of Labour and Exchange', by remarking that his preceding results 'lead directly to the well-known law, as stated in the ordinary language of economists, that value is proportional to the cost of production' (p. 200) – although he is quick to stress that it is *marginal* labour costs which are involved (and to point up the connection with the theory of rent) (pp. 201–2). Both consumption and production adapt to relative prices and it is this 'complicated double adjustment' of quantities (p. 202) which leads price ratios to equal *both* marginal utility ratios *and* marginal labour cost ratios. This mutual relationship is heavily emphasized by Jevons in his eighth section, 'Relations of Economic Quantities', where it is stated in successive sentences, for example, that '*value is proportional to cost of production*' and that 'values per unit are directly proportional to the final degrees of utility' (p. 204). As Jevons stressed some pages later, however, in the section 'Joint Production', a necessary condition for the proportionality of values to marginal labour costs is that labour be free to vary the relative outputs of the things in question (p. 210), an observation which has a direct bearing on Wicksteed's subsequent remarks on the 'value of labour power'.

We may conclude this section by noting some interesting remarks by Collison Black on the second half of Jevons's chapter V. Black observes that while Jevons 'does not explicitly face the question of whether there can be production by labour alone he certainly gives minimal attention to the role of cooperating factors . . . Jevons is in fact dealing with the case of what Karl Marx called "simple commodity production" in which the problems of organization and entrepreneurship do not arise' (p. 25). He goes on to remark that Jevons 'almost implicitly' assumes increasing labour costs and 'certainly does not examine the possibility of constant or increasing returns' (ibid.). As we shall see, Wicksteed too says little of non-labour inputs in his critique but, even if he was Jevons's one true disciple, he does take labour costs to be constant.

**III**

The first volume of *To-Day* was published in May-September 1883, with the sub-title 'A Monthly Gathering of Bold Thoughts' and contained, among other things, translations from parts of the 1872 French edition of Marx's *Capital* I. (Engels was not happy about the quality of these translations.) At the end of 1883, however, publication of the journal was taken over by H. H. Champion, who also published *Justice* – the journal of the Democratic Federation and then of the SDF – from the beginning of 1884 (Pelling, 1979, p. 24). Volume II (new series) of *To-Day* was sub-titled 'The Monthly Magazine of Scientific Socialism' and was edited by E. Belfort Bax (who was also an editor of *Commonweal* and of *Justice*) and J. L. Joynes (with whom, it will be recalled, Wicksteed had collaborated in the founding of the Land Reform Union). In No. 1, January 1884, the editors declared that ' "TO-DAY" will be an exponent of scientific socialism' and that issue contained, indeed, contributions from Hyndman, William Morris, Edward Aveling and Eleanor Marx. Subsequent issues in 1884 contained not only further pieces by these four leading socialists but contributions from, among others, Stewart Headlam, Belfort Bax, Paul Lefargue, Edward Carpenter, George Bernard Shaw, Havelock Ellis, Ferdinand Freiligrath and Sydney Olivier. It can hardly be questioned, then, that in publishing his critique in the October 1884 issue of *To-Day*, Wicksteed was keeping company with the leaders of 'advanced thought' in Britain and hardly doubted that that critique was, therefore, read by those leaders. Indeed, the first item in the issue for January 1885, which contained Shaw's Comment on Wicksteed, was signed by 'The Executive Council of the Social-Democratic Federation'. Later volumes of *To-Day* contained articles by Henry George (April 1886), H. H. Champion (October 1886) and Graham Wallas (March 1889), in addition to pieces by authors already referred to. It became more Fabian in orientation, its final editor being Hubert Bland, whom Bernstein referred to, in a letter to Babel of 20 October 1898, as 'the acute Fabian Hubert Bland' (Gay, 1952, p. 61 and n. 29). Volume XI, No. 68 was transmogrified into *The International Review*, No. 1, July 1889, edited by Hyndman – this No. 1 was also the last number.

**IV**

Wicksteed begins his '*Das Kapital*: a Criticism' by saying, 'I have long wished to lay before the disciples of Karl Marx certain theoretical objections to the more abstract portion of *Das Kapital* which suggested themselves to me on my first reading of that great work, and which a patient and repeated study of it have failed to remove' (p. 705). (Wicksteed's article originally appeared on pp. 388–409 of the October 1884 issue of *To-Day* but page references given here will be to the more accessible reprint in Wicksteed, 1933.) Unfortunately, he does not explain what he intends by 'have *long* wished'; as was seen above, it was no more than two years earlier that Wicksteed had discovered Jevonian theory, the clear basis for his critique of Marx's value theory. We can be more certain that Wicksteed's reference to Marx's 'great work' was intended straightforwardly. He also writes of 'the great Socialist thinker' and of 'so profound and abstruse a work as *Das Kapital*' (p. 710); he twice praises Marx's analysis, in the later part of Volume I, of accumulation and unemployment (pp. 707, 724); and the long footnote on pp. 707–8, his distinction between communistic, patriarchal and commercially organized societies on p. 718 and, indeed, the general tenor of Wicksteed's whole critique indicates clearly that the critique was grounded in a careful and subtle appreciation of Marx's work. That appreciation was, of course, not based on an English translation, for the first such translation of *Capital* I appeared only in 1887 – Wicksteed writes (p. 706, n. 1), 'I cite from the second German edition (1872), which is probably the one in the hands of most of my readers. References to the French translation are added in square brackets.' (Not surprisingly, Wicksteed does not discuss any differences between Chapter 1 of the first German edition and the opening chapters of the second German and the first French editions.) Since Volume II was not published in German until 1885, and Volume III until 1894, Wicksteed naturally refers only to Volume I, and he makes clear that 'I speak, of course, of the single volume published' (p. 707). It is thus not surprising – but is still important to note – that Wicksteed's criticism of Marx's theory has nothing whatever to do with the (subsequently notorious) 'transformation problem'. In Wicksteed's view, a fatal flaw in Marx's value theory can be found *within* the very first chapter of *Capital* I itself.

After presenting a clear, accurate and fair statement of some of Marx's arguments, Wicksteed summarizes as follows:

> First. The (exchange) value of a ware is determined by the amount of labour needed on the average to produce it.
> Second. There is such a degree of correspondence between the value of a ware and its average selling price, that for theoretical purposes we must assume that nominally wares are bought and sold at their values.
> Third. Labour-force is (in our industrial societies) a ware subject to the same laws and conditions of value and exchange as other wares. (p. 710)

And he observes, 'Against the second (when a correct definition of value has been reached) I have nothing to urge. It is the first and third that I wish to test' (ibid.) – although it transpires that his test of the third claim involves little more than an application of his rejection of the first.

Wicksteed *accepts* Marx's claim that (in Wicksteed's words), 'the fact of two wares being exchangeable . . . implies of necessity both . . . that they are *not identical* . . . and that they are different manifestations or forms of *a common something* (else they could not be equated against each other). In other words, things that are exchangeable must be *dissimilar in quality*, but yet they must have some common measure, by reduction to which the equivalent portion of each will be seen to be *identical in quantity*' (pp. 710–11). (On Wicksteed's acceptance of this claim, see also pp. 712, 713. In stark contrast to Wicksteed's position is that adopted by Böhm-Bawerk in his critique of Marx, *History and Critique of Interest Theories* (chapter XII, B, b), also of 1884. Böhm-Bawerk accepts Marx's claim about the necessary existence of a 'common something' *purely* for the sake of the argument, making it perfectly clear that he really sees no basis for the claim.) Wicksteed disposes quickly of the 'qualitative dissimilarity' – which lies in different 'use-values' in Marx's terms 'or, as I should express it, *commodities differ one from another in their specific utilities*' (p. 711) – in order to concentrate on the central question, 'What is the *common something* of which each ware is a more or less?' (ibid).

Wicksteed first sets out Marx's answer to this question, namely that various wares 'are all products of abstract human labour' (p. 711; Wicksteed makes it very clear that, according to Marx, the heterogeneity of specific types of labour must be abstracted from). He then remarks, 'Now the leap by which this reasoning lands us in labour as the sole constituent element of value appears to me so surprising that I am prepared to learn that the yet unpublished portions of *Das Kapital* contain supplementary or elucidatory matter which may set it in a new light' (p. 712). But with respect to Volume I, Wicksteed continues, 'Marx himself introduces a modification into his result (or develops a half-latent implication in it), in such a way as to vitiate the very analysis on which that result is founded' (ibid.). For only a few pages after Marx has stated the common element to be abstract labour,

we find the important statement that *the labour does not count unless it is useful*. . . . Simple and obvious as this seems, it in reality surrenders the whole of the previous analysis. . . . If only useful labour counts, then when the wares are reduced to mere indifferent products of such labour in the abstract, they are still *useful* in the abstract, and therefore it is not true that 'nothing remains to them but the one attribute of being products of labour' . . . for the attribute of being useful also remains to them. In this all wares are alike. (ibid.)

Wicksteed now presses his point harder. Marx uses reproducible wares in his examples,

But for all that his analysis is based on the bare fact of exchangeability. This fact alone establishes . . . heterogeneity and homogeneity. Any two things which normally exchange for each other, whether products of labour or not . . . must have that 'common something' in virtue of which things exchange and can be equated with each other. . . . Now the 'common something', which all exchangeable things contain, is neither more nor less than abstract *utility*, *i.e.* power of satisfying human desires. (p. 713)

Not surprisingly, Wicksteed immediately rejects any suggestion that

there is no common measure to which we can reduce the satisfaction derived from such different articles as Bibles and brandy, for instance (to take an illustration suggested by Marx), for as a matter of fact we are all of us making such reductions every day. If I am willing to give the same sum of money for a family Bible and for a dozen of brandy, it is because I have . . . found them equivalent. In economic phrase, the two things have equal abstract utility for me. In popular (and highly significant) phrase, each of the two things is *worth* as much to me as the other. (p. 713)

(The commensurability of such disparate items as Bibles and brandy was to remain a central emphasis in Wicksteed's later *Alphabet* (1888) and *Common Sense* (1910).)

While Wicksteed had described himself, on his opening page, as 'making no illusions to myself as to the probability of serious and matured convictions being shaken, on either side, by such a controversy' (p. 705), he now allows himself the (optimistic) observation:

I venture to think that if any student of Marx will candidly re-peruse the opening portion of *Das Kapital*, and especially the remarkable section on 'the two-fold character of the labour represented in wares' . . . he will be compelled to admit that the great logician has at any rate fallen into formal (if not, as I believe to be the case, into substantial) error, has passed unwarrantably and without warning, from one category into another, when he makes the great leap from specific utilities into objectivised abstract labour . . . and has given us an argument which can only become formally correct when so modified and supplemented as to accept *abstract utility* as the measure of value. (p. 714)

Having demonstrated, to his own satisfaction, the error in Marx's argument, Wicksteed proceeds to devote several pages to arguing that the Jevonian theory is more general and, more particularly, that it therefore *includes*, under appropriate conditions, the possibility that relative commodity prices will be proportional to labour costs. This naturally reminds one of the argument, cited above, which Jevons put forward in chapter V of his *Theory of Political Economy*. And it is, indeed, in this context that Wicksteed makes his main references to Jevons. He proposes, as an objection to his own argument, that 'if owing to some new invention A could be made henceforth with half the labour that it requires to make B it would still perform the same service for me as it did before, and would therefore be equally useful *but its exchange value would be less'* (p. 715). And he then remarks:

> It is the complete and definitive solution of the problem thus presented which will immortalize the name of Stanley Jevons, and all that I have attempted or shall attempt in this article is to bring the potent instrument of investigation which he has placed in our hands to bear upon the problems under discussion. Under his guidance we shall be able to account for the *coincidence*, in the case of ordinary manufactured articles, between 'exchange value' and 'amount of labour contained', while clearly perceiving that exchange value itself is always immediately dependent, not upon 'amount of labour', but upon abstract utility. (ibid.)

Wicksteed is sensitive to Marx's concern with the relevance of social context for the form of economic phenomena and begins the present stage of his argument by saying that, 'Exchange value is a phenomenal manifestation (conditioned by our present social and industrial organization) of *equivalence of utility*, which equivalence of utility would, and does, exist even under industrial conditions which render its manifestation in the particular form of exchange value impossible' (p. 716). Citing Marx's own quip that 'since Political Economy delights in Robinsoniads, let us begin with Robinson on his island', Wicksteed accepts Marx's invitation and explains why Robinson Crusoe would so allocate his labour time that the marginal utilities of his various products would be proportional to their respective marginal labour costs (pp. 716–17). He then turns to 'the case of an industrial community the labour of which is directed to the immediate supply of the wants of its own members, without the intervention of any system of exchange' (p. 717). Making no reference to any input other than labour, and assuming *constant* labour costs, Wicksteed supposes that one coat costs eight times the labour that one hat costs but that, in an initial situation, an extra hat would have the same utility as an extra coat. (Here, as in the *Alphabet* (1888), Wicksteed speaks of diminishing marginal utility; in the *Common Sense* (1910) only equivalence at the margin is referred to.) More labour would be directed to the production of hats and less to that of coats; if this reallocation of labour be pushed to the point at which an extra hat would have half the utility of an extra coat, it should still be pushed yet further (p. 717). 'Equilibrium' will be established only when labour is so allocated that an extra hat would have one-eighth of the utility of an extra coat. 'But observe a coat is not worth eight times as much as a hat to this community, because it takes eight times as long to make it (that it always did, even when *one* hat was worth as much to the community as a coat) – but the community is willing to devote eight times as long to the making of a coat, because when made it will be worth eight times as much to it' (p. 718).

'The transition to the industrial conditions under which we actually live is easy', Wicksteed continues (ibid.), but unfortunately he is, in fact, much less explicit in the ensuing paragraph than he was in his discussion of the hypothetical 'hat and coat' society. Making no reference to any conditions of production, he confines himself to saying little more than that in 'a commercially organized society' (ibid.) the (exchange) values of A and B will be equal when A and B are of equivalent utility to a purchaser of both, just as A and B will be of equal 'worth' under that same condition whether the society be commercially organized or not. In compensation, however, Wicksteed then remarks that 'One point remains to be cleared up' (p. 719), and he proceeds to stress the importance of the 'margin of supply' (ibid.) and to illustrate his argument by analysing the response to 'an improvement in the manufacture of watches . . . which saves twenty-five per cent of the labour' (p. 720), reducing the labour cost from twelve days to nine. The initial equilibrium price of a watch is taken to be £10. As flow supply increases, 'The value of watches has fallen, *not because they contain less labour*, but because the recent increments have been *less useful*, and . . . the utility of the last increment determines the value of the whole' (pp. 720–1). The new equilibrium price of a watch will be £7:10s – i.e. 75 per cent of the initial £10 – 'yet it is not worth £7:10s, neither more nor less, because it contains nine days of a certain quality of labour, but men are willing to put nine days and no more of such labour into it, because when made it will be worth £7:10s., and it will be worth that sum in virtue of its utility at the margin of supply which . . . determines its exchange value' (p. 721). It will be clear that Wicksteed here again assumes *constant* labour costs, unlike Jevons, and that he ignores all non-labour inputs (unless the twelve days and the nine days of labour are vertically integrated quantities, any other primary inputs are free, and either interest charges are zero or the new 'time-structure' of the labour inputs is the same as the old one. With other assumptions, a 25 per cent saving in the labour inputs would not lead to a 25 per cent reduction in the price of a watch). Note too that Wicksteed implicitly takes other prices to be unchanged; and that in the *Alphabet* Wicksteed was decidedly cautious about any interpretation of the money price of a commodity as its marginal 'social' utility (1888, pp. 78, 86–8). Within these limits, however, Wicksteed has now extended the conclusion drawn from his Robinsonaid and from his 'hat and coat' society to a commercial society.

Wicksteed now concludes his 'test' of the first proposition which he had attributed to Marx by arguing that not only does the theory of diminishing marginal utility account fully for the relative values of articles that can be indefinitely multiplied by the application of labour (p. 721) but that it *also* provides an explanation of the (changing) relative values of those things, such as 'specimens of old china, pictures by deceased masters, and to a greater or lesser degree, the yield of all natural or artificial monopolies' (p. 722), 'the number and quality of which labour is powerless to affect' (ibid.). (Wicksteed does not explain in what sense he sees 'the yield of . . . monopolies' as being not variable by labour input.) Such things are exchanged and must therefore be regarded as containing the 'common something', Wicksteed insists: 'I cannot see how any analysis of the act of exchange, which reduces the "common something" implied in that act to *labour* can possibly be applied to this class of phenomena' (ibid.).

Having dismissed, to his own satisfaction, the first proposition – that (exchange) value is proportional to average labour input – Wicksteed deals far more rapidly (arguably, too rapidly) with the third proposition – that the (exchange) value of labour-power is determined in just the same way as that of other wares (commodities). Relative exchange values of freely reproducible things will tend to equality with the corresponding relative labour costs, he reiterates:

> But if there is any commodity C, to the production of which a man who has labour at his disposal can *not* direct that labour at his will, then there is no reason whatever to suppose that the value of C will stand in any relation to the amount of labour which it contains. . . . Now this is the case with labour-force in every country in which the labourer is not personally a slave . . . therefore, there is no economic law the action of which will bring the value of labour-force, and the value of other commodities, into the ratio of the amounts of labour respectively embodied in them. It appears to me, therefore, that Marx has failed to indicate any immanent law of capitalistic production by which a man who purchases labour-force at its value will extract from its consumption a surplus value. (p. 723)

Wicksteed concludes by praising the 'contributions of extreme importance' which Marx has made 'in the latter portion of the published volume of *Das Kapital*' – adding that he 'cannot see that they stand in any logical connection with the abstract reasoning of his early chapters' (p. 724).

## V

It may be useful here to consider certain passages in Volumes I and III of *Capital* – the latter not known to Wicksteed at the time of his criticism, of course – which seem to bear on the issues raised by Wicksteed. It is readily confirmed, first of all, that Marx did indeed take 'use-value' to be an important 'background' condition. Thus, 'A thing can be a use-value without being a value. This is the case whenever its utility to man is not mediated through labour. Air, virgin soil, natural meadows, unplanted forests, etc. fall into this category. . . . Finally, nothing can be a value without being an object of utility. If the thing is useless, so is the labour contained in it; the labour does not count as labour, and therefore creates no value' (I, p. 131; page references to *Capital* I and III are to the Penguin editions of 1976 and 1981, respectively). Again, commodities 'must stand the test as use-values before they can be realized as values. For the labour expended on them only counts in so far as it is expended in a form which is useful for others. . . . The owner of a commodity is prepared to part with it only in return for other commodities whose use-value satisfies his own need' (I, pp. 179–80). Nor does Marx give only an 'individual purchaser' dimension to the importance of use-value. In discussing the social allocation of labour between the various spheres of production, he insists that, 'Use-value still remains a condition' (III, p. 774) and argues that, 'Only such-and-such a quantity of [necessary labour-time] is required in order to satisfy the social need. The limit in this case emerges through the use-value. Under the given conditions of production, society can spend only so much of its total labour-time on one particular kind of product' (III, pp. 774–5). As is already implied by Marx's reference to virgin soil, unplanted forests, etc. cited above, use-value here is not related only to final consumption goods. Non-produced inputs are said to be use-values (I, p. 131 and many places in III, Part Six, on Ground-Rent); the now-famous 'Results of the Immediate Process of Production' (I, pp. 948–1084) is replete with references to the use-values of produced inputs; and Marx writes of labour-power that, 'its use-value consists in the subsequent exercise of that power' (I, p. 277).

In discussing 'The Process of Exchange', Marx writes at one point that, 'Things are in themselves external to man, and therefore alienable. In order that this alienation [*Verausserung*] may be reciprocal, it is only necessary for men to agree tacitly to treat each other as the private owners of those alienable things' (I, p. 182). Presumably Marx does not really mean that ownership is a strictly sufficient condition for reciprocal alienation; each thing owned must also be a potential use-value for its initial non-owner. 'Nothing is settled with the legal power of these persons to use and misuse certain portions of the globe. The use of this power depends entirely on economic conditions, which are independent of their wills. The legal conception itself means nothing more than that the landowner can behave in relation to the land just as any commodity owner can with his commodities' (III, p. 753). Nevertheless, when land is both owned and useful, 'the earth is bought or sold just like any other commodity' (III, p. 762). If the earth in question should be virgin soil (see III, p. 807 on the price of untilled land), then something not produced by any labour has a price, an exchange-value in terms of gold. Hence 'abstract-labour content' is not a 'common something' inherent in *all* things subject to exchange.

What was Marx's view of such phenomena and of their relation to his insistence that 'abstract-labour' is the basis of 'value' and hence of exchange-value? Part Six of Volume III, from which the above references to land are taken, was of course written before Volume I was published in 1867 – probably in 1864/1865, in fact. Moreover, Volume I itself contains references to things having a price but no value. Already in Chapter 3 one reads that 'Things which in and for themselves are not commodities, things such as conscience, honour, etc., can be offered for sale by their holders, and thus acquire the form of commodities through their price. Hence a thing can, formally speaking, have a price without having a value' (I, p. 197). After some nonsense about such prices being 'imaginary, like certain quantities in mathematics', Marx writes that 'the imaginary price-form may also conceal a real value-relation or one derived from it, as for instance the price of uncultivated land, which is without value because no human labour is objectified in it' (ibid.). And later in the same chapter Marx, with dramatic quotations from both Sophocles and Shakespeare in support, notes that even Phoenician virgins and the bones of the saints come to have a price (I, p. 229). Hence we cannot answer our question by the simple expedient of supposing that Marx became aware of the phenomena at issue only after publishing Volume I.

Unsurprisingly, Marx recognized clearly the role of 'nature' in the production of wealth:

Use-values . . . are combinations of two elements, the material provided by nature, and labour. If we subtract the total amount of useful labour of different kinds . . . a material substratum is always left. This substratum is furnished by nature without human intervention. . . . Labour is therefore not the only source of material wealth, i.e. of the use-values it produces. As William Petty says, labour is the father of material wealth, the earth is its mother. (I, pp. 133–4)

Since non-produced inputs from 'nature' are essential in the production of use-values but do not themselves incorporate 'abstract labour', it is appropriate that Marx's Volume III, Part Six, 'The Transformation of Surplus Profit into Ground-Rent', should contain a number of observations on the relations between use-value, labour and exchange-value. (It may be noted that, according to Engels, the material incorporated in this section of Volume III had been left by Marx in a relatively finished form; see III, p. 96.)

Near the beginning of Part Six, Marx notes that the price of a piece of land is the ground-rent capitalized at the rate of interest (III, p. 760; the point is repeated at pp. 763, 807, 911–12). Such a price, he affirms, is 'a category that is *prima facie* irrational, in the same way that the price of labour is irrational, since the earth is not the product of labour, and thus does not have a value' (III, p. 760). (Marx waxes even more indignant about the 'irrationality' of a price of land at III, p. 914.) And a few pages later he suggests that,

we must keep in mind . . . that the prices of things that have no value in and of themselves – either not being the product of labour, like land, or which at least cannot be reproduced by labour, such as antiques, works of art by certain masters, etc. – may be determined by quite fortuitous combinations of circumstances. For a thing to be sold, it simply has to be capable of being monopolized and alienated. (III, p. 772)

In discussing differential rent, in the context of factories powered by waterfalls or by steam, Marx then writes: 'Use-value is altogether the bearer of exchange-value but not its cause. If the same use-value could be obtained without labour, it would have no exchange-value. On the other hand, however, a thing cannot have exchange-value without having use-value, i.e. without being such a natural bearer of labour' (III, p. 786). 'The price of the waterfall, besides, is altogether an irrational expression concealing a real economic relationship. The waterfall, like the earth in general and every natural force, has no value, since it represents no objectified labour and hence no price, this being in the normal case nothing but value expressed in money. Where there is no value, there is *eo ipso* nothing to be expressed in money' (III, p. 787). Differential rent, more generally, Marx takes to have two bases, location and fertility (III, p. 789), where fertility refers to 'the difference in the natural fertility of soil types' (III, p. 797), i.e., to difference in use-value. Straying briefly into Volume III, Part Seven, we may note also Marx's remark that, 'Value is labour. So surplus-value cannot be earth' (III, p. 954).

Marx refers at one point to 'a genuine monopoly price, which is determined neither by the price of production of the commodities nor by their value, but rather by the demand of the purchasers and their ability to pay, consideration of which therefore belongs to the theory of competition, where the actual movement of market prices is investigated' (III, p. 898). And a few pages later, he writes that, 'by monopoly price here we mean any price determined simply by the desire and ability of the buyer to pay, independently of the price of the product as determined by price of production and value. A vineyard bears a monopoly price if it produces wine which is of quite exceptional quality but can be produced only in a relatively small quantity' (III, p. 910). Later, in Part Seven, Marx seeks to put a quantitative limit on monopoly prices: 'A monopoly price for certain commodities simply transfers a portion of the profit made by the other commodity producers to the commodities with the monopoly price. Indirectly, there is a local disturbance in the distribution of surplus-value among the various spheres of production, but this leaves unaffected the limit of the surplus-value itself' (III, p. 1001).

With respect to the 'third proposition' which Wicksteed attributes to Marx, we may note that Chapter Six of Volume I is entitled 'The Sale and Purchase of Labour-Power', no reference being made in this title to the *production* of labour-power. Within this chapter, Marx refers to labour-power as a 'peculiar commodity' (I, p. 274), refers to 'the peculiar nature of labour-power as a commodity' (I, p. 277) and then writes yet again of 'this peculiar commodity' (I, p. 279); three times within this short but crucial chapter of only eleven pages, Marx marks the 'peculiarity' of this commodity. But he simply asserts, very quickly, that, 'Like all other commodities it has a value' (I, p. 274), while it is hardly self-evident, in fact, that labour-power either is a commodity or has a value *when the terms 'commodity' and 'value' are used in Marx's sense*. One might ask: is labour-power produced for the purpose of exchange? Is it produced in profit-maximizing, cost-minimizing capitalist industries? Why can it be said to have a value equal to that of its 'produced inputs' – real wage goods – with no direct labour element to be included (I, p. 274)? Marx might seem merely to side-step the fact that labour-power, unlike commodities in general, is not produced by capitalist industries, by writing, 'Given

the existence of the individual, the production of labour power consists
in his reproduction of himself or his maintenance' (ibid.).

We do not know of any comment by Wicksteed on the above
passages – or any others – from Volume III but it is, of course,
tempting to ask how he would have responded to them. The sensible
answer is: 'We do not know.' A rash answer is that the following
responses would at least have been in keeping with the general tenor
of Wicksteed's writings. Marx clearly recognizes that the possession
of use-value is a necessary condition for the possession of exchange
value. He acknowledges too that untilled land, Phoenician virgins,
rare wines, antiques and, indeed, many 'monopolized' things have
exchange-value without possessing value (in Marx's sense). Hence,
Wicksteed could have argued, Marx says, albeit only implicitly, that
the possession of use-value might be a possible candidate for being a
'common something' involved in all exchangeable things, while
'abstract labour' is certainly not such a candidate. Marx's own discussions of land suffice to show that his derivation, from the mere
fact of exchange, of abstract labour as the 'common element' was
illegitimate. While it is true that Marx views the price of land as the
capital value of rents, and treats both rents and the interest rate as
being related – even if indirectly – to value quantities, the fact remains
that land itself has exchange-value but not value. Even *if* it is true
that 'most' exchange involves commodities produced for sale, Wicksteed might conceivably have continued, Marx's 'derivation' was
flawed in principle. And as a matter of fact, the purchase and sale of
land (broadly interpreted) and of labour-force, neither of which is
produced for sale under competitive pressures, are far from unimportant. The only genuinely interesting question is how Marx both recognized all the relevant phenomena and adhered so firmly to his 'abstract
labour argument', not merely using it but insisting on its necessity in
scientific political economy.

We shall not be so rash as to speculate on how Wicksteed might
have responded to that 'genuinely interesting question' but some possible lines of reply on behalf of Marx may be hinted at here, albeit
only briefly, since their proper development and evaluation would
require a major work in itself. It might be questioned, first, whether
Marx's argument about the 'common something' in the first chapter
of *Capital* I is really 'based on the bare fact of exchangeability'. That
chapter is, after all, entitled 'The Commodity', and a commodity, for
Marx, is not *any* object of exchange but is, much more specifically,
an object produced by labour for the purpose of exchange. Throughout
his chapter 1 discussion, therefore, Marx is considering only objects

which are, by definition, both products of labour and use-values for someone other than the producers (or, at the very least, objects which the producers expect to be use-values for others). In the context of *that* discussion, then, it would not be legitimate to fault Marx's 'logic' by pointing to the existence (as Marx does himself later on) of exchanged objects not produced by labour; that would be pointing – it might be urged – not to a logical error on Marx's part but to the need for, or possibility of, a more wide-ranging discussion of exchange-value. It might then be argued further that, since Marx rejects all particular useful properties of commodities as a possible 'common something' (I, p. 127) and continues: 'If then we disregard the use-value of commodities, only one property remains, that of being products of labour' (I, p. 128), Marx's 'logic' is sound *if* he has some good substantial or methodological ground for denying the concept of 'abstract utility'. This line of thought could, of course, become a defence of Marx's chapter 1 argument, against Wicksteed's critique, *only* when such a substantial or methodological ground were produced and convincingly defended.

Rather than seeking to defend Marx's chapter 1, some might content themselves with trying to explain why Marx argued as he did. Thus attention might be drawn, for example, to Marx's interesting list, at the conclusion of chapter 1 of *A Contribution to the Critique of Political Economy*, of what he saw as the four principal problems raised by serious critics of Ricardo: 'Since the determination of exchange-value by labour-time has been formulated and expounded in the clearest manner by Ricardo, who gave to classical political economy its final shape, it is quite natural that the arguments raised by economists should be primarily directed against him' (Marx, 1971, p. 61). The four major problems are, in Marx's view, that of explaining wages, that of explaining the existence of a surplus, that of relating supply-and-demand considerations to the determination of exchange-value by labour-time and, finally, that of explaining how such things as land can possess exchange-value while containing no labour-time (ibid., pp. 61–3). In each case, Marx seems to take the labour-time explanation of exchange-value as *given* and to see the problem in terms of reconciling the phenomenon in question with that given explanation; this last is unquestioned, taken for granted. It might then be suggested that 'all' that Marx was seeking to do in chapter 1 of *Capital* I (which can, after all, be seen as a direct descendant of the *Contribution to the Critique*) was to provide a 'logical' background to the *already accepted* theory of Ricardo for the case of freely reproducible commodities; that Marx was not there even attempting a real 'proof' of the labour-time theory. It will be clear that, however interesting or correct this account may be as an explanation of *why* Marx argued as he did in chapter 1, it does nothing to *defend* Marx's argument against Wicksteed's critique. If there is a defence against that critique, it must be found elsewhere.

## Acknowledgements
I thank the staff of Dr Williams's Library, London, the John Rylands Library, Manchester, and the Manchester College Library, Oxford, for their assistance and the Leverhulme Trust for the award of a Research Grant, in Autumn 1983, which greatly facilitated much of the work on which this paper is based. I am grateful to M. Blaug, D. Elson, H. Kurz, P. Leeson, C. Levy, A. Roncaglia and S. Rigby for their reactions to a previous draft. Particular thanks are also given to M. Evans, T. Peach and B. Schefold for their influence on section V of the present version. I need not state who is responsible for the remaining shortcomings.

A longer version of this paper, including further discussion of the *To-Day* debate, of George Bernard Shaw and of Eduard Bernstein, was published in my *From Exploitation to Altruism*, Polity Press, Cambridge, 1989; I am grateful to Polity Press for permission to publish the present version.

## References
Collini, S. 1979, *Liberalism and Sociology*, Cambridge University Press, Cambridge.
Gay, P. 1952, *The Dilemma of Democratic Socialism: Eduard Bernstein's challenge to Marx*, Columbia University Press, New York.
Herford, C. H. 1931, *Philip Henry Wicksteed. His Life and Work*, Dent, London and Toronto.
Hobsbawm, E. J. 1979, *Labouring Men. Studies in the history of labour*, Weidenfeld & Nicolson, London.
Jevons, W. S. 1970, *The Theory of Political Economy* (1871), ed. R. D. Collison Black, Penguin Books, Harmondsworth.
Marx, K. H. 1971, *A Contribution to the Critique of Political Economy* (1859), Lawrence and Wishart, London.
— —1976, *Capital*, Volume I (1867), Penguin Books, Harmondsworth.
— —1981, *Capital*, Volume III (1894), Penguin Books, Harmondsworth.
Pelling, H. 1979 (2nd edn), *The Origins of the Labour Party, 1880–1900* (1954) Oxford University Press, Oxford.
Thompson, E. P. 1977, (revised edition), *William Morris. Romantic to Revolutionary* Merlin Press, London.
Wicksteed, P. H. 1888, *The Alphabet of Economic Science. Part I. Elements of the theory of value or worth*, Macmillan, London.
— —1933, *The Common Sense of Political Economy*, Volume II (1910), ed. L. Robbins, Routledge, London.
Wolfe, W. 1975, *From Radicalism to Socialism: Men and ideas in the formation of Fabian socialist doctrines, 1881–1889*, Yale University Press, New Haven, Conn.

# 7 Tugan-Baranovsky, Russian revisionism and Marxian political economy

## M. C. Howard and J. E. King

### I. Introduction

Today the term 'revisionism' is frequently identified with the criticism of Marxian orthodoxy which emerged within the German Social Democratic Party (SPD) during the 1890s. This reflects the dominant position of German social democracy in the Second International, both practically and ideologically. It had the largest mass membership and its theoreticians, most notably Karl Kautsky, defined the orthodox position on the development of advanced capitalism and the appropriate strategy through which socialism could be achieved.[1] The first serious attempt to 'revise' doctrine at the centre of the socialist movement has naturally been seen by intellectual historians to be of paramount importance, and has come to be widely accepted as defining 'revisionism' itself. However, there was a Russian counterpart to the German school represented by the so-called 'legal Marxists'.[2] It is now recognized that the Russian revisionists began questioning basic principles as early as 1890, while Bernstein – the principal German revisionist – was still an orthodox Marxist.[3] What we argue here is that their criticisms were also more acute than those of the Germans, and that revolutionary Marxism within Russia was significantly influenced by them.[4] In addition, Russian revisionism anticipated viewpoints that would characterize much of 'western Marxism' in the twentieth century.

'Legal Marxism', from which Russian revisionism emerged, was a response to the populist socialism which dominated the intelligentsia in the latter half of the nineteenth century. Populism was a diffuse movement and represented a unity only in so far as it embodied a hostility to capitalist development, and a disposition to base progress upon the traditional institutions of Russian economic life. There was considerable diversity of opinion as to what exactly constituted 'progress', how it was best achieved, the extent to which capitalism posed a threat, and the health and adaptability of non-capitalist institutions.[5] But in the last two decades of the century populist ideology achieved greater coherence, with the argument that Russian capitalist development was blocked, so that comprehensive emulation of Europe was not only undesirable but also impossible. If Russia were to survive as a sovereign power, economic evolution had therefore to be predominantly non-capitalist. The alternative was a subordination to Western nations, perhaps even formal colonization.

The populists' economic arguments are outlined in the next section. Here we note only that they were bound to be opposed by all Marxists, for whom, and despite Marx's own sympathy for populist doctrine,[6] progress towards socialism depended upon the prior development of capitalism. If Russian capitalist development were indeed blocked, a socialist Russia would be impossible. From the beginning of the 1880s with the work of Plekhanov, Axelrod and Zasulich,[7] orthodox Marxists began to criticize populism systematically, and during the 1890s there was a 'great debate' which finally secured the victory of the Marxists at the level of ideas. It is here that the legal Marxists came to prominence, but they also began critically to examine orthodox Marxism itself. Thus, rather paradoxically, Russian revisionism was born within a concerted attempt to defend Marxism against populist socialists. Perhaps because of this tension, it proved to be intellectually more vibrant than the work of Bernstein and his associates.

The two principal theorists of Russian revisionism were Peter Struve and Mikhail Tugan-Baranovsky, and Struve is often considered to be pre-eminent.[8] So far as Marxian political economy is concerned, however, we argue in the following sections that Tugan represented the main theoretical force. Certainly Struve played the major role in organizing the literary forces of Russian social democracy in the 1890s, and his intellectual development was more complex than that of Tugan. But the arguments of Tugan-Baranovsky against both populism and orthodox Marxian political economy were stronger than those of Struve,[9] and Tugan is more accurately described as a genuine revisionist, for he remained committed to socialism throughout his life, while Struve and the other legal Marxists became liberals or conservatives after 1900.[10] For these reasons we focus upon the work of Tugan-Baranovsky.[11]

Mikhail I. Tugan-Baranovsky was born in 1865 at Solyonoye in the Ukraine. By birth he was half-Ukrainian and half-Tartar, as well as possibly of aristocratic lineage. He held degrees in natural science, law and economics, and began working within a Marxist framework of analysis as early as 1890. His revisionism was evident from the outset, but became more pronounced in the early part of the twentieth century after he had left social democratic politics. Once Tugan's works became accessible, with the publication of translations after

1890, German theorists took him very seriously indeed.[12] In the last decade of his life he became deeply committed to the cooperative movement and to Ukrainian nationalism. In 1917 he served as Finance Minister in the provisional Ukrainian government. He died in January 1919.

In the history of economic thought, Tugan is recognized to be important for his analysis of cyclical fluctuations.[13] Here we argue that he exercised a significant influence within Marxism itself. In the next section it is shown how Tugan's analysis of Tsarist industrialization emphasized exactly those 'peculiarities' of the process which Trotsky took to be the material basis of his theory of 'permanent revolution', which was by far the most perceptive political work of revolutionary Marxism in Russia. Following on from this, it is argued in section III that Tugan-Baranovsky's theory of aggregate demand not only represented the strongest refutation of populist economics, but also underpinned the arguments of Preobrazhensky for 'primitive socialist accumulation' in the 1920s.

There is little difficulty in establishing the importance of Tugan's ideas in each of these cases for the parallels are clear and Tugan's originality pronounced. It is, however, not possible to support *textually* the claim that he directly influenced Trotsky and Preobrazhensky. Revolutionary Marxists regarded orthodoxy as a serious matter. This meant that they could not admit to any connection to revisionists without seriously weakening their own position within socialist ranks. But, even if this were thought to throw into doubt the actual link of Tugan-Baranovsky's analysis to that of Bolshevik theorists, it would nevertheless remain true that central themes of leading Russian Marxists were anticipated by Tugan.

The same holds true for the argument of section VI, where it is maintained that Tugan's socialism was based upon positions which were later characteristic of 'western Marxism'. Tugan-Baranovsky's viewpoint was also more secure than that of much twentieth-century Marxism, since it rested upon his penetrating critique of Marx's 'laws of motion'. Many theorists of western Marxism took it for granted that the socialist movement could not be anchored in economics; Tugan, by contrast, *argued* that it could not, because Marx's treatment of capitalist dynamics was seriously deficient. His reasoning is outlined in section IV.

Tugan-Baranovsky's revisionism was not, however, an unqualified success. As is shown in section V, the major weakness of his work lies in price theory. He seems to have misunderstood the intricate structure of Marx's own value analysis, and his attempted reconcili-

ation of utility theory with a cost of production approach is a super-
ficial eclecticism. This aside, the overall importance of Tugan-Baranovsky in the history of Marxism and revisionism is pivotal, and has been
underestimated by intellectual historians.

## II. The 'peculiarities' of tsarist economic development

In the last two decades of the nineteenth century the principal economic theorists of populism, Vasily Vorontsov and Nikolai Danielson,
both appealed to the same basic theory; capitalist economic relations
necessarily generated an 'under-consumption' and this made a full
development of capitalism in Russia impossible. In its pure form capitalism would stagnate; only factors extraneous to capitalist social
relations could offset this and allow growth. Surplus value could not
be completely realized within a fully capitalistic economy. Workers'
consumption demand was insufficient because the rate of exploitation
was positive, and the shortfall could not be made good by capitalists
because surplus value was in part used for accumulation, or saved.
To ensure full realization of surplus value, a capitalist economy needed
a specific type of market system: one in which there were external
sources of consumption demand.

This was a general theory of capitalism, and not an analysis of the
specific deficiencies of its Russian variant. But the populist economists
applied it to Russia by denying that capitalism there could tap sufficient sources of external consumption demand. Russia's 'late start'
meant that foreign markets were already monopolized by the more
developed nations. Russian capitalism, it was held, was only maintained in its present degenerate form by the artificial stimulus of tsarist
fiscal policy. Ultimately, the state's resources would prove insufficient
to maintain even this parasitic status quo. Unless the strategy of
attempting to follow Western Europe were abandoned, sustained and
comprehensive economic development would prove impossible. Russia
had to follow her own 'special path' of progress distinct from that of
the West.[14]

The counter-arguments of the Marxists were stated by many authors,
but Tugan-Baranovsky and Lenin towered above the others in the
consistent discipline and thoroughness of their analyses, and of the
two Tugan's was superior. There was also a significant difference in
focus. Whereas Lenin concentrated on the development of capitalism
in agriculture, Tugan dealt with industrial development. His exposure
of the deficiencies in under-consumptionism is dealt with in section
III; here we concentrate upon his account of tsarist industrialization.[15]

*The Russian Factory in the Nineteenth Century*, first published in

1898, still remains one of the most impressive analyses of industrialization in terms of historical materialism.[16] It traced the economic history of Russia from the time of Peter the Great, with the principal concern being to undermine the populists' allegation that industrialization was 'artificial' in character. At the same time Tugan explained the dependent nature of the revival of small-scale industry which Vorontsov appealed to as evidence for the potential vibrancy of non-capitalist forms.

Tugan emphasized that the industrial modernization implemented by Peter was crucial to the survival of Russia as an independent political entity, the value of which the populist economists were not prone to dispute.[17] Moreover, he argued that the capitalist features of this industrial expansion could not have been avoided, as the populists believed. Imported means of production and skilled labour from the more advanced West were an absolute necessity, and economy required that they be organized in large-scale factories.[18] The new factories, in turn, depended upon the expertise and resources of merchant capitalists; no other group could have acted as a substitute.[19] Furthermore, since a free labour market was underdeveloped, the state had to intervene on an extensive scale, and in a coercive manner, so as to provide the requisite labour-power.[20] Tugan then went on to show that, in the nineteenth century, a further development of capitalist relations was required to sustain the process. In particular, the bonded labour which had facilitated early achievements became a barrier to further advance, and a general reform of serfdom was required to provide wage labour on a more extensive scale.[21] He claimed that the growth of small-scale industry, to which populists pointed as evidence of an alternative to capitalism, was a response to, and dependent upon, large-scale industry. Production that had initially been confined to factories, because it required economic use of the scarce skills of imported labour from the West, was eventually taken up by small domestic producers. And much of their output served the needs of large-scale industry, while the distribution system was dominated by merchant capital.[22]

The 'forced' nature of tsarist modernization was generally appreciated by Russian Marxists;[23] the originality of Tugan's treatment lay in his concentration upon industrial development, in the sophistication of his argument, and in his recognition that 'late starters' were impelled to depart very substantially from reliance upon the spontaneous forces of civil society. The state had to take a leading role; capital and technology could only be procured on the requisite scale through imports; and overt coercion had to replace an absent market discipline.[24] In consequence, modernization took the form of 'uneven and combined development'.

It was exactly this that constituted the material basis for Trotsky's theory of 'permanent revolution', which was first outlined in 1906. Trotsky was undoubtedly influenced by others, but his notion of 'revolution in permanence' really amounted to an analysis of the social and political implications of the form of industrialization which Tugan had described.[25] In particular, he showed that the pattern of the tsarist 'reconstruction from above' dramatically expanded the size of the proletariat, while minimizing the formation of an urban bourgeoisie and petty-bourgeoisie within Russia, and that the Russian proletariat had 'modern' features due to the emphasis upon large-scale productive units. Dependence on the West had, by contrast, increased the importance of bourgeois rentiers in Europe, and held back proletarian development as investment resources were transferred to Russia. In any revolutionary conflict with Tsarism – and such a confrontation was taken to be self-evident by virtually the entire Russian intelligentsia – it would be the working class that would be the dominant force. Hence its class interest would be triumphant, so that the transition to socialism via a bourgeois republic would be impossible.[26] The inhibitions of socialist revolution in Europe, which had arisen in part because of Russian development, would then be overcome through the power provided by the Russian breakthrough. As is now widely recognized, Trotsky's conception of the Russian revolutionary process proved to be essentially correct.[27] What has not been recognized is how it rested upon those features brought to the fore in Tugan-Baranovsky's economic analysis.

Tugan did not elaborate his analysis to cover social and political variables due partly to his overriding interest in countering populist economics. This concern with populism also generated an inappropriate reaction on his part: he stressed that Russia's unique pattern of modernization would ultimately bring its future history into conformity with that of Western Europe via integration into the world market.[28] This also explains why, although Tugan noted that the peculiarities of nineteenth-century development resulted in a fusion of western liberalism with traditional Russian ideas, he failed to appreciate that the same might be true for Marxism.[29] His exposure of the limitations of Marxist doctrine (outlined in section IV below) may have operated to reinforce this blind-spot. After the intellectual defeat of populism, however, the revolutionary implications of the different 'special path' which Tugan had perceived provided the materialist foundation for that strand in Bolshevik politics which achieved dominance in 1917.

**III.   The 'production of means of production by means of production'**
Bolshevik strategy after the revolution also had a basis in Tugan's
economics. Again, this originated in the 'great debate' between populists and Marxists during the 1890s. Tugan-Baranovsky provided the
strongest argument against the claim that under-consumption would
ultimately constrain Russian capitalism.[30] And, in the 1920s, it was
the same relationships to which Preobrazhensky appealed to justify
the rapid expansion of the socialist industrial sector against Bukharin's
claim that this would run aground on the insufficient purchasing power
of the peasantry. Bukharin took a position very similar to the populists; like them he was defeated intellectually, and Tugan's economics
were crucially important in both cases.

Tugan-Baranovsky was the first to see the significance of Marx's
reproduction models for the problem of effective demand,[31] and so
great was his admiration that he always considered Quesnay and Marx
to be superior theorists to Smith, even after he had jettisoned Marxist
politics.[32] In the reproduction models, Tugan rightly saw a framework
by which the sectoral interconnections of an economy became susceptible to rigorous analysis. He used them to formulate a theory of
cyclical oscillations and organize his account of fluctuations in the
British economy. In the process he provided a critique of under-
consumptionism, placing emphasis instead upon the concept of 'disproportionality' between sectors as the central factor operating to cause
varying growth rates through time. In doing so he joined to the
reproduction models two other themes found in Marx (but which Marx
had treated separately): that capitalist production was production for
profit, not production oriented to providing use values, and that technical progress had a labour-saving bias, reflected in a rising organic
composition of capital.[33]

According to Tugan the demand for industrial output in capitalist
development stemmed increasingly from industry itself. The only problems that could arise would be from 'disproportionalities' between
sectors, but he adduced reasons for believing that proportionality
would ultimately be restored through the automatic operation of
market forces.[34] Capitalism could thus be viewed as involving the
'production of means of production by means of production'. Consumption demand provided no constraint so long as proportionality
was maintained. Tugan, in fact, imagined it possible for there to be
a virtually automated economy where machines produced machines,
and consumption was almost completely eliminated.[35] As will be seen
in section VI below, Tugan was not enamoured by this prospect, nor

by the process through which it might come about, but he did believe that it represented the logic of a capitalist economy.

As such it provided a compelling refutation of Vorontsov's and Danielson's under-consumptionism. True, Tugan's argument was abstract and did not incorporate those features specific to Russian development, but the populists' stance was similarly grounded in a highly theoretical argument.[36] And although it caused problems for the orthodox Marxists too (see section IV below) it was this very generality that allowed Tugan's argument to have an influence within Marxism. It became obviously applicable to the situation of the NEP, and it underlay the fierce argument between Bukharin and Preobrazhensky as to the possibilities and constraints on industrial development posed by peasant agriculture.

In a very real sense this was a repeat of the debates of the 1890s. Bukharin argued for gradual industrial advance, on the grounds that rapid expansion would run into a 'sales crises' because of inadequate demand arising from the limited consuming power of the peasantry.[37] Somewhat paradoxically, his overall scheme for socialist development depended on Lenin's 'On Cooperation', which bore the influence of Tugan's work on cooperatives. However, after Lenin's death Bukharin launched a sustained attack on the 'super-industrializers', behind whom he identified the economics of Tugan.[38] He was right to do so. Preobrazhensky's position did indeed rest on Tugan's ideas. He devalued the economic importance of consumer demand, saw the possibility of industry's 'self-development', and extended the analysis of the reproduction models which Tugan had brought to prominence.[39] The debt to Tugan-Baranovsky becomes even clearer when it is realized that the famous Feldman growth model of 1928 merely formalized aspects of Preobrazhensky's 'primitive socialist accumulation', indicating the intersectoral requirements for an ever-increasing weight of capital goods in national output.[40]

### IV. The contradictions of capitalism

Tugan's attack on the under-consumptionism of the populists was generally accepted by Russian Marxists in the 1890s.[41] It was clearly the most powerful of all the arguments employed against the belief that Russian capitalism was 'blocked'.[42] Nevertheless Tugan's theory constituted part of his own revisionism, and this created problems for the orthodox. There were elements of under-consumptionism in *Capital*,[43] and Tugan charged that Marx, like the populists, had fallen under the influence of 'Sismondianism'.[44] Moreover, under-consumptionist ideas formed the backbone of the dominant theory of capitalist crises in the work of social democratic theorists of the Second International.[45] Thus Tugan's refutation of populism also incorporated an attack upon orthodox Marxism.

During the 1890s this did not produce a controversy within Russian social democracy analogous to that in Germany, precisely because both the orthodox Marxists and revisionists were under threat from populism. At this time the legal Marxists also accepted a central tenet of Plekhanov, the need for a bourgeois-democratic revolution against Tsarism.[46] In consequence they had no truck with the social democratic reformists who challenged Marxian orthodoxy after 1898. For these reasons there was a closing of the ranks, and internal disputes were subdued. After 1900 the legal Marxists left the social democratic movement altogether. With the orthodox theorists preoccupied with the challenge by reformists, and then with the split between Bolsheviks and Mensheviks, there was no systematic engagement with critics of Marxism.

What criticism the orthodox did level at Tugan-Baranovsky was not especially acute. Plekhanov and Lenin charged that Tugan had drawn extreme and unwarranted conclusions from an essentially valid argument against Populism. There was substance in this allegation, but it was asserted, not argued, and rested on nothing more substantial than quotations from Marx.[47] True, Lenin did go beyond this by pointing out that under-consumption could be interpreted as a form of disproportionality, involving an imbalance between departments I and II, and was thus in principle consistent with Tugan's crisis theory. However, Lenin's point was a purely formal one, as he offered no convincing reasons as to why this particular form of disproportionality was more likely than any other. Kautsky, and later Bukharin, added nothing to this.[48] Nor did Hilferding: in fact, his work showed signs of being influenced by Tugan.[49] Rosa Luxemburg went a little deeper when she accused Tugan of undertaking a mere 'arithmetical exercise', having failed to explain what motivated capitalists to invest endlessly.[50] But the basis of her criticism was her own theory of accumulation, and therefore lacked coherence. Only in the light of Keynes were Marxists convincingly able to maintain that her erroneously-based critique did have a kernel of truth.[51] This is not surprising. The Marxists themselves lacked precisely what was needed to treat the problem of under-consumption: a coherent theory of effective demand. As we have indicated in section III, this lacuna hindered Bukharin during the controversies of the 1920s. It also plagued all Marxists in coming to an adequate appreciation of the world depression in the 1930s.[52]

During the 1890s Tugan's revisionism also extended to include a critique of Marx's theory of profit. In fact, this was implicit in his account of capitalist growth. If capitalism might become automated while continuing to accumulate with an expanding capital goods sector, exploited labour could not form the sole source of profit. Nevertheless, Tugan missed this implication of his treatment of reproduction, and his criticism of Marx's theory of profit centred on the alleged tendency for the rate of profit to fall. He located a serious logical error in Marx's exposition of this law.

Marx had argued that technical progress increased the relative size of constant capital, and since only labour-power generated surplus value even an increase in the rate of exploitation would not compensate for a higher organic composition of capital.[53] However, Tugan maintained that only if the rate of profit rose (or at least remained constant) would there be an incentive for capitalists to adopt new technologies. He provided numerical examples to illustrate this point, and concluded that the rate of profit could not fall as a result of genuine technical progress.[54]

There are deficiencies in Tugan's objections. He did not take cognizance of the complexity of Marx's argument, which was that a technical change would appear profitable to individual capitalists at the initial price vector, but its adoption by all capitalists would alter prices so as to reduce the general rate of profit. Also Tugan's examples did not deal with a multi-commodity economy, which was the context in which Marx had treated the law. The three-sector model used by Tugan assumed equal organic compositions of capital, and was in consequence really a one-commodity economy.[55] Thus his critique was not general, since it involved only a 'special case' refutation. Apart from these limitations, however, Tugan's position was sound. It would be fully vindicated by subsequent proofs that cost-reducing innovations must raise the rate of profit, so long as real wages remain unchanged (as Marx's argument assumed). In fact, critics of the law of the falling rate of profit did not surpass Tugan's treatment until the work of Shibata in the 1930s, and not conclusively so until the 1950s and 1960s when rigorous demonstrations of Marx's errors were provided by Samuelson and Okishio.[56]

Tugan's critique of Marx's theory of the falling rate of profit, however, made virtually no impact on orthodox Marxists. This reflected the dominance of under-consumptionist theories of crises. Only with the publication of Henryk Grossmann's *The Law of Accumulation and the Breakdown of the Capitalist System* in 1929 did the law play a significant role in Marxian economics, and even then widespread adoption had to await the 1970s.[57] Nevertheless, it is to Tugan's enduring intellectual credit that he indicated that this line of development was a blind alley.

Tugan-Baranovsky coupled his attack on Marx's profit theory with a harsh evaluation of the associated theory of wages. Although less original here, his argument posed a much greater threat to Marxist politics.[58] As we have already seen, Tugan accepted that technical change was predominantly labour-saving but he recognized that its effects in generating an excess supply of labour (and hence a depressive effect upon wages) would be most pronounced as the capitalist organization of production replaced pre-capitalist forms. Mechanization then would greatly increase the labour-force available for capitalist employment by making profitable the utilization of female and child labour. However, when capitalism succeeded in becoming the dominant mode, this dramatic increase in labour power would cease, and working-class organizations would be better placed to capture some of the productivity increases in the form of higher wages.[59] Following Struve, Tugan also pointed out that this was no bad thing for socialism; an impoverished mass would be unable to achieve the status of a ruling class and usher in a new civilization.[60]

Neither the orthodox Marxists in Germany nor those in Russia responded adequately to these criticisms.[61] Plekhanov and Lenin both interpreted Marx as arguing that immiseration was relative, not necessarily absolute, and pointed out that statistics on distribution were in accord with this view.[62] Leaving aside the question of whether or not relative immiseration was, in fact, the doctrine Marx consistently espoused, to claim that it was did not contradict anything that the revisionists said, as Tugan in fact pointed out.[63] Furthermore, Tugan actually understated the deficiencies in Marx's theory of wages because he took it for granted that technical progress had a pronounced labour-saving bias. When Marxists did finally accept that this was erroneous, they would restate Tugan's criticism with even more force.[64]

By the early 1900s Tugan-Baranovsky had reached the conclusion that the economic contradictions of capitalism were far less dramatic than Marx had imagined. The tendency for the rate of profit to fall was non-existent, immiseration was but a half-truth, and although cyclical crises continued they were not well explained by Marxian economics, nor could they be expected to become ever more severe.[65] But, at the same time, Tugan's reading of Marx, especially on the nature of the accumulation process, and of the utopian socialists, had convinced him of the irrationality of capitalism. In consequence, he departed from social democracy, but he did not cease to be a socialist. He believed that the basis of a viable socialist strategy could not be narrowly economic but must instead be explicitly ethical. Here he pointed forward to tendencies that would grow within Marxism after World War I. Before we consider this, however, it is important to recognize that Tugan had his own blind-spots. They were most manifest in his discussion of value theory, as some orthodox Marxists realized.

## V.   Tugan-Baranovsky's treatment of value theory

Marx's theory of value is now known to be seriously flawed. But the really important deficiencies were not exposed until the 1960s and 1970s, and this was often undertaken by Marxists themselves.[66] Earlier critics had perceived problems with the original form of the theory, but they had not recognized that their objections could be overcome through a reformulation of Marx's ideas, as later proposed by Bortkiewicz and Seton.[67] Tugan-Baranovsky was no exception here, and his critique of Marx's theory of value, together with his own analysis of price determination, was defective.

Tugan identified what he believed to be an 'inner contradiction' in Marx's notion of value. 'According to Marx, value is objectified labour. But, as Marx expressly recognizes, price does not equal labour value. And labour cannot objectify itself in anything, if not in price. Hence value is not objectified labour.' The consequence is that Marx 'lives in a fantasy world, which bears no relation to the real world. Real phenomena – like the price of land – are described as imaginary, while entirely imaginary concepts – like the "exchange value" which plays no part in exchange relations – are proclaimed as the key to the highest economic wisdom.'[68] Here Tugan seems to have misunderstood Marx's argument, which rested upon his distinction between 'appearance and reality'.[69] What Tugan-Baranovsky referred to as Marx's 'fantasy world' was for Marx the 'reality' behind 'appearances', and Marx would have considered Tugan to be misled by 'appearances'. Since the core of Marx's doctrine – that equilibrium prices and property incomes can be derived from labour values – may be established under fairly general assumptions, Tugan's criticism was not well founded. His problem was in great part terminological. Tugan interpreted the concept of value to mean 'evaluation', and on this understanding maintained that it must be subjective in nature.[70] Marx, of course, had required a commodity to have use-value; but apart from this he had not included any use-value reference in his concept of value, so Tugan's depiction was wholly misguided.

However, he did not propose a complete abandonment of a labour theory of value in favour of neoclassical utility analysis. Instead, he sought a reconciliation on the grounds that neoclassical economics had itself neglected the supply side, and hence the role of cost. In Tugan's view real economic life had both a subjective and objective aspect, and value theory must also be two-dimensional. Economic action involved both the (subjective) goal of utility maximization and (objective) changes to the external world. Tugan concluded that equilibrium required (for each pair of commodities) equality between the ratio of their marginal utilities and the ratio of their labour costs. Labour was not the substance of value, as Marx had maintained, but the most important determinant of the average price of the majority of commodities.[71] Here Tugan used 'labour cost' as an index of cost of production. He believed that Ricardo had been right both to recognize that labour would not be the only cost, and to argue that treating costs as composed of labour alone would be sufficiently accurate for all practical purposes.

A similar synthesis was proposed at the time by the German conservative W. Mühlpfort and (in a rather different form) by Alfred Marshall, doyen of English liberal economics, and more recently by Leif Johansen and Michio Morishima.[72] For Tugan it proved to be a path full of pitfalls, and Bukharin showed no clemency in exposing them. Neoclassical value theory rested upon a liberal conception of the relation between society and the individual which was at odds with that of Marxism, Bukharin argued. Its concepts could not simply be appended to those of Marx without undermining the coherence of the whole.[73] Tugan did, in fact, recognize that the 'social' perspective of Marx was very different from that of the neoclassicals, but he wrongly believed that the distinction was not relevant to value theory.[74] Bukharin's criticism was actually reinforced by some neoclassical economists, who argued that utility theory was self-sufficient; it needed no supplementation by an 'objective' theory of costs, since utility considerations governed supplies as much as demands.[75] Modern neoclassical theory no longer makes reference to non-utility costs, and non-neoclassical theorists have jettisoned 'costs of production' as a concept appropriate for a purely objective theory of value.[76] Furthermore, Austrian neoclassicism, the principal influence upon Tugan, was precisely that form of subjectivist theory which came most into conflict with his theory of accumulation. Austrian theory traced the value of capital equipment to the contribution which it made to the production of consumption goods.[77] Accumulation was thereby made dependent upon consumption demand and, as Bukharin pointed out, this contradicted Tugan's own position in the analysis of reproduction, where consumption demand received no special status.[78] In addition, Bukharin might have noted – if he had not been equally confused on the issue – that the neoclassical conception of demand precluded the type of demand deficiencies that underlay Tùgan's theory of cyclical crises.[79] In addition, the Austrian perspective should have alerted Tugan to the impossibility of any magnitude of labour acting as an index of costs, for costs will vary with the dates at which labour is applied.[80]

Tugan's treatment of value theory was thus the weak point of his revisionism. He misunderstood the nature of Marx's theory, his criticisms were not robust, and he embraced an ill-conceived eclecticism which confused the real issues dividing the 'objective' from the 'subjective' approaches in the formulation of economic theory.[81] Tugan's attempt to incorporate subjectivism into Marxism, however, was more soundly based in his treatment of the transition of socialism, for it followed from his more acute criticism of Marx's treatment of the contradictions of capitalism.

## VI. Tugan-Baranovsky and modern socialism

Tugan did not accept that capitalism had any system-destroying contradictions. But he did believe the 'production of machines by ever more machines' to be an expression of the very essence of capitalism, and one that was incompatible with treating human beings as ends, rather than as means. This scepticism as to the 'breakdown' of capitalism and neo-Kantian ethics resulted in his articulating socialist viewpoints which Marxists would adopt only many decades later.

He repudiated the 'inevitabilism' that characterized the 'scientific socialism' of the German SPD. 'Humanity will not receive Socialism as the gift of the blind, elemental economic forces. It must consciously work and struggle for the new social order.'[82] This struggle, Tugan believed, would have to be ethically based and focused upon the irrationality of capitalism, where the purposes and requisites of life had become transposed. He was thus led to emphasize the themes of alienation and fetishism which he found in Marx, and which orthodox Marxists ignored, and to argue that the critique of capitalism found in the work of the utopian socialists was at least equal to that of Marx, a point which orthodoxy totally repudiated.[83]

Tugan's perspective was very different, too, from that which characterized the revisionism of Bernstein, where socialism was often perceived in inevitabilist terms, as the logical culmination of bourgeois liberalism. It was Tugan's orientation that was to become increasingly evident with the rise of 'Western Marxism'. Marxists like Lukacs, Gramsci and the Frankfurt School thinkers repudiated the primacy of economics, emphasizing instead the importance of superstructural

forces in bringing about the realization of socialism, whose desirability
– rather than inevitability – was emphasized.[84] An explicit ethical
orientation now dominates some schools of Marxism.[85] The humanism
of the 'Young Marx', of which Tugan would, of course, have been
unaware, played an important role in bringing about this reorientation.
Since it is precisely here that the dehumanizing effect of capitalist
production is the major theme, it is not surprising that Marxists in the
twentieth century have moved towards Tugan's position.

There is in this another link with Bolshevism. Lenin's theory of the
non-spontaneous nature of socialist consciousness, his treatment of
party organization, and his belief in the necessity of a vanguard of
committed idealists, extended well beyond the voluntarist dimension
of Plekhanov's orthodoxy.[86] Gramsci described the achievement of
Bolshevism as a 'revolution against *Capital*',[87] and after 1917 these
elements of Leninism came to make their own impact upon Marxism
in the West, contributing to the repudiation of determinism as it was
understood by the mainstream of the Second International. In this
important sense the work of Tugan-Baranovsky and Lenin had similar
effects despite their very different strategies for achieving socialism.

There is, however, one dimension of Tugan's socialism which was
not at all modern. He shared with the classical Marxists a disposition
towards centralism in socialist organization. Of all the 'laws of motion'
enunciated by Marx, Tugan considered the 'centralization of capital'
alone to be soundly based.[88] Together with his hostility to the 'anarchy
of the market', and to the irrational drive for accumulation within
capitalism, this worked towards his acceptance of centralized planning.
He did note the political dangers involved with this concentration of
power, and he did favour cooperative organization of the actual units
of production, but he also considered fully decentralized forms of
socialist organization to be impossible.[89] In consequence, like all theorists of the era of the Second International, he failed to anticipate the
economic problems that would arise within command economies.[90]
Thus the contradictions of 'actually existing socialism' were unanticipated by both orthodox Marxism and its most perceptive socialist
critic.

## Notes

1. See Howard and King (1989c, chapters 4 and 5).
2. On the nature of 'legal Marxism' and the 'legal Marxists', see Kindersley (1962).
3. Kindersley (1962, pp. 47, 112, 124, 204); Pipes (1970, p. 107); Kowal (1965, chapter IV).
4. Ultimately the perspective of German revisionism became influential within the SPD, but only very much later; see Howard and King (1988a; 1989c, chapter 14).

5. On Russian populism, see Mendel (1961); Walicki (1969); Wortman (1967); Venturi (1960).
6. For Marx's views on Russia, see Shanin (1983) and Howard and King (1989c, chapter 7).
7. Howard and King (1989b and 1989c, chapter 8).
8. See, for example, Kindersley (1962); Pipes (1970); Von Laue (1956).
9. For example, Struve's chief economic argument against populism made a major (and erroneous) concession to his opponents. On this, see Bulgakov (1897) and Luxemburg (1911), pp. 292–8.
10. Kindersley (1962); Pipes (1970; 1980); Kowal (1965).
11. For the influence of Struve on Russian Marxists, see Howard and King (1988b; 1989a; 1989c, chapters 9–11).
12. Bernstein (1905; 1909); Kautsky (1901–2; 1908); Schmidt (1901); Bauer (1906–7); Boudin (1907); Pannekoek (1910).
13. Hansen (1951, p. 281); Hutchinson (1953, p. 377); Schumpeter (1954, p. 1126); Kowal (1973); Amato (1984).
14. Vorontsov (1882); Danielson (1893).
15. Lenin's criticism of populism is considered in Howard and King (1989c, chapter 9).
16. The *Russian Factory* went through three editions between 1898 and 1907. There was a German translation based on the second Russian edition of 1900, published in the same year. References here are to the English translation of the third Russian edition, published in 1907, but designated as Tugan-Baranovsky 1898.
17. Tugan-Baranovsky (1898, pp. 1–43).
18. Ibid., pp. 14, 204.
19. Ibid., pp. 1–43.
20. Ibid., pp. 16–20.
21. Ibid., pp. 21–2, chapters 2–5 and 9.
22. Ibid., pp. 1–43.
23. For the views of Plekhanov and Lenin, see Howard and King (1988b; 1989b; 1989c, chapters 8 and 11).
24. Tugan-Baranovsky (1898, pp. 53, 297, and chapter 12).
25. Trotsky (1906). For an account of what is known about the influences on Trotsky, see Howard and King (1989c, pp. 229–32).
26. Trotsky (1906; 1930; 1932–3, chapter 1).
27. See, for example, Molyneux (1981); Löwy (1981); and Knei-Paz (1979). Gerschenkron (1966) and Moore (1967) are also relevant.
28. Tugan-Baranovsky (1898, pp. 94–5, 257, 268).
29. Ibid., chapters 8 and 13.
30. Tugan-Baranovsky first dealt with under-consumption and crises in Tugan-Baranovsky (1894a). A second edition appeared in 1900, and a third in 1914. The second edition was translated into German in 1901, and is referred to here as Tugan-Baranovsky (1894b). The third edition has been partially translated into English as Tugan-Baranovsky (1894c).
31. Marx presented his reproduction models in Marx (1885, chapters XX–XXI). For an analysis of these models see Howard and King (1985, pp. 181–93).
32. Kowal (1965, p. 212).
33. Marx (1867, pp. 152, 592); Howard and King (1985, pp. 195–7).
34. Tugan-Baranovsky (1894c).
35. Tugan-Baranovsky (1894b, pp. 230–1).
36. There are deficiencies in Tugan's argument, but they are subsidiary to our concerns here; see Howard and King (1989c, pp. 171, 178).
37. Bukharin (*Selected Writings*, part II).
38. Nove (1971); Kowal (1965, pp. 1, 15–16, 22–3, 27, 43n.79, 69, 74f); Bukharin (1924); (*Selected Writings*); Cohen (1980, chapter VI).
39. Preobrazhensky (1922; *Crisis*; 1926); Howard and King (1989c, chapter 15).

40. Feldman (1928). For an exposition of the Feldman model, see Nove and Nuti (1972, pp. 13, 149–72).
41. See Lenin (*Collected Works*, volume III); and Howard and King (1989c, chapter 9).
42. Howard and King (1989c, chapters 9 and 10).
43. Marx (1985, p. 320; 1894, pp. 244, 250, 256–8, 304–5, 484); Howard and King (1985, pp. 216–18).
44. Tugan-Baranovsky (1894b, p. 203); Kowal (1973, p. 308); Amato (1984, pp. 15–16).
45. Howard and King (1989c).
46. Howard and King (1989b; 1989c, chapter 8).
47. Plekhanov (*Selected Philosophical Works*, volume II, p. 491, 552); Lenin (*Collected Works*, volume I, p. 87, volume II, p. 166, volume III, pp. 45, 54, volume IV, p. 46).
48. Kautsky (1901–2, p. 117); Bukharin (1924).
49. Hilferding (1910, pp. 243, 285, 420, 421).
50. Luxemburg (1913, p. 315).
51. Robinson (1951); Kalecki (1971, pp. 146–55); Sweezy (1942, chapter X).
52. See Howard and King (1990).
53. Marx (1894, chapters XIII-XIV); Howard and King (1985, pp. 200–7).
54. Tugan-Baranovsky (1894b, chapter 7; 1905, pp. 174–85).
55. Garegnani (1970).
56. Shibata (1934; 1939); Okishio (1963); Samuelson (1957); Howard and King (1991).
57. Grossman (1929); Howard and King (1988c; 1989c, chapter 16; 1991, chapters 6 and 15).
58. Howard and King (1989c, chapter 4); Kindersley (1962).
59. Tugan-Baranovsky (1898, pp. 351–2; 1910, chapter II); Kowal (1965, chapter V).
60. Tugan-Baranovsky (1910, pp. 78–9); Kindersley (1962).
61. For the German response, see Howard and King (1989c, chapter 4).
62. Plekhanov (*Selected Philosophical Works*, volume II, p. 537); Lenin (*Collected Works*, volume I, p. 470, volume IV, pp. 106, 201, 233, 310).
63. Tugan-Baranovsky (1910, chapter II); Kowal (1965, chapter V).
64. Sweezy (1968); Meek (1968); Howard and King (1985, chapter 12). For an assessment of Marx's theory of technical change, see Blaug (1960); and for a neoclassical view of the effect of industrialization on wages, see Hicks (1969).
65. Tugan-Baranovsky (1894c; 1910, chapter III); Kowal (1965, chapter VI and VII).
66. Steedman (1977); Roemer (1981).
67. The most famous was that by Böhm-Bawerk; see Howard and King (1989c, chapter 3); Bortkiewicz (1907); Seton (1957).
68. Tugan-Baranovsky (1905, pp. 140, 142, 166–74).
69. On this distinction, see Cohen (1978, appendix I), and Howard and King (1985, pp. 31–2, 48–9, 52, 59, 63, 75, 103, 140, 144–5, 167, 170, 176).
70. Kowal (1965, chapter IV).
71. Tugan-Baranovsky (1906; 1905, pp. 154–65). For neoclassical influences on other legal Marxists, see Kindersley (1962, pp. 154–72).
72. Howard and King (1987); Marshall (1890); Johansen (1963); Morishima (1973).
73. Bukharin (1914, pp. 163–72).
74. Tugan-Baranovsky (1910, pp. 30–1); Kowal (1965, chapters IV and V).
75. Timoshenko (1954); Walsh (1970).
76. Sraffa (1960, pp. 8–9).
77. Howard (1980; 1983, chapter 11).
78. Bukharin (1924, pp. 218–19).
79. Howard (1983, pp. 164–77).
80. Howard (1980).
81. Howard (1983, pp. 143–4, 153–5).
82. Tugan-Baranovsky (1905, pp. 236–9; 1910).

83. Tugan-Baranovsky (1910); Kowal (1965, pp. 64–6, 105, 118, 127f, 381).
84. Anderson (1976); Kolakowski (1978); McLellan (1979); Merquior (1986).
85. Elster (1985); Roemer (1988); Howard and King (1989d; 1991, chapter 17).
86. Lenin (*Collected Works*, volume V, pp. 349–520, volume XXXIII, pp. 487–502); Plekhanov (*Selected Philosophical Works*, volume II, pp. 283–315); Harding (1983).
87. Gramsci (*Selections*, pp. 34–7).
88. Tugan-Baranovsky (1910, chapter II).
89. Tugan-Baranovsky (1910, parts II and III).
90. Nove (1983).

## References

Amato, S. 1984, 'Tugan-Baranovsky's theories of markets, accumulation and industrialization', in Koropeckyj (1984).
Anderson, P. 1976, *Considerations on Western Marxism*, New Left Books, London.
Bauer, O. 1906–7, 'Mathematische Formeln Gegen Tugan-Baranovsky', *Die Neue Zeit* 26, pp. 822–3.
Bernstein, E. 1905, 'Tugan-Baranovsky's Marx-Kritik', *Dokumente des Sozialismus, Hefte für Geschichte, Urkunde und Bibliographie des Sozialismus* 5, pp. 418–21.
— 1909, 'Tugan-Baranovsky als Sozialist', *Archiv für Sozialwissenschaft und Sozialpolitik* 28, pp. 786–96.
Blaug, M. 1960, 'Technical change and Marxian economics', *Kyklos* 13, pp. 495–509.
Bortkiewicz, L. Von 1907, 'On the correction of Marx's fundamental theoretical construction in the third volume of "Capital" ', in Sweezy 1969, pp. 199–221.
Boudin, L. S. 1907, 'Mathematische Formeln Gegen Karl Marx', *Die Neue Zeit* 26, pp. 524–35, 557–67, 603–10.
Bulgakov, S. N. 1895, 'Trety tom "Kapitala" K. Marksa', *Russkaya Mysl* 3.
— 1897, *O Rynkakh pri Kapitalisticheskom Proizvodstve*, M.I. Vodovozovoj, Moscow.
Bukharin, N. I. 1914, *The Economic Theory of the Leisure Class*, introduced by D. Harris, Monthly Review Press, New York; 1972.
— 1982, *Selected Writings on the State and the Transition to Socialism*, ed. R. B. Day, Spokesman, Nottingham. These articles were written between 1915 and 1929.
— 1924, *Imperialism and the Accumulation of Capital*, ed. by K. Tarbuck, Monthly Review Press, New York; 1972.
Cohen, G. 1978, *Karl Marx's Theory of History: A Defence*, Princeton University Press, Princeton, N.J.
— 1980, *Bukharin and the Bolshevik Revolution*, Oxford University Press, Oxford.
Danielson, N. F. 1893, *Ocherki Nashego Poreformennogo Obschchestvennogo Khozyaystva*, A. Benke, St Petersburg. (Danielson wrote under the pseudonym Nikolai-on).
Eagly, E. V. (ed.) 1968, *Events, Ideology and Economic Theory*, Wayne State University Press, Detroit, Mi.
Eissenstat, B. W. (ed.) 1971, *Lenin and Leninism*, Heath, Lexington, Ky.
Elster, J. 1985, *Making Sense of Marx*, Cambridge University Press, Cambridge.
Feldman, G. A. 1928, 'K Teorii Tempov Narodnogo Dokhoda', *Planovoe Khoziaistvo*, November and December, pp. 146–70, 151–78.
Garegnani, P. 1970, 'Heterogeneous capital, the production function and the theory of distribution', *Review of Economic Studies* 37, pp. 407–36.
Gerschenkron, A. 1966, *Economic Backwardness in Historical Perspective*, Harvard University Press, Cambridge, Ma.
Gramsci, A. 1977, *Selections from the Political Writings, 1910–20*, Lawrence & Wishart, London.
Grossman, H. 1929, *Das Akkumulations – und Zusammenbruchsgesetz des Kapitalistischen Systems (Zugleich eine Krisentheorie)*, C. I. Hirschfeld, Leipzig.
Hansen, A. H. 1951, *Business Cycles and National Income*, Norton, New York.
Harding, N. 1983, *Lenin's Political Thought*, Macmillan, London.

## 100  Classicals, Marxians and Neo-Classicals

Hicks, J. R. 1969, *A Theory of Economic History*, Oxford University Press, Oxford.
Hilferding, R. 1910, *Finance Capital*, ed. T. Bottomore, Routledge & Kegan Paul, London; 1981.
Howard, M. C. 1980, 'Austrian capital theory: an evaluation in terms of Piero Sraffa's "Production of Commodities by Means of Commodities" ', *Metroeconomica* 32, pp. 1–23.
—1983, *Profits in Economic Theory*, Macmillan, London.
Howard, M. C. and King, J. E. (eds) 1976, *The Economics of Marx*, Penguin, Harmondsworth.
—1985, *The Political Economy of Marx*, 2nd edition, Longman, Harlow.
—1987, 'Dr. Mühlpfort, Professor von Bortkiewicz and the "Transformation Problem" ', *Cambridge Journal of Economics* 11, pp. 165–8.
—1988a, 'The revival of revisionism: the political economy of German Marxism, 1914–1929', *European History Quarterly* 18, pp. 409–26.
—1988b, 'Lenin's political economy, 1905–1914: The "Prussian" and "American" paths to the development of capitalism in Russia', *Historical Reflections* XV, pp. 1–31.
—1988c, 'Henryk Grossman and the breakdown of capitalism', *Science and Society* 52, pp. 290–309.
—1989a, 'Russian revisionism and the development of Marxian political economy in the early twentieth century', *Studies in Soviet Thought* 37, pp. 15–37.
—1989b, 'The political economy of Plekhanov and the development of backward capitalism', *History of Political Thought*, pp. 329–44.
—1989c, *A History of Marxian Economics: Volume I, 1883–1929*, Macmillan, London and Princeton University Press, Princeton, N.J..
—1989d, 'Rational choice Marxism', *Review of Social Economy*, December, pp. 392–414.
—1990, 'Marxian economics and the great depression', *History of Political Economy* 22, pp. 46–62.
—1991, *A History of Marxian Economics: Volume II, 1930–1990*, Macmillan, London and Princeton University Press, Princeton, N.J.
Hutchison, T. W. 1953, *Review of Economic Doctrines*, Clarendon Press, Oxford.
Johansen, L. 1968, 'Labour theory of value and marginal utilities', *Economics of Planning* 3, pp. 89–103.
Kalecki, M. 1971, *Selected Essays on the Dynamics of the Capitalist Economy, 1933–1970*, Cambridge University Press, Cambridge.
Kautsky, K. 1901–2, 'Krisentheorien', *Die Neue Zeit* 20, pp. 37–47, 76–81, 110–18, 133–43.
—1908, 'Verelendung und Zusammenbruch: die Neueste Phase des Revisionismus', *Die Neue Zeit* 26, pp. 540–51, 607–12.
Kindersley, R. 1962, *The First Russian Revisionists*, Clarendon Press, Oxford.
Knei-Paz, B. 1979, *The Social and Political Thought of Leon Trotsky*, Clarendon Press, Oxford.
Kolakowski, L. 1978, *Main Currents in Marxism*, Volume III, Oxford University Press, Oxford.
Koropeckyj, I. S. (ed.), 1984, *Selected Contributions of Ukrainian Scholars to Economics*, Harvard University Press, Cambridge Ma.
Kowal, L. I. 1965, 'Economic doctrines of M. I. Tugan-Baranovsky', unpublished Ph.D. thesis, University of Illinois.
—1973, 'The market and business cycle theories of M. I. Tugan-Baranovsky', *Rivista Internazionale di Scienze Economiche e Commerciale* 4, pp. 307–30.
Lenin, V. I. 1960–70, *Collected Works*, Progress Publishers, Moscow.
Löwy, M. 1981, *The Politics of Combined and Uneven Development*, Verso, London.
Luxemburg, R. 1913, *The Accumulation of Capital*, Routledge & Kegan Paul, London; 1951.
Marshall, A. 1890, *Principles of Economics*, Macmillan, London.
Marx, K. 1867, *Capital*, Volume I, Lawrence & Wishart, London; 1970.

—1885, *Capital*, Volume II, Lawrence & Wishart, London; 1970.
—1894, *Capital*, Volume III, Lawrence & Wishart, London; 1972.
McLellan, D. 1979, *Marxism After Marx*, Macmillan, London.
Meek, R. L. 1968, 'Discussion of Sweezy's Paper', in Eagly 1968, pp. 120–3.
Mendel, A. P. 1961, *Dilemmas of Progress in Tsarist Russia*, Harvard University Press, Cambridge, Ma.
Merquior, J. 1986, *Western Marxism*, Paladin, London.
Molyneux, J. 1981, *Leon Trotsky's Theory of Revolution*, Harvester Press, Brighton.
Moore, B. 1967, *Social Origins of Dictatorship and Democracy*, Penguin, Harmondsworth.
Morishima, M. 1973, *Marx's Economics: A Dual Theory of Value and Growth*, Cambridge University Press, Cambridge.
Nove, A. 1971, 'Lenin and the New Economic Policy', in Eissenstat 1971, pp. 155–71.
—1983, *The Economics of Feasible Socialism*, George Allen & Unwin, London.
—and Nuti D. M. (eds) 1972, *Socialist Economics*, Penguin, Harmondsworth.
Okishio, N. 1963, 'A mathematical note on Marxian theorems', *Weltwirtschaftliches Archiv* 91, pp. 287–98.
Pannekoek, A. 1910, 'Herrn Tugan-Baranovsky's Marx-Kritik', *Die Neue Zeit* 28, pp. 772–83.
Pipes, R. 1970, *Struve: Liberal on the Left*, Harvard University Press, Cambridge, Ma.
—1980, *Struve: Liberal on the Right*, Harvard University Press, Cambridge, Ma.
Plekhanov, G. V. 1974–81, *Selected Philosophical Works*, Progress Publishers, Moscow.
Preobrazhensky, E. A. 1922, *From N.E.P. to Socialism*, trans. B. Pearce, New Park Publications, London; 1973.
—1980, *The Crisis of Soviet Industrialization: Selected Essays*, ed. D. A. Filtzer, Macmillan, London. These articles were written in the 1920s.
—1926, *The New Economics*, trans. B. Pearce, Oxford University Press, Oxford; 1965.
Robinson, J., 'Introduction' in Luxemburg 1913, pp. 13–28.
Roemer, J. 1981, *Analytical Foundations of Marxian Economic Theory*, Cambridge University Press, Cambridge.
—1988, *Free to Lose*, Harvard University Press, Cambridge, Ma.
Samuelson, P. A. 1957, 'Wages and interest: a modern dissection of Marxian economic models', *American Economic Review* 47, pp. 884–912.
Schmidt, C. 1901, 'Zur Theorie der Handelskrisen und der Ueberproduktion', *Sozialistische Monatshefte* 9, pp. 669–82.
Schumpeter, J. A. 1954, *A History of Economic Analysis*, George Allen & Unwin, London.
Seton, F. 1957, 'The "transformation problem" ', *Review of Economic Studies* 24, pp. 149–60. Reprinted in Howard and King 1976 pp. 162–76.
Shanin, T. (ed.), 1983, *Late Marx and the Russian Road: Marx and the Peripheries of Capitalism*, Routledge & Kegan Paul, London.
Shibata, K. 1934, 'On the law of decline in the rate of profit', *Kyoto University Economic Review*, July, pp. 61–75.
—1939, 'On the general profit rate', *Kyoto University Economic Review*, January, pp. 40–66.
Sraffa, P. 1960, *The Production of Commodities by Means of Commodities*, Cambridge University Press, Cambridge.
Steedman, I. 1977, *Marx After Sraffa*, New Left Books, London.
Sweezy, P. M. 1942, *The Theory of Capitalist Development*, Monthly Review Press, New York; 1968.
—(ed.) 1949, *Karl Marx and the Close of His System*, Kelly, New York.
—1968, 'Karl Marx and the Industrial Revolution', in Eagly 1968, pp 107–19.
Timoshenko, V. P. 1954, 'M. I. Tugan-Baranovsky and Western economic thought', *Annals of the Ukrainian Academy of Arts and Sciences in the United States* 3, pp. 803–23.
Trotsky, L. 1906, *Results and Prospects*, in Trotsky 1930 pp. 29–122.

—1930, *The Permanent Revolution*, Pathfinder Press, New York; 1969.

—1932-3, *The History of the Russian Revolution*, Pluto, London; 1977.

Tugan-Baranovsky, M. I. 1894a, *Promyshlennye Krizisy v Sovremennoi Anglii*, I. N. Skorokhodova, St Petersburg.

—1894b, *Studien zur Theorie und Geschichte der Handelskrisen in England*, G. Fischer, Jena; 1901.

—1894c, 'Periodic industrial crises', *Annals of the Ukrainian Academy of the Arts and Sciences in the United States*, 1954, 3, pp. 745–802.

—1898, *The Russian Factory in the Nineteenth Century*, Irwin, Homewood, Il; 1970.

—1905, *Theoretische Grundlagen des Marxismus*, Dunker und Humblot, Leipzig.

—1906, 'Subjektivismus und Objektivismus in der Wertlehre', *Archiv für Sozialwissenschaft und Sozialpolitik* 22, pp. 557–64.

—1910, *Modern Socialism in its Historical Development*, Swann Sonnenschein, London.

Venturi, F. 1960, *Roots of Revolution*, Weidenfeld & Nicolson, London.

Von Laue, T. H. 1956, 'Legal Marxism and the "Fate of Capitalism in Russia" ', *Review of Politics* 18, pp. 23–46.

Vorontsov, V. 1882, *Sud'by Kapitalizma v. Rossii*, M. Stasjulevic, St Petersburg (Vorontsov wrote under the pseudonym 'V.V.').

Walicki, A. 1969, *The Controversy Over Capitalism*, Oxford University Press, Oxford.

Walsh, V. 1970, *Introduction to Contemporary Microeconomics*, McGraw-Hill, New York.

Wortman, R. 1967, *The Crisis of Russian Populism*, Cambridge University Press, Cambridge.

# 8 John Strachey: the making and unmaking of an English Marxist, 1925–40

*Noel Thompson*

This paper considers certain salient themes in the economic writing of John Strachey,[1] one of the most prominent intellectuals of the left in inter- and postwar Britain, and specifically his birth, death and resurrection as a liberal socialist in the interwar period. The story is an interesting one in itself but it is also interesting for what it reveals of the pressures, perils and dilemmas confronting the British left intelligentsia between the wars.

Any assessment of John Strachey's contribution to British socialist thinking must begin with *Revolution by Reason* (1925),[2] a work which in the last two decades has received a fair measure of approbatory attention from historians of economic thought. However, while recognizing its merits, commentators have none the less largely failed to grasp the distinctive nature of Strachey's intellectual achievement, a failure which, for the most part, stems from a failure to comprehend the theoretical terrain occupied by late nineteenth- and early twentieth-century socialist political economy.

There is little space in this paper to do justice to the disparate and conflicting strains of that corpus of thought,[3] but as a generalization it is fair to say that the three main elements of which it is comprised – Fabian socialism, Marxian socialism and Guild socialism – had this in common, they all condemned the anarchy of the market and sought to replace it by the rational, purposive, collective control of economic activity. For Marxian socialists such as H. M. Hyndman, this would be effected by the state; for Guild socialists by producers' and consumers' guilds individually or in concert, and for the Fabian socialists by the incremental advance of municipal, national and consumer co-operative control.

There were two major consequences of this rejection. First, socialist writers were forced to confront the complex problems involved in economic calculation under marketless socialism – problems with which they were ill-equipped to deal and which left them a ready victim for the theoretical axe wielded by Hayek and von Mises in the 1920s. Secondly, and for the purposes of this paper more importantly,

socialist political economy turned its back on the transformative potentialities of the market, i.e. it failed to grasp the ways in which the
market might be utilized to give effect to socialist economic policies.

It is in this context that *Revolution by Reason* should be set, for it
is here that the distinctive nature of Strachey's contribution to socialist
economic thinking becomes most apparent. For, while he accepted
the fundamentals of the late nineteenth- and early twentieth-century
socialist critique of the market, Strachey none the less understood
how it could be used for socialist purposes. It is this which allowed
him to chart a *via media* between the vapid rhetoric of the revolutionary left and the insipid incrementalism of the Fabian right of the
labour movement.

So why was Strachey able to break the mould? Here it is important
to highlight the young Strachey's intellectual debts. He was, and
remained throughout his life, a synthetic rather than an original
thinker and to understand his intellectual trajectory one must be clear
at each point in time the minds and the systems of thought exerting
the greatest gravitational pull. In 1925 two stand out – J. M. Keynes
and J. A. Hobson. From the first he derived his monetary theory and
a realization of the socialist potentialities of monetary policy; from
the latter he seems to have assimilated a macroeconomic critique of
capitalism which saw general economic depression as the inevitable
consequence of an imbalance between the producer and consumer
goods sectors of the economy; an imbalance which in turn stemmed
from the maldistribution of wealth in favour of those – the rich – with
a high propensity to save and invest. Strachey was to describe his
critique of capitalism as 'the classical Marxian case against private
ownership',[4] yet neither the exploitation theory he expounds nor the
theory of capitalist crisis he builds upon it were distinctively Marxian.
On the contrary, the theory of capitalist crisis he expounds in chapter
8 of *Revolution by Reason* is clearly Hobsonian. Further, as Strachey
was to admit in a letter to Palme Dutt (written in 1931), he had not,
in 1925, actually read Marx's *Capital*.[5] If Marx was influential, therefore, it was influence of the most general kind. There is nothing
distinctively Marxian about *Revolution by Reason*.

Thus it was the influence of Keynes and, almost certainly, the
influence of Hobson or, to put it another way, it was the influence of
two of the most intellectually distinguished 'new liberals'[6] of the period
that was fundamental and it was undoubtedly this that gave *Revolution
by Reason* its distinctive, market-accommodating, liberal socialist,
theoretical thrust and flavour.

What, therefore, did Strachey believe could be done to transform a capitalism violently imploding under the pressure of a deficient demand for final goods into a socialism which would work economically and command and continue to command the allegiance of the electorate? As, for Strachey, capitalism's fundamental flaw lay in a chronic tendency to deficient aggregate demand, the way forward seemed, necessarily, to lie in expanding the purchasing power of the masses. In *Revolution by Reason* this was to be effected through 'a public banking system capable of giving such accommodation to industry as will enable it to increase the purchasing power of the workers' and 'an Economic Council' which would ensure the use of such credit facilities 'by forcing up . . . money wages and other receipts . . . of the working-classes' by means of minimum wage legislation and/or the disbursement of family allowances.[7]

Crucial to the success of such a strategy was the expansion of production *pari passu* with demand and to ensure this Strachey believed it would be necessary to effect a restructuring of the nation's industrial base. This would be the responsibility of the Economic Council which would use the leverage provided by a public banking system, to grant the financial assistance necessary to meet statutory wage obligations only on condition that capitalist producers 'accept [ed] the Council and co-operated logically with it in a general policy of National Planning'.[8]

The key to this transformative strategy and, indeed, much of its political and social appeal lay in its use of the market. Thus the incorporation of the market avoided, as Strachey saw it, the over-concentration of economic power which characterized state socialism and so any suggestion of the coercive conscription of labour or the imposition of a particular basket of goods and services on the consumer. Planning there would be, but it would be planning in response to the expressed needs of the working classes mediated by the market rather than planning imposed by state or municipal bureaucracy. 'We prefer', wrote Strachey, 'to let citizens express their real wants by giving them purchasing power' rather than having those wants decided by the 'economic dictatorship' of an 'all-wise Government'. For Strachey, to begin by nationalizing and then planning 'the organization of supply' was 'to begin at the wrong end' for it would result in 'an all-wise Government provid[ing] only those things it thinks its citizens *might* want. We prefer to let those citizens express their real wants by giving them purchasing power.'[9] Such enhanced purchasing power would give to the working classes, through the medium of the market, real control over the nation's resources. Power to the working classes meant power in their pocket to purchase.

Planning would therefore be 'planning not in the abstract, but to meet demand. . . . There is an essential difference between planning to meet a genuine spontaneously manifested, new demand and planning to give people what the Government thinks they ought to want.'[10] Thus with increased working class purchasing power the market could be relied upon to transmit to the Economic Council the information to guide its acceleration of a structural change which would gear production to the maximization of social welfare rather than the satisfaction of bourgeois or bureaucratic whim. In this context the market could also be relied upon to generate full employment.

Violent social upheaval could therefore be avoided by a revolution that utilized not *force majeure* but the proletarianized forces of a sanitized market. We have, therefore, in *Revolution by Reason*, something that might legitimately be referred to as a market or liberal socialist strategy. Along with this went an emphasis on consumer sovereignty, the circumscription of the economic power wielded by the socialist state, an economic pluralism which accepted the existence of considerable autonomy for a range of privately owned enterprises and also a willingness to allow the market (the foreign currency market) to establish and vary the international value of sterling. We have, in short, a willingness to accommodate the market and certain associated liberal principles within a socialist vision of the future.

By 1927, however, Strachey had largely abandoned this position and in an article published in the *Socialist Review* (July 1928), we even find him alluding to his past errors as a 'currency crank'. In a short paper such as this, it is impossible to discuss at length the reasons for his abandonment of the 1925 proposals but both objective and ideological factors were important. Objectively, the return to the Gold Standard and the defeat of the General Strike cast doubt, to say the least, on the viability of a strategy based on monetary expansion, floating exchange rates and high statutory wages. In addition the rejection by the 1927 Labour Party Annual Conference of the ILP Living Wage proposals suggested that a radical, expansionary, economic strategy of the kind which Strachey had himself proposed was not within the realm of practical politics. For a time, therefore (1927/8) Strachey moved towards a fuller acceptance of the Marxian critique of capitalism and thus to a position which implied the futility of the kind of economic tinkering he had been advocating in *Revolution by Reason*. Yet it must be stressed that it was the critical and not the prescriptive aspect of Marxism which Strachey took on board, for he still looked to the possibility of implementing an economic strategy which would smooth the road to socialism and avoid the chasm of revolution. Thus he continued to believe in the possibility of a non-violent revolution by reason and in a critical review of Palme Dutt's *Socialism and the Living Wage*, Strachey argued that it was important to 'regard the revolution not as a single dramatic act which will some-day take place, but as a mighty process of change and struggle which is going on to-day *and will go on for many decades to come* all around us'.[11]

Strachey's election to Parliament in 1929 was a political confirmation of this position, involving as it did an acceptance of the constraints imposed on any advance towards socialism by the political and parlia-mentary realities confronting a minority Labour government. In addition election led, once again, to a close working relationship with Oswald Mosley who had Strachey as his parliamentary private sec-retary. In such political circumstances pragmatism and expediency rather than purity of doctrine and analysis were at a premium and inevitably it was the influence of the pragmatist Mosley rather than the philosopher Marx which exerted the greatest gravitational pull upon Strachey's own thought. The power of this pull is most clearly evidenced in a pamphlet which Strachey wrote with Aneurin Bevan, W. J. Brown and Allen Young in February 1931 entitled *A National Policy* which, in effect, represents a defence of the 'Manifesto' which Mosley had published in December 1930 in the hope of winning round the Labour Party to employment policies of a more active, interventionist nature.

The key ingredients of *A National Policy* were these. There was to be a National Economic Planning Organization which would be responsible for the formulation of a National Plan. This would then be executed by a National Investment Board which would be respon-sible for initiating, coordinating and controlling an industrial rationaliz-ation and reorganization strategy. Thus it would 'control and coordi-nate investment . . . at present made under the auspices of the government or local authorities'; it would, in certain circumstances, determine the location of firms, 'what form of capital equipment indus-tries used' and where financial assistance would be directed to particu-lar industries. Finally, it would 'set on foot new capital projects throughout the whole field of industry which would not, under present circumstances, be undertaken'.[12] The whole 'plan' was also to be implemented behind protectionist barriers. Thus protection was seen as 'the only possible answer' if the country were 'consciously to choose the forms of production best suited to it and to see that those industries were permanently established here, protected from the interference of quite arbitrary external factors' and in this context a policy of imperial preference was suggested.[13]

Perhaps the most obvious feature of *A National Policy* is Strachey's preparedness to compromise socialist principle for strategic reasons. Thus he accepted that 'Questions of the ultimate goal of society' were to be 'excluded' from the pamphlet, while any question of the public control of economic activity was to be decided on an *ad hoc* basis and 'not by reference to preconceived ideas as to the form of Social Organization which is ultimately desirable'.[14] Yet it is important to note too that the pamphlet represents a significant retreat from Strachey's earlier preparedness to utilize the transformative potentialities of the market for socialist purposes. Thus there is the acceptance of protection; there is the idea of organizing economic activity by reference to a preconceived economic plan; there is, following from this, the physically and economically directive role of the National Investment Board and there is the absence of any mention of letting market forces, through flotation, determine the international value of sterling. Here, however, the main point to stress is that while planning in 1926 was seen as responsive, planning in 1931 is seen as directive. Thus reorganization of the supply side in relation to a preconceived economic plan is given priority over any idea of planning in response to consumer demand. Consumer sovereignty had, in effect, been abrogated.

This retreat from the centrality of the market can, I think, be explained by reference to a number of factors none of which there is space, in a paper such as this, to discuss at any length. To begin with there are the economic and psychological consequences of the Wall Street Crash which were sufficient to shake anyone's faith in the market as a regulative mechanism let alone someone as alive as Strachey to a market economy's deficiencies. Secondly, in Britain, the high and, after 1929, the rapidly rising level of unemployment reinforced any scepticism about the equilibrating properties of the market. Thirdly, and related to this, the very magnitude and immediacy of the problem of unemployment in Britain seemed to preclude a solution of the roundabout kind which utilized the intermediation of the market in the way that Strachey had suggested in 1925. What was needed was immediate, direct action of a kind which could only be undertaken by the state. Fourthly, as there was a desperate need to galvanize the Labour Party into action and as an expansionary strategy of the kind proposed by Strachey in *Revolution by Reason* had made no headway in the Party some alternative had to be suggested. Fifthly, given the manifest need in 1929–31 to maintain international confidence and thence Labour's freedom of manoeuvre, any strategy which had as its *fons et origo* a 'high' level of wages was, given its unacceptability to the international financial community, simply not practicable. Finally, given that Strachey and Mosley were hoping for a measure of cross-party support, a strategy with minimum wage legislation at its heart was not what was required and, in the absence of such legislation, a transformative use of the market of the kind previously envisaged, was no longer possible.

By early 1931 we have, in Strachey, a man near the end of his tether or, at least, a man who had stretched the tether of his socialist principles to breaking point in an effort to produce a practical policy capable both of mitigating the problem of unemployment and securing parliamentary support. It was likely, therefore, that the Labour Party's rejection of the Mosley Manifesto would have profound repercussions and this it certainly did. Mosley and Strachey left the Labour Party and launched the New Party. Under the leadership of Mosley, however, the Party took an increasingly rightward direction in the summer of 1931 and, by August, Strachey was forced to abandon it and search for another vehicle to translate his political and economic philosophy into effective practice.

1931 was the year of crisis for Strachey. He was a man who needed three things – 'a faith to fight for', a guru to expound it and a party to translate it into action. In 1931 he lost all three. British social democracy manifested the bankruptcy of its economic thinking, Mosley showed himself to have feet of clay or worse, and the Labour Party was revealed as impotent in the face of domestic and international pressures. It is this, surely, which explains the appeal of the British Communist Party to Strachey for what it did was to restore all that he had lost. Marxism-Leninism gave him his faith, the Kremlin canon lawyers became his mentors and the Party provided him with the political vehicle he required to translate his new faith into effective political practice.

Given the circumstances of Strachey's conversion to Comintern communism it is understandable that he should have embraced it as much for psychological or spiritual as for intellectual reasons; and certainly it was, for Strachey, as much a faith as an intellectual system. What occurred after August 1931 was not a conversion to Marxism as an explanation of history or as a way of reasoning or as a means of comprehending the laws of capitalist development, but a conversion to Marxism-Leninism as a total, scientifically rigorous and infallible system of explanation which gave the certainty of right answers in an uncertain world. This was the visceral appeal, this the fatal attraction of Comintern communism; it held out the possibility of making order out of the chaos of betrayal and lost illusions.

Yet the costs of this psychological fix were high. If Strachey gained the security which came with certainty it was the security of the walled enclosure. From 1932 at least until 1937 Strachey became, in effect, a popularizer who consciously, if temporarily, abandoned his capacity for independent thought. He was a brilliant popularizer, a forceful and lucid popularizer and a popular popularizer but a popularizer none the less. The flexibility and fertility of Strachey's prescriptive thinking in the period 1925–31 is absent from works such as *The Nature of Capitalist Crisis* (1935) and *The Theory and Practice of Socialism* (1936). Thus in place of the formulation of policies which, whatever their failings, did address contemporary economic ills and the afflictions of labour, we are treated in the works of Strachey's Comintern period to the enervating repetition of the communist mantra that profit-oriented production must give way to a system of planned production for use. Rhetoric replaced strategy; the chanting of the witch doctor replaced the scalpel of the surgeon. More specifically we have in works like the *Theory and Practice of Socialism* an unnerving return to the flawed fundamentals of the constructive or, more accurately, unconstructive political economy advanced by British Marxists prior to 1914. Thus the market was entirely banished from Strachey's economic prescriptions. There was to be no such Trojan horse admitted within the walls of the New Jerusalem. In its place, argued Strachey, 'We must find some other mechanism of regulation' and, as he saw it, 'the sole alternative method by which complex, highly developed economic systems can be regulated is by means of the deliberate decisions of some central body as to what goods, and how many shall be produced. This organization of production by means of such conscious decisions is called a system of planned production for use.'[15] 1936 therefore represented both the high watermark of Strachey's uncritical acceptance of Marxism-Leninism-Stalinism, as a science of society, and the low watermark of the relevance of his writings to contemporary policy debates. Thereafter, and certainly from 1938 onwards, if the god did not fail, his infallibility did at least seem to fray a little at the edges.

This is not immediately apparent when we peruse the pages of *What are We to Do?* (1938). On the contrary, the first part of the work is given over to a devastating, orthodoxly communist and entirely predictable attack upon the Fabian social democracy of the British labour movement. In addition, the final chapter of the work eulogizes the idea of a 'new model' (i.e. Communist) Party characterized both by the objective rigour of its analysis and an unquestioning acceptance of the Party line by its 'battle-hardened cadres'. This, together with a vanguardist interpretation of the Party's political role, leaves the reader in little doubt that Strachey had ingested, and was still in the process of regurgitating, a substantial part of the six-volumes of *Lenin's Selected Works* cited in the bibliography. In these and other respects, therefore, one may look in vain for any fissures in the adamantine orthodoxy of Strachey's position. Thus the political philosophy, the political party and the intellectual freedoms permitted by social democracy all stand condemned.

Yet *What are We to Do?* is different from works such as *The Nature of Capitalist Crisis* and *The Theory and Practice of Socialism* for, if the orthodoxy of Strachey's communism is not in doubt, communist orthodoxy itself had changed or changed at least in this respect – the vituperative, social-fascist castigating, revolutionary communist Mr Hyde had, in the words of Arthur Koestler, given place to the 'gentle, bedside-mannered, communist Dr. Jekyll who was . . . a freedom-loving, anti-fascist, popular-front democrat'.[16] Now the emergence of the Popular Front and the British Party's adherence to it may be interpreted as a change in tactics, but for Strachey and others it had important ideological implications. Thus while in the mid–1930s Strachey would and could contemplate no alternative to existing economic arrangements other than a 'planned system of production for use', he was now obliged to formulate a popular front economics which could command the support of all 'progressive political forces'. As Strachey put it (writing in 1938), 'if for good or evil we have adopted People's Front Politics we must have a People's Front economics also. If we do not the result will not be that we avoid being involved in a reformist economic policy, but that we get involved in a thoroughly bad reformist policy.'[17] Strachey had, therefore, to turn his attention back once again to the period of transition; to devising a medium-term, reformist economic strategy which would, at least temporarily, permit the survival of capitalism and which, by preventing its catastrophic demise, would stem the advance of fascism.

Two things followed. First, as regards economic prescriptions, Strachey had to re-enter the realm of the politically possible and economically feasible, focusing once again on the economic short run. Secondly, and following from this, Strachey had to re-shelve the sacred texts and begin reading the economic works of those who, often for very different reasons, sought to prevent at least the violent overthrow of capitalism. This Strachey duly did.[18]

So what was to be done? Here Strachey made no pretence to prescriptive originality, pointing out that almost all the measures which he was advocating 'found a place . . . in the official Labour Party programme. The measures have been familiar features of Labour and to some extent Liberal programmes for many years.' They included first, the distribution of 'increased purchasing power amongst the wage-earning population by way, mainly, of increased social service provision and minimum wage legislation', the funds being found 'either by the employing capitalists by way of an increased wages bill or out of taxation imposed by the Government on the same class'; and secondly, the provision of 'work and, therefore, wages for the mass of the workers' and there followed the conventional list of capital projects such as roads, railways, land reclamation, housing, etc. The third component of the strategy involved the reorganization of industry and here Strachey argued for the creation of a National Investment Board to effect the public control or nationalization of industries such as mining and armaments.[19]

Now in the mid-thirties, Strachey had rejected such an expansionary programme on the grounds that it failed to resolve capitalism's central contradiction, namely that it was caught between the Scylla of a falling rate or profit which imperilled its dynamism and the Charybdis of under-consumption which periodically threatened its stability. Thus in the mid–1930s he argued that any attempt to escape from under-consumption crises by way of increased government expenditure or higher wages would imperil the dynamism of capitalism by accelerating the fall in the rate of profit, whereas the neo-classical strategy of increasing profits by lowering wages would, in addition to intensifying class conflict, precipitate or exacerbate a crisis of deficient demand.

Now this position, articulated most fully and clearly in *The Nature of Capitalist Crisis*, can also be found in *What are We to Do?* However, in addition to such bald statements of despair, there are also indications in the 1938 work of some light at the end of the reformist tunnel. Thus Strachey accepted that it was 'quite possible that social reforms by widening the market and so making it possible for the capitalists to use all their capital, would actually increase the *total amount* of profit and interest which the capitalists would receive',[20] i.e. there existed the possibility of everyone or nearly everyone being a winner as a result of the expansionary strategy which he was proposing. Yet for all that Strachey was none the less quick to emphasize that popular front economics would not provide a permanent means of escape for capitalism, for capitalists would still tend to react in such a way as to imperil the system's vitality. 'Experience indicates', he wrote, 'that the capitalists will not . . . be willing to take a lower rate of return on their money' because 'The fact that' this would be accompanied by an increase in *their* market will always appear as a dim, questionable, theoretical sort of consideration which no practical man would be willing to take into account. For the increase in costs inevitably comes first. The employer is faced with the necessity of producing more money to pay out to his workers and for the raw materials at the end of the week. He will not [therefore] be in any mood to listen to arguments about his money flowing back to him by way of an increased demand for goods.[21]

However, despite this continuity of pessimism, Strachey had shifted his position. In the mid–1930s Strachey had dismissed the efficacy of a reformist strategy on the grounds of economic logic alone, now the case for pessimism rested more precariously upon a particular interpretation of the behavioural psychology of the capitalist. The bars of the logical prison which Strachey himself had constructed were at last beginning to bend.

In fact, in the business of bending, Strachey went further than this and argued that it might after all be possible to persuade certain groups of capitalist producers of the benefits accruing from popular front economics and so maintain their animal spirits. Here it was important to dissipate their fears of imminent liquidation and persuade them that in the medium term their autonomy would be guaranteed and indeed bolstered by the economic policies of a popular front government. So by 1938, Strachey had taken the first important steps back towards the road of liberal socialism and in that respect *A Programme for Progress* (1940) while it certainly marked his formal and irrevocable rupture with British communism, simply continued a process of intellectual liberation already begun.

Reviewing *A Programme* in *Labour Monthly* in June 1940, J. R. Campbell, a member of the British Communist Party, wrote that 'Strachey [was] going back to the "inevitability of gradualness", to the step by step transformation of capitalism into socialism with Keynes instead of Sidney Webb as the prophet of this stale rehash reformism'. He had, to quote Campbell again, 'come precious near to inventing one of those Social-Democratic utopias like the I.L.P. Living Wage Plan of 1926–29'.[22] Leaving aside the small fact that Webb had not supported the ILP Living Wage strategy and that if Strachey had 'invented' such a strategy it was for the second time, it is fair to say that Campbell had hit the nail accurately on the head. Of course, what was wrong about *A Programme for Progress* for the communists was not the theoretical coherence or otherwise of its economics as its timing. The world had moved on since 1938. The Popular Front was a dead duck and so, for the British Communist Party, was popular front economics.

Yet, if *What are We to Do?* marked a significant advance along the road to *A Programme for Progress*, it is important to note three important features of the latter work which distinguish it from the former. First, there was the explicit and generous use of Keynesian sources. Most obviously, Strachey drew upon J. M. Keynes' *General Theory* (1936) but he also cites and uses, among other works, James Meade's *Consumers' Credit and Unemployment* (1938) and Douglas Jay's *The Socialist Case* (1937). In this context too it is interesting to note that while Lenin is cited he occupies a relatively minor place in the index. Secondly, though I do not have time to develop this point, Strachey in the 1940 work subjected the Marxian perception of the economic tendencies making for the historical transience of capitalism to critical scrutiny. In particular, he questioned the existence of ineradicable tendencies to increasing immiseration and for the rate of profit to fall. Thirdly, he showed how the economic policies he proposed would allow capitalism to extricate itself for some considerable time from the deficient demand or deficient profitability dilemma.

So how was this to be done? How could the government pursue expansionary economic policies without rising costs and jeopardizing profitability. Here, as Campbell rightly pointed out, we are back with the 'social democratic utopias' of the ILP. First, and most importantly, the government should, through the medium of a public banking system, create the funds necessary either to embark upon a capital investment programme itself or to provide finance for those entrepreneurs who were willing 'to produce either independently or in conjunction with the government, the roads, schools, hospitals and houses which the nation required'.[23] Secondly, Strachey argued for a government-financed increase in consumption through the medium of increased old age pensions, family allowances and unemployment benefits.[24] Along with these specific proposals it is also interesting to note there went an emphasis upon the principle of consumer sovereignty of a kind which was last to be found in *Revolution by Reason* and a concomitant acceptance that the market might be used as a means of gauging how best to use resources. 'Let the consumer choose,' Strachey exhorted. 'Give twenty shillings to an unemployed man, an old age pensioner . . . or best of all to the mother of a large family of small children and . . . Each shilling will be used to buy and ultimately . . . will cause to be produced exactly those goods and services which best satisfy the most urgent needs of consumers.'[25] For Strachey such a deliberate creation and direct and indirect expenditure of funds by the government would provide a means of eliminating deficient demand without at the same time raising costs or depressing the rate of profits.

The second way in which expansion might be funded without imperilling the dynamism of the economic system was by way of redistributive taxation. This policy had been vetoed in the mid–1930s on the grounds that the increased taxation which it assumed, in falling necessarily on the economic surplus, would inevitably impinge upon profits. Now, however, Strachy disaggregated the Marxian concept of surplus, and identified interest and rent as constituent elements which might be tapped without squeezing profit margins or depressing the expectations of capitalist producers.[26]

With *A Programme for Progress*, therefore, Strachey had come full circle, returning to the policies and by implication some of the principles of liberal socialism. Thus the state by marrying social welfare objectives with a macroeconomic stabilization policy was seen as giving positive content to the ideal of economic liberty. At the same time, such a strategy would be pursued in the context of a mixed economy where private enterprise enjoyed and indeed would be guaranteed a significant measure of autonomy and where the transformative potential of the market was recognized and exploited. Thus state and consumer expenditure, mediated by the market, would be used to guide resources into socially beneficial lines of economic activity. In addition, it could be used to preserve that full employment equilibrium which had so manifestly eluded governments adhering to orthodox principles of fiscal management in the interwar period. With *A Programme for Progress* we are back once again in the realm of the possible or, as Comrade Campbell put it, 'in spite of a qualification inserted here and there throughout the book', *A Programme* represented, 'a fundamental abandonment of the positions of Revolutionary Marxism'.[27] It did indeed. The market had been rehabilitated, its socialist potential recognized, a realistic economic strategy based upon a positive notion of liberty had been formulated and Strachey had escaped at last from the endlessly revolving prayer wheel of Comintern communism.

**Acknowledgement**

Research for this paper was facilitated by a research grant from the British Academy.

**Notes**
1. For biographical information on Strachey, see H. Thomas (1973).
2. Strachey's *Revolution by Reason: an Outline of the Proposals Submitted to The Labour Movement by Sir Oswald Mosley* (1925) was, as the full title suggests, the amplification of proposals contained in a short pamphlet with the same title written

by Oswald Mosley and published some months earlier. However, both pamphlet and book, though different in minor respects, are quite clearly the product of a joint intellectual enterprise.

3. For a fuller treatment of the Marxian socialist and Fabian socialist critique of the market, see my *The Market and its Critics: socialist political economy in nineteenth century Britain*, pp. 216–25, 250–72.
4. J. Strachey (1925, p. 23).
5. See Thomas, (1973, p. 113).
6. Though I accept Michael Freeden's distinction between 'centrist' (Keynes) and 'new' or 'left' liberalism (Hobson), a distinction for which he makes a convincing case. (Freeden, 1986).
7. J. Strachey (1925, pp. 128, 133ff.).
8. Ibid., pp. 135–6, 162.
9. Ibid., pp. 149–50.
10. Ibid, p. 179.
11. J. Strachey (1927, p. 9; emphasis added).
12. Bevan, Brown, Strachey and Young (1931, pp. 33–5).
13. Ibid., pp. 12, 25–6.
14. Ibid., pp. 6–7.
15. J. Strachey (1936, p. 28).
16. Koestler, (1983, p. 335).
17. See Thomas, (1973, p. 175).
18. It was, for example, in 1937 that Strachey read Keynes' *General Theory* and Douglas Jay's *The Socialist Case*.
19. J. Strachey, (1938, pp. 339n., 338–67).
20. Ibid., p. 341.
21. Ibid., p. 342.
22. J. R. Campbell (1940, pp. 361–3).
23. Strachey, (1940, pp. 54–5).
24. Ibid., pp. 95–6.
25. Ibid., pp. 94–6.
26. Ibid., pp. 154.
27. Campbell (1940, p. 363).

## References

Bevan, A., Brown. W. J., Strachey, J. and Young, A. 1931, *A National Policy: An account of the Emergency Programme Advanced by Sir Oswald Mosley*, London.

Campbell, J. R. 1940, 'Immediate programme or social democratic utopia', *Labour Monthly* 22, pp. 361–3.

Freeden, M. 1986. *Liberalism Divided: A Study of British Political Thought 1914–1939*, Oxford University Press, Oxford.

Jay, D. 1937, *The Socialist Case*, Faber, London.

Koestler, A. 1983, *Arrow in the Blue*, Hutchinson, London.

Strachey, J. 1925, *Revolution by Reason: An Outline of the Proposals Submitted to the Labour Movement by Sir Oswald Mosley*, London.

—1927, 'Notes', *Socialist Review*, November, pp. 1–9.

—1936, *The Theory and Practice of Socialism*, Gollancz, London.

—1938, *What are We to Do?*, Gollancz, London.

—1940, *A Programme for Progress*, Gollancz, London.

Thomas, H. 1973, *John Strachey*, Methuen, London.

Thompson, N. 1988, *The Market and its Critics: Socialist Political Economy in Nineteenth Century Britain*, Routledge, London.

# 9 Alternative visions of the entrepreneur: Cantillon, Say, Dupuit

*Robert B. Ekelund, Jr and Robert F. Hébert*

## Early visions: Cantillon and Say

Richard Cantillon (*c*. 1680–1734), businessman, financier and economist, was the first writer to place the entrepreneur at the centre of a formal theory of markets. He depicted the entrepreneur as the *modus operandi* of the competitive process, a key figure who functions as a catalyst and a market intermediary. Cantillon's entrepreneur scouts the economic landscape, sniffs out profitable opportunities, estimates possible demand, directs resources to meet profit objectives and lives with the risk of possible failure.

In this pioneer formulation, the entrepreneur confronts uncertainty to a limited extent. Faced with the general lack of information about certain aspects of supply and demand (e.g. weather, population changes, consumer spending patterns), Cantillon's entrepreneurs 'buy at a certain price and . . . sell at an uncertain price', but they take each product as given. A farmer-entrepreneur might choose between producing wheat or oats based on their relative prices, but in either case, the form and substance of the crop is known. In other words, Cantillon regarded the entrepreneur as a price strategist, not a product strategist.[1]

J. B. Say (1767–1832) also made the entrepreneur the fulcrum of economic enterprise and organization. Allowing that the entrepreneur might also be a capitalist, Say nevertheless defined entrepreneurship in terms of a person's abilities and/or responsibilities as manager and decision-maker. Following Cantillon, Say regarded the entrepreneur's function as inherently risky. Say made entrepreneurship part of a larger concept, *industrie*, which he posed as a substitute for Adam Smith's use of 'labour'. Say (1821, p.xxxvii) argued that '*industry* is a more comprehensive and significant term than labour' because in addition to physical exertion, it embraces functions involving human skill, judgement and ingenuity. Say made the entrepreneur a member of the *industrieux*:[2] his role is to coordinate economic resources and combine them into a utility-creating process, and he faces uncertainty regarding 'the causes and circumstances that facilitate demand'.

The basic limitation of Say's theory is that his entrepreneur operates within a stationary equilibrium setting characterized by the equality of product prices with their costs of production. Although the entrepreneur can exercise judgement within the production process, he is unable to see beyond that process to the discovery of new processes or to changes inspired by different social structures. Specifically, Say's theory leaves no room for demand *discovery*, an important entrepreneurial function. Say was rather sanguine concerning the abilities of entrepreneurs in this regard. He believed that they commonly know little of the cause and circumstances that facilitate demand and, furthermore, he accused entrepreneurs of myopia and misdirection in attempting to learn (Say, 1821, p. 132).

**Dupuit on utility, demand and entrepreneurship**
On the one hand, Jules Dupuit (1804–66) absorbed vital lessons from Cantillon and Say, but on the other hand, he made the concept of entrepreneurship more robust. His vision of entrepreneurship is encased within a pragmatic analysis of utility and demand.

*Utility, product quality and the competitive process*
Dupuit's contributions to comparative statics establish him as an early and important 'neoclassical' economist, but they also divert attention from his keen understanding of the dynamics of the competitive process, in which the entrepreneur plays a crucial role. It is not common knowledge that Dupuit went beyond static analysis (which he believed to be a mere abstraction of market operations) to a view of competition that stressed interactions between gradations of product quality and nominal market prices. Dupuit broadened the dimensions of competition by defining and elaborating the connection between (marginal) utility and demand. This link is fundamental and crucial to everything he did in economics. In Dupuit's economic theory demand presupposes utility, and he never tired of stressing the point that 'there is no utility other than that which people are willing to pay for' (Dupuit, 1844, p. 96). He argued correctly that the maximum sacrifice in terms of money that individuals were willing to give was the best estimate of the utility of the object (Dupuit, 1844, p. 89).

Dupuit thought of goods as combinations of utility-producing characteristics rather than as one-dimensional 'lumps' of utility. He defined quality attributes broadly to include any product or service element that augments consumers' utility, or that avoids disutility by reducing waiting time or transactions costs. Furthermore, Dupuit understood the concept of a full-price market equilibrium wherein (e.g. in the case of transportation) waiting time is minimized through a scheme of product differentiation (cf. Ekelund and Shieh, 1986). Dupuit (1844, p. 100) asserted that quality dimensions are basic to the definition of a 'good', and that each product is capable of many variations:

> Very infrequently does a modification of the productive process . . . not also change the quality of the product; the latter becomes better or worse, larger or smaller, lighter or heavier, quicker or slower, and so on. Now all these qualities have a value which must be recognized in the calculation of utility.

Clearly, dynamic competition is an ongoing process of creating new combinations of utility-producing characteristics which will reward the creator with increased profits.

*Demand discovery and the role of the entrepreneur*
Within this dynamic, competitive process, Dupuit made the entrepreneur responsible for 'demand discovery'. The entrepreneur must estimate the utility that individuals or groups of individuals attach to goods or services. Since each good or service is potentially comprised of a number of utility dimensions, the entrepreneur's function is fairly sophisticated. It requires the 'production' of utility beyond what is attributed to the mere physical dimensions of the product. The entrepreneur must be skilful at creating utility through market segmentation, quality variation, and all manner of product differentiations. He must be able to identify and supply the commodity characteristics (convenience, time savings, physical properties, etc.) that consumers are willing to pay for.

Dupuit (1849, pp. 26, 31) held that such talent is relatively rare; it is in part *sui generis*, but it may also be acquired and enhanced:

> It takes a special skill to ascertain by certain indicators the importance of the service rendered, to define these clearly and classify them methodically in a schedule of prices that relates the price to that importance. Although this special skill is mainly a natural gift, it can, like any other skill, be greatly enhanced by study, observation, theory, and experience.

Dupuit was the first writer to argue that the entrepreneur is someone who manipulates prices *and* product characteristics, experimenting in order to find profitable combinations of elements that make up a successful product. Cantillon (and Say) told us that the entrepreneur does not know the demand function for each (monolithic) product he sells, but Dupuit told us that the entrepreneur does not even know the product itself! In other words, it is the duty of the entrepreneur to formulate a product and sales strategy. This necessarily enlarges the realm of uncertainty faced by the entrepreneur, but Dupuit was not daunted by the problem. He wrote:

> Ignorance of the law of consumption is no obstacle to the rational calculation of prices. Probability rather than certainty may render the problem more difficult, but it also lends new charm to the solution. All business calculations turn on conjectures about the law of consumption on the one hand, and on the means of making consumers pay for the utility of the products . . . on the other. But *in the producer's uncertain world the solution depends both on his skill in guessing the needs of the consumers and on his imagination in devising a method of making them pay as much as possible.* (Dupuit, 1849, p. 12; italics in original)

This insight led Dupuit to explore complex sales strategies such as price discrimination, but it also sensitized him to the importance of product differentiation that creates, in the subjective judgement of the consumer, an increase in utility. Dupuit recognized that different demand elasticities exist among consumers, and that this could be 'exploited' to the gain of both sellers *and* buyers:

> The same merchandise, disguised in diverse stores under various forms, is often sold at very different prices to rich people, to well-to-do people, and to poor people. There is the fine, the very fine, the extra fine, and the super fine which, although drawn from the same barrel, present no real difference except that of the superlative on the label and the price which is written on it. Why? Because the same thing has a very different utility value for the consumer. If there was only an average price, there would be a loss for all those who would deprive themselves of this product because they attach an inferior utility to this price, and a loss for the salesman who would be paid by many of the buyers only a very small part of the utility of the service rendered. (Dupuit, 1853, p. 177).

The important point for Dupuit was what effect product differentiation had upon total sales. He took it as self-evident that consumers' total utility would rise if the number of goods or services purchased increased.

Dupuit's analysis brought him to the threshold of modern microeconomic theory in several respects. He perceived the fact that transaction costs accompany all exchange, and he suggested that the entrepreneur must account for such costs in setting nominal prices. In the case of transport, Dupuit (1849, pp. 159ff; 1854, p. 343) advised that in certain instances nominal rates might be lowered to offset such 'customer costs' as slow-moving trains, inconvenient departures and arrivals, passenger congestion, and the high opportunity costs of alternative modes of transport. Thus the responsibility of devising a full-scale 'products policy' is two-pronged: the entrepreneur must ascertain the optimal (and variable) physical characteristics of a good; *and* he must discover and account for customer opportunity costs in devising the price or set of prices that maximise utility. In sum, Dupuit envisaged nothing less than what we now call a full-price competitive model, within which he gave the entrepreneur a prominent role.[3]

## Conclusion

After 1870, economics gradually and systematically shifted emphasis away from the *transformation* of resources into utility towards the *distribution* of utility under conditions of competitive market exchange. In the process, the role of the entrepreneur was gradually squeezed out of economic theory.[4] Few economists of the twentieth century tried to reverse the dominant view that microeconomics is (unilaterally) the theory of price. The most notable exceptions were Joseph Schumpeter (1883–1950) and Frank Knight (1885–1962).

Schumpeter (1926) was the first economist of the modern era to see beyond the narrow limits of mere price uncertainty and clearly to identify the role of the entrepreneur with the creation of new products. He linked the entrepreneur to innovation, by which he meant a change in the form of the production function, and he gave the entrepreneur a key role in the theory of economic development. Moreover, Schumpeter extended the entrepreneur's range of action to include quality variations of existing goods as well as creation of new goods. However, he minimized the role of uncertainty, declaring unequivocally that 'the entrepreneur is never the risk-bearer'.

Frank Knight (1921) recognized the limitations of purely deterministic price-theoretic models. While admitting that the price system effectively allocates resources among alternative uses, he argued that it does not establish the *pattern* of alternative uses. According to Knight the pattern of alternative uses is determined by the entrepreneur. However, Knight had little to say about what constitutes a product, or about the entrepreneur's role in discovering the bundle of attributes that compromises a product's ability to convey utility to its users.

Among contemporary writers, Israel Kirzner (1973; 1985) currently leads the effort to restore the entrepreneur to a prominent place in economic theory. Kirzner's discussion of 'demand discovery' concentrates on the *price*-equilibrating actions of the arbitrageur/entrepreneur, thus implying a given set of goods whose prices are brought into competitive equilibrium by the entrepreneur (i.e. Cantillon's original notion). The wider range of entrepreneurial activity that encompasses product formation and marketing strategy remains underdeveloped in contemporary economics despite Dupuit's early conceptual insights on the scope of entrepreneurship.

Dupuit's frequent and first-hand experience with specific market behaviour, especially the economics of transport and service enterprises schooled him in the wider context of competition and entrepreneurship. His integration of the theories of consumer behaviour and entrepreneurship culminated an early French tradition that linked entrepreneurship to uncertainty. Cantillon and Say singled out and analysed certain effects of price uncertainty in competitive markets. Dupuit enriched their analyses by exploring the consequences of product uncertainty as well as price uncertainty. He was led to this subject by his original discovery of the utility foundations of demand. Dupuit understood that the demand function, conceived as the embodiment of consumers' utility, is merely an abstract notion until it is discovered by entrepreneurs who are willing to bet on their judgement. To him, therefore, the theory of consumer behaviour could not be compartmentalized. Even though entrepreneurs are profit-motivated, they play a vital (and joint) role with consumers in effecting (aggregate) utility-maximization.

**Notes**
1.  Cantillon (1931, pp. 51, 121) noted that the entrepreneur 'can, of course, fix a price and stand out against selling unless he gets it, but if his customers leave him to buy cheaper from another, he will be eaten up by expenses while waiting to sell at the price he demands, and that will ruin him as soon as or sooner than if he sold without profit'. He summed up the consequences wryly: 'It often happens that sellers who are too obstinate in keeping up their price in the market, miss the opportunity of selling their produce or merchandise to advantage and are losers thereby. It also happens that by sticking to their prices they may be able to sell more profitably another day.'
2.  See James (1977). Say (1821, p. 329) divided the *industrieux* into *savants* (scientists), *entrepreneurs* (managers) and *ouvriers* (workers), but he noted that sometimes a manufacturer acts as a 'man of science . . . and . . . [an] entrepreneur too'.
3.  Space limitations prevent a more detailed and elaborate analysis of Dupuit's highly original view of entrepreneurship, which anticipated neoclassical insights of the modern era, particularly Kelvin Lancaster's (1966) attempted revision of the theory of consumer behaviour. A more detailed treatment of these matters is contained in Ekelund and Hébert (1988).
4.  The traditional story in the history of economic thought is that, after Say, further contributions to the theory of entrepreneurship languished until Schumpeter resurrected the concept and gave it a starring role in his *Theory of Economic Development* (1911). This conventional wisdom constitutes a serious abridgement of actual developments in the history of economic analysis. For a detailed treatment of the historical development of entrepreneurship, see Hébert and Link (1988).

**References**
Cantillon, R. 1931, *Essai sur la nature du commerce en général*, trans. H. Higgs, Royal Economic Society, London.

Dupuit, J. 1844, *De la mesure de l'utilité des travaux publics*, in *De L'utilité et de sa mesure*, ed. M. de Bernardi, La Riforma Sociale, Torino, 1933.

—, 1849, *De l'influence des péages sur l'utilié des voies de communication* in *De'L'utilité et de sa mesure*, ed. M. de Bernardi, La Riforma Sociale, Torino, 1933.

—, 1853, *De l'utilité et de sa mesure. De l'utilité publique*, in *De L'utilité et de sa mesure*, ed. M. de Bernardi, La Riforma Sociale, Torino, 1933.

—, 1854, 'Péage', in *Dictionnaire de l'économie politique*, eds C.Coquelin and C. Guillaumin, Paris, Guillaumin, 1853, II, pp. 339–44.

Ekelund, R. B. Jr and Shieh, Y. N. 1985, 'Dupuit, spatial economics and optimal resource allocation: a French tradition', *Economica* 53, pp. 483–96.

— and Hébert, R. F., 1988, 'Entrepreneurship as demand discovery: Dupuit's "characteristics" theory of consumer behavior', unpublished manuscript.

Hébert, R. F. and Link, A. N., 1988, *The Entrepreneur: Mainstream Views and Radical Critiques*, 2nd edn. Praeger, New York.

James, M. 1977, 'Pierre-Louis Roederer, Jean-Baptiste Say, and the concept of *industrie*', *History of Political Economy* 9, pp. 455–75.

Kirzner, I. M., 1973, *Competition and Entrepreneurship*, University of Chicago Press, Chicago.

—, 1985, *Discovery and the Capitalist Process*, University of Chicago Press, Chicago.

Knight, F. H. 1921, *Risk, Uncertainty and Profit*, Harper & Row, New York.

Lancaster, K. J. 1966, 'A new approach to consumer theory', *Journal of Political Economy*, 74, pp. 132–57.

Say, J. B. 1821, *A Treatise on Political Economy*, trans. C. R. Prinsep from the 4th French edn, Augustus Kelley, New York, 1971.

Schumpeter, J. A. 1926, *The Theory of Economic Development*, trans R. Opie from the 2nd German edn, Harvard University Press, Cambridge, Mass., 1934.

## 10 The synoptic edition of the *Eléments d'Economie Politique Pure*

### Claude Mouchot and Pierre-Henri Goutte

In January 1988, the Centre A. & L. Walras of the University Lumière in Lyon, published Volume VIII of the *Œuvres économiques complètes d'Auguste et de Léon Walras: Eléments d'économie politique pure*[1], in the form of a synoptic edition of the five editions written by Léon Walras.

We propose to present in this paper Volume VIII and the choices that directed how this edition was compiled. In order to throw light on the problems that were posed by this choice, we must briefly set out the development of the *Eléments* in the course of the successive editions. This history of the *Eléments* has no pretence to be exhaustive: rather it will situate the main amendments that were important to the synoptic edition. Then we shall explain the solutions we adopted; and lastly, we shall introduce the complementary elements that we have added to this volume, in particular the *Abrégé des éléments d'économie politique pure*.

**The development of the *Eléments***
Walras introduced into his successive editions, and especially into the second and fourth editions, considerable amendments to his work. We have felt it necessary to situate them in essential continuity, in the mind of the author: 'my doctrine of today is just the same as my doctrine [of 1874–7].'[2] Thus according to Walras the amendments that he introduced did not modify his theory; they only improved it.

*The first edition (1874–7)*
The first edition of the *Eléments* was published in two installments. The first, on 27 July 1874, included:

I Objet et divisions de l'éconnomie politique et sociale
II Théorie mathématique de l'échange
III Du numéraire et de la monnaie.

The second of 6 September 1877, included:

124

IV  Théorie naturelle de la production et de la consommation de la richesse
V   Conditions et conséquences du progrès économique
VI  Effets naturels et nécessaires des divers modes d'organisation économique de la société.

We shall only note here that these titles call for only two 'Theories': exchange and production; the developments on capitalization and credit, on the one hand, and on money, on the other hand, doubtless not seeming sufficiently elaborated to L. Walras: he did not call them 'theories'.

*The second edition (1889)*
Published in July 1889, it differed considerably from the first edition. First there was a complete renewal of the study of money, in Part V (and no longer III), under the title: 'theory of money'; he substituted 'for the demonstration based on the consideration of the "circulation à desservir" . . . the demonstration based on the consideration of the "encaisse désirée" '.[3] Two points are of note here. First, the development of his conception of the part played by money in pure theory; in fact the summary of the 29th lesson in the first edition reads: 'there is every reason for gathering into a single theory the pure theory and the applied theory of the circulation of the social wealth' [p. 540 of the synoptic edition]; the summary of the corresponding lesson of the second edition (37th lesson) is modified thus: 'we will have the pure theory of money followed immediately by its theory of application' [p. 540]. Thus one can observe Walras's conceptual evolution. But – and this is the second point – this evolution was incomplete: first he kept in *pure* economy 'Four lessons of applied theory [of money]';[4] then, and in particular, 'the equation equality of supply and demand of money was always set apart and empirically'.[5]
    Let us note then that, in respect of money, we need to have at our disposal two parallel texts: the first edition and the second edition.
    Following that, there is a considerable reorganization of the Parts 'in order to mark better the order of the four big problems of which I have spoken [problems of exchange, of production, of capitalization and credit, and of money]'.[6] In particular, a passage from Part V (1st edn) became the 'theory of capitalization and credit' (Part IV). Thus, from the second edition onwards the essential structure of the work is in place. This is to be found again in the synoptic edition by the frequence and importance of texts common to editions 2–5 (we have noted: 5th edn, the edition of 1926; see below: the 'edition définitive').

Lastly, we draw attention to the introduction of the 'Théorème de l'utilité maxima des capitaux neufs'[7] 'which really forms the crowning of the whole structure of mathematical economics, as the "théorème de la satisfaction maxima" forms its basis'.[8]

It is necessary too to note another very important point: the criticism of Walrasian 'tatonnement' by Joseph Bertrand[9] in 1883. Bertrand later showed by various examples that the equilibrium of production is undefined on a real market. Walras answered that 'on the theoretical market . . . exchange remains not yet settled until the increase or the decrease has brought about the equality of supply and demand', [10] but it was not until the 4th edition that he introduced the 'tatonnement' with pledges, which, according to him, overcame that criticism.

### The third edition (1896)

This edition was more or less a reprint of the second edition. Walras made no secret of this: he reproduced in the third edition the Preface to the second, and the Preface to the fourth edition begins thus: 'This 4th edition . . . is in fact only the 3rd, the one which bore that figure (1896) having been made with copies left over from the 2nd (1889)' (p.XXVI of the synoptic edition).

There were however, two important changes. First, the omission of the four lessons of the applied theory of money, noted above, which would later be partly re-used in the *Etudes d'économie politique appliquée*. Next, the introduction of the third appendix: I. Geometrical theory of price determination; II. Observations on the principle of the theory of prices by MM. Auspitz and Lieben; III. Note on the refutation of the English theory of rent by M. Wicksteed.

This appendix opens the well-known quarrel about the theory of marginal productivity between Walras and Barone.

The third edition thus set the following problems for the synoptic edition: how to deal with the texts which had been re-used in the *Etudes d'économie politique appliquée*; and what was to be done with a text that only appeared in this edition: Appendix III.

### The fourth edition (1900)

This was published in September 1900 and introduced four important changes.

First, money was at last completely linked to the whole of the procedure. Thus he wrote in March 1899: 'I will have completely solved the problem which consists [ . . . ] of establishing rationally a complete equilibrium of economic society at a given moment.'[11]

The synoptic edition has therefore had to place in parallel three different texts, concerning money.

Then, this linking of money to the rest of the construction led him to modify the organization of the Parts. If we leave aside the division into two Parts of the theory of exchange (two commodities; several commodities), which was more pedagogically than conceptually necessary the general equilibrium builds itself, step by step, in Parts II – VI by the successive solution of the 'four big problems of political economy'. What is more, 'all dynamic [Parts VII and VIII] [is] thus clearly put after the static'.[12] This new organization led him to break up the former Part IV (in the 3rd edn.) which is used partly in Part V (the 4th edn.) and partly in Part VII (the 4th edn.).

(It should be noted that the synoptic edition makes possible an uninterrupted reading of each edition in spite of all these reorganizations of Parts.)

Then again, 'as to what concerns production . . . the preliminary "tatonnements" for the establishment of equilibrium [are] no longer made effectively but with pledges'.[13]

This new presentation of the 'tatonnement' established the theoretical character of the Walrasian market; it thus constituted an answer to Bertrand's criticism but, as Professor D. A. Walker notes, it no longer had the power to explain economic reality.[14]

Lastly, the omission of Appendix III which was approved by K. Wicksell,[15] must be noted. It was replaced by § 326, which constitutes the presentation of the theorem of marginal productivity. Walras clearly attributed to Barone the corresponding equation.[16]

*The 'Edition définitive' (posthumous: 1926)*

This only differed from the fourth edition by the introduction of two notes dated 1902,[17] of which the first especially (§ 326) brought in a modification of the text. He took as his own the theory of marginal productivity, explaining himself clearly on that matter in this note: and in § 326 again, the affirmation of using up the output between the producing services. William Jaffé called this edition the '4th definitive'.

This brief outline of the development of the *Eléments* is necessary in order to understand the problems set by our synoptic edition: additions, omissions and reorganizations were numerous; nevertheless, we had to produce a work that was both readable and that gave all the variants in the clearest possible way to make it easy for the reader.

**The synoptic edition**

*The general organization of the volume*
First of all Walras's work in its most finished form, that is to say the
'Edition définitive' (which we call the fifth edition) had to be readily
accessible. Therefore, this edition is reproduced continuously throughout the work. The four preceding editions are introduced when they
differ from the fifth as variants of this fifth edition, and parallel to it.

One of the first problems was that of the reorganization of the Parts
– and also of the lessons – carried out by Walras in the second and
fourth editions. We solved this problem in two ways: first, by using
and reproducing the 'Table of corresponding Sections, Lessons and
Parts' elaborated by Jaffé in *Elements of pure economics*; this magnificent work greatly facilitated the job for us as the correspondences and
transfers of texts was provided for us ready-made; and second, by
carrying over as the beginning of each Part and Lesson, the numbers,
titles and summaries of *all* the editions. This practice often leads to
repetitions, but it allows, where necessary, the specification of differences where they exist. On the other hand, the fact that a Part or a
Lesson has been only partially re-used in that place is also made clear.
A note indicates, in this case, where the rest of this Part or Lesson
can be found; thus allows a continuous reading of any of the editions.

A second problem was the risk of having four variants of the same
text. That did not happen owing to the fact that there are considerable
similarities, noted above, between the second and third editions, and
the fourth and fifth. As a result, we have a maximum of three parallel
texts, in particular those on money, as has been seen.

Lastly, we have omitted two texts, important by their length: the
mathematical introduction – 'Des fonctions et de leur représentation
géométrique. Théorie mathématique de la chute des corps.' – which
was in the second and third editions, and which appears in *Oeuvres
économiques complètes*, Vol. VII, *Mélanges d'économie politique et
sociale*; and the 39th and 40th Lessons of the 2nd edition which appear
in *Oeuvres*, Vol X, *Etudes d'économie politique appliquée*. (Both
changes Walras carried out himself.) We have, nevertheless, reproduced the summaries of these two lessons in the place where they
would logically have appeared.

(We have kept on the 37th and 38th Lessons of the second edition
because of their parallelism with Lessons 29, 31 and 32 of the first
edition.)

*Variants of considerable volume: from one paragraph to several pages*
An *added text* (which did not appear in the first four editions) is
indicated by a vertical line in the left margin, with the indication of
the editions in which it appears (see case 1, example 2 and 3 in Annex,
p. 132). This is a case for Appendices I and II.

A *modified text* carries the same indications: a vertical line in the
left margin with an indication of the editions in which it appears. It
is thus always placed on an odd-numbered page, and the former
variant is placed opposite, on the even-numbered page, boxed (see
case 2 in Annex, p. 134) This is the case especially for the texts
concerning money which have needed two different borderings (1st
edition, and 2nd and 3rd editions).

An *omitted text* (i.e. which appeared only in the first four editions)
is inserted in the text of the fifth edition in the place which it had in
those editions. It is then boxed, with the indication of the editions in
which it figured; it is reproduced in smaller print. This is the case,
e.g., for the 28th Lesson of the 1st edition, the 37th and 38th Lessons
of the 2nd edition, and the Appendix III of the 3rd edition.

*Variants of small volume: from one word to a few lines*
These are put in footnotes which are referred to by letters (a, b,
c, . . . ) in the text. This notes system and other symbols are explained
in the Annex.

**Complementary elements**

*The* Abrégé des Eléments d'économie politique pure
We decide to include the *Abrégé* in this volume as more than 90 per
cent of this work is used again in identical form from the *Eléments*
or from Appendix I, as Walras clearly states in his Foreword. We
have therefore set out a table of corresponding Sections, Lessons and
Parts between the *Abrégé* and the fifth edition of the *Eléments*. In
this table the sections noted in italics draw attention to a difference
– minor or major – with the text of the *Eléments*; the whole of these
differences is then specified, lesson by lesson, in the following pages.

*The terminologies*
We have reproduced the *Terminologie* for the fourth edition of the
*Eléments* and that of the *Abrégé*, drawn up by Walras, the manuscripts
of which are to be found in the Bibliothèque cantonale et universitaire
de Lausanne.[18]
The quite exceptional character, in Walras's day, should be noted

of this indication of 'key terms' in his works, as too, the precision of his bibliographic references.

These *Terminologies* will be of particular use to us in setting the thematic indexes which are to be found in Volume XIV of the *Oeuvres*.

### The Annexes

We have recalled briefly in the annexes the history of the editions of the *Eléments* (with the list of reviews kept by Walras) as well as that of the *Abrégé*.

### The notes of William Jaffé

From the beginning of our project we felt it necessary to introduce in this volume the 'Translator's notes' of *Elements of pure economics*, both to pay tribute to the one who did so much to make known the ideas of the Master of Lausanne and to acknowledge that our edition owed much to that book and also to acknowledge the irreplaceable tool that the *Correspondence and Related Papers of Léon Walras* represents. We wish to thank Professor D. A Walker, once again, for allowing us to reproduce them.

We have differentiated between his notes on the one hand, simple directions for reading matter (bibliographic references, references to another part of the text, etc., which are set at the bottom of the pages with the indication: [W. J.]: and on the other, analyses of the contents, which have been placed at the end of the book.

Thus we have kept to the principle we had set ourselves at the beginning of our project: to give the reader the texts of Auguste and Léon Walras, independently of the criticism, positive or negative that they gave rise to.

### Notes

1. Volume VII, *Mélanges d'économie politique et sociale*, was published in 1986. See Claude Hébert and Jean-Pierre Potier (1987), 'The surprising history of the *Mélanges d'économie politique et sociale*, a previously unpublished work by Léon Walras', *History of Economics Society Bulletin* IX(1), Autumn pp. 67–79.

    See also Pierre Dockès and Jean-Michel Servet 1987. 'Notes on the history of publications and reserves of the Walras Archives', *Papers of the XIVe Meeting of the History of Economics Society*, 20–22 June, 4, pp. 1427–39.
2. *Oeuvres économiques complètes*, vol. VIII, *Eléments d'économie politique pure*, Paris, Economica, 1988; Prefaces to the second and fourth editions, pp. 10, 11.
3. Preface to the second edition, pp. 4, 6.
4. Preface to the second edition, p. 4; these are Lessons 37 – 40.
5. Preface to the fourth edition, p. 9.
6. Preface to the second edition, p. 8.
7. Lesson 26 of the second edition, pp. 406–26.

8. *Correspondence of Léon Walras and Related Papers* 1965, ed. William Jaffé, North-Holland, Amsterdam, 3 vols; vol. II, letter 859, p. 277.
9. *Journal des savants*, September 1883, pp. 499–508.
10. 'Un économiste inconnu: Hermann-Henri Gossen', *Journal des économistes*, 4th séries, 30 (4) August 1885, pp. 68–90.
11. *Correspondence*, vol III, letter 1396, p. 66.
12. Ibid., letter 1423, p. 89.
13. Preface to the first edition, pp. 5, 7.
14. Donald A. Walker 1987, 'Walras's theory of tatonnement', *Journal of Political Economy* 95 (4), August pp. 758–74.
15. *Correspondence*, vol. III, letter 1461, p. 126.
16. *Oeuvres*, vol. VIII, *Eléments*, p. 590.
17. Ibid., pp. 591, 637.
18. Cotation: IS 27 V a 17.

*Case No. 1: there is no boxed text on the left hand page*

*Exemple 1*

Une seule minute pour faire l'échange[2]. Mais, en bonne logique, il faut aller du cas général au cas particulier, et non du cas particulier au cas général comme un physicien qui, pour observer le <sup>d</sup>ciel<sup>d</sup>, choisirait avec soin un temps couvert au lieu de profiter d'un <sup>e</sup>soir<sup>e</sup> sans nuage<sup>f</sup>.

---

*dd 1–3: soleil.*
*ee 1–3: ciel.*
*f 1  : fin de la 9<sup>e</sup> leçon.*

*Exemple 2*

2–5 | Or il est très évident que le maximum d'utilité à obtenir ainsi n'est pas le maximum relatif de la libre concurrence, compatible avec cette condition que tous les échangeurs donneront et recevront ‹librement› des deux marchandises dans une proportion commune et identique, mais un maximum absolu qui ne tient nul compte de la condition d'unité de prix ‹et d'égalité de l'offre et de la demande effectives à | 4–5 ce prix et qui, ainsi, supprime la propriété›.

4–5 | 1. Voyez *Etudes d'économie sociale. Théorie de la propriéte.* 4.

Text common to the five editions (as there is no vertical line to the left) except:
*dd 1–3*: the first three editions read '*soleil*' instead of the word 'ciel';
*ee 1–3*: likewise they read 'ciel' instead of 'soir'.
Note [2] draws attention to a note of W. Jaffé, at the end of the book.

This text appears only in the 2nd–5th editions vertical line to the left and indication: 2–5.
The word '*librement*' and the expression '*et d'égalité ... propriété*' appears only in the 4th and 5th edition: vertical line to the right and indication: 4–5.
Note 1 appears only in the 4th and 5th editions.

*Exemple 3*

2–5 | Ainsi se résoudrait le problème qui consiste, – *Etant données deux marchandises* (A) *et* (B) et les courbes d'utilité ou de besoin de ces deux marchandises pour chacun des échangeurs[f], ainsi que la quantité possédée par chacun des porteurs, à déterminer les courbes de demande[g].

f 2–4: ou les équations de ces courbes.
g 2–4: ou leurs équations.

Text appearing only in the 2nd–5th editions.
f 2–4: 2nd–4th editions used, in addition, the expression 'ou les équations de ces courbes';
g 2–4: likewise they use in addition 'ou leurs équations'.

*Case No. 2: there is a boxed text on the left hand page*

1-3

244. On a d'abord, pour un individu quelconque, l'équation d'échange des services contres les produits et services consommables et contre le revenu net

$$o_t p_t + \ldots + o_p p_p + \ldots o_k p_k + o_{k'} p_{k'} + o_{k''} p_{k''} + \ldots$$
$$= d_a + d_b p_b + d_c p_c + d_d p_d + \ldots + d_e p_e \ (§ 242).$$

Et, la condition de satisfaction maxima (§ 80) étant toujours la condition déterminante d'offre des services et de demande des produits et de revenu net, on a aussi, entre ces quantités demandées et les prix, les équations:

$$\varphi_t \, (q_t - o_t) = p_t \varphi_a \, (d_a),$$
..............
$$\varphi_p \, (q_p - o_p) = p_p \varphi_a \, (d_a),$$
..............
$$\varphi_k(q_k - o_k) = p_k \varphi_a \, (d_a),$$
$$\varphi_{k'} \, (q_{k'} - o_{k'}) = p_{k'} \varphi_a \, (d_a),$$
$$\varphi_{k''} \, (q_{k''} - o_{k''}) = p_{k''} \varphi_a \, (d_a),$$
..............

← 4-5

|2-3

240. On a d'abord l'équation

[1]  $E = F_a \, (p_t \ldots p_p \ldots p_k, p_{k'} \ldots p_{k''} \ldots p_b, p_c, p_d \ldots i)$,

soit 1 équation d'excédent total du revenu sur la consommation (§ 238).

241. On a d'ailleurs, pour un individu quelconque, l'équation d'échange des "services[a] contre les capitaux[b] et les produits ‹et services› consommables

$$o_t p_t + \ldots + o_p p_p + \ldots + o_k p_k + o_{k'} p_{k'} + o_{k''} p_{k''} + \ldots$$
$$= f_a \, (p_t \ldots p_p \ldots p_k, p_{k'}; p_{k''} \ldots p_b, p_c, p_d \ldots i)$$
$$+ d_a + d_b p_b + d_c p_c + d_d p_d + \ldots$$

Et, la condition de satisfaction maxima (§ 80) étant toujours la condition déterminante d'offre positive ou négative des services[b] et de demande des produits, on a aussi, entre ces quantités offertes, ces quantités demandées et les prix, les équations

$$\varphi_t \, (q_t - o_t) = p_t \varphi_a \, (d_a),$$
..............
$$\varphi_p \, (q_p - o_p) = p_p \varphi_a \, (d_a),$$
..............

*aa 1*: revenus producteurs
  *b 1*: producteurs

Key to the notes:
*aa 1*: 1st edn used the expression *'revenus pro-ducteurs'* instead of the word *'services'*.
*b 1*: 1st edn adds *'producteurs'*:
–6th line: *'capitaux producteurs'*
–12th line: *'services producteurs'*
The vertical line to the right, marked 2–3, draws attention to the fact that the words: ‹*et services*› appear only in the editions 2 & 3.
← shows the beginning of the boxed text; . . . indicates that this text is continued on the following page; when it is finished,
→ shows the return to 5th edn.

This text only appears in the 4th and 5th editions: this is what is indicated by the vertical line to the left and the indication 4–5 at the beginning of this line.
It replaces the corresponding text from the first three editions which appears, bordered and with indication of the edition 1–3 on the lefthand facing page.

# 11 L. E. von Mises on consumer sovereignty

## R. A. Gonce[1]

### I

The genius who inspires much of the contemporary Austrian economic theorists' work is L. E. von Mises. Setting aside his beliefs about philosophy and method, and looking at his version of substantive Austrian economic theory, what identifies it? The thesis of this essay is that the idea of consumer sovereignty, assured by a principle of harmony of rational interests in the long run, but endangered by a notion of entrepreneurial driving-force, is the overarching doctrine identifying it. The paper will glance at the history of the idea, proceed to Mises's use of it, and arrive at an assessment of his contribution.

### II

' "Consumer sovereignty" is one of those concepts that flourish and are widely influential long before they are explicitly recognized and named.'[2] The belief that effective consumer demand directs production and distribution, suggested in Adam Smith's work, was denied by socialists, culminating in Karl Marx, who maintained that private ownership over capital goods gives capitalists the power to dominate the social order and to suppress others' freedom. But emboldened by the new subjective theory of value of the 1870s, the idea began to revive and grow. In 1911, Frank A. Fetter claimed that in a market economy consumer demand amounts to a 'democracy of valuation' and 'dictates the direction of industry'.[3] In the 1920s the great debate over the theoretical possibilities of socialism was underway, and Mises was at work developing his own version of Austrian economic theory. In 1922, he referred to the *Herrschaft* of the consumers,[4] and elaborated on the notion as the years went by. In the 1930s, while the great debate was still vibrant, his ideas influenced W. H. Hutt and F. C. Benham, who named and treated theoretically the idea of 'consumer sovereignty', Hutt doing so in some detail.[5] Their work set off critical discussions by J. Viner in 1938 and L. M. Fraser in 1939. In the 1930s the critics were wondering: could the notion be convincing in the face of externalities, imperfect consumer rationality, variations in the

*136*

distribution of income among consumers, real costs, monopoly, mass production of standardized products, and selling efforts?

In those times Mises was producing his massive treatise *Nationalö-konomie* (1940). In its revised edition, *Human Action* (1949), created in and for America during World War II and the onset of the Cold War, and later slightly revised (1963, 1966), he further developed and completed his own version of Austrian economic theory that bears the idea of consumer sovereignty as its hallmark.[6]

## III

The heart of his argument is that if strict *laissez-faire* capitalism exists, wherein the state enforces juristic laws that leave the operation of natural laws unhampered, then consumer sovereignty will rule over all, with the rational interests of all other classes being harmonized with it in the long run. In more detail, the consumers' rational wants, as expressed by effective consumer demand in product markets, ulti-mately (the exact meaning of 'ultimately' being left unclear) will deter-mine all prices; self-interested entrepreneurs, factor owners, savers and investors will voluntarily and rationally calculate and choose courses of action in light of price facts; and so effective consumer demand will govern 'all economic phenomena'[7] and optimally satisfy itself.[8]

To prove this he adopts a method involving his conception of ration-alism (renamed 'apriorism'), abstraction (renamed the 'method of imaginary constructions') so that he can begin with one isolated indi-vidual and build up theory be restoring complexities stage by stage, and 'ratiocination' so that he can work out theorems. By this method he sets up his axioms in a theory of sociology (renamed 'praxeology'), and elaborates in detail their economic meaning in his version of Austrian economic theory (renamed 'catallactics').

His praxeology concerns isolated man, society, social order and the case of strict *laissez-faire* capitalism (called 'pure capitalism' and renamed the 'unhampered market economy').[9] Natural inequality, self-interest, autonomous rationality and libertarianism mark man, he con-tends. It is axiomatic that rational self-interest rules human action. Society is an unplanned outcome of rational self-interests. Natural laws (renamed 'praxeological laws'), grounded in the nature of man and the nature of the material world, constitute the social order.[10] In keeping with them, external freedom, division of labour, private ownership, exchange, competition and, apparently, capitalism exist. By the case of pure capitalism Mises means a state practising strict *laissez-faire* by enforcing juristic laws that ratify the praxeological laws but leave their operation unhampered, and that are so perfect as to allow no externalities to exist.[11] In this case of pure capitalism the praxeological laws will confer sovereignty upon the consumer interest. And they will bring about a harmony of the rational interests of all men in the long run;[12] implicitly, they will bring all other classes' interests into harmony in the long run with the sovereign consumers' interest.

Upon this theory of 'praxeology' he builds up, stage by stage, his own version of Austrian economic theory. The most relevant of these stages to begin with concerns the national economy in abstraction from economic growth, money, and international trade. Within it exist product markets and within them individuals with a consumer interest. The consumer interest, he holds, is egoistic, and 'stony-hearted' towards the feelings of others.[13] It desires leisure and the consumption of as many good quality and low-cost goods and services as possible. Implicitly, such consumption requires purchasing power obtained by work done in available employment opportunities. Explicitly, Mises allows that the consumer interest also wishes to consume in the sense of enjoying certain forms of work and certain desired working conditions.[14]

This consumer interest reveals itself in effective consumer demand. Disaggregating to one individual consumer, effective demand depends upon preferences manifesting autonomous rationality, considerable but less than perfect knowledge, subjective values, and mobility unimpeded by any product or brand loyalties; and it depends upon possession of purchasing power.

The ideas of power, coercion, freedom and equality are related, and now Mises defines these terms and draws some distinctions. In the political domain the state has power of coercion, and he narrowly defines coercion to mean physical force or the threat of it, exerted by a person or persons, applied directly to another, overriding the other's autonomous rationality, compelling certain action. Coercion suppresses external freedom. External freedom means solely absence of coercion, and its existence calls for neither possession of power nor any equality in the distribution of power. Efforts to redistribute power to achieve equality will conflict with external freedom.[15] In the economic domain 'all power is vested in the consumers'.[16] Their purchasing power by definition can exert 'indirect' or 'financial' or 'catallactic' pressure, but not coercion.[17] Thus it cannot suppress external freedom. Since it is not power of coercion it is not power at all. And so in the economic domain there is 'no compulsion and coercion',[18] and praxeological freedom is undiminished.

Effective consumer demand for the aggregate of all individuals in a given market results from an aggregation of preferences, and from some distribution of purchasing power among individuals. As an aggregate its effect is analogous to that of rule by majority.[19]

Entrepreneurs and the firms they organize face this effective consumer demand. Solely one interest motivates entrepreneurs: it is rational, long-run profit-maximization noted by Mises in abstraction from any trade-offs involving leisure or risk-aversion.[20] The firms the entrepreneurs organize are non-bureaucratic, wholly responsive to their will.[21] Hence the entrepreneurs' interest and their ability to execute it remain perfectly intact.

Several conditions force the entrepreneurial interest into harmony in the long run with the consumer interest. Consumers have considerable but less than perfect knowledge, they are rational, and their preferences are mobile. Competition in the structural sense prevails in the long run, competition being defined to mean the existence of many buyers and sellers, product differentiation, and no barriers to entry. Monopoly, a condition that can allow the entrepreneurial and consumer interests to conflict,[22] is held to be a rare case of little importance.[23] And competition in the behavioural sense Mises defines to mean 'catallactic' – as distinguished from 'biological' – competition, signifying conduct including only rivalrous efforts better to serve the consumer sovereignty and excluding all exploitative and anti-competitive acts.[24] These conditions impose catallactic pressure compelling the entrepreneurs to realize that superior service to consumers is the only way to secure their own profit interest, that any pursuit of their interest in conflict with the consumer interest (such as sloth resulting in inefficiency and high costs, poor quality products, fraudulent selling efforts, and so on) will bring its own punishment in the long run. These conditions cause the entrepreneurs to be powerless. They compel them to be 'subservient' and 'unconditionally' obedient to the consumer sovereignty, to be its virtual 'mandataries'.[25]

Price formation and resource allocation in product markets are aspects of a 'market process'. Competitive, initial prices exist, ultimately determined by the consumer sovereignty; real costs exert no influence for they do not exist, costs being opportunity costs reflective of consumers' preferences. Monopoly pricing is a rare case of little importance. So also is price discrimination.[26] In light of these competitive, initial, but now just past prices entrepreneurs form expectations (renamed 'appraisements') about future prices. How these are formed Mises briefly describes but does not explain theoretically.[27] Though they calculate upon expectations, entrepreneurs calculate with undiminished efficiency.[28] They make production decisions and carry out selling efforts. Though information may be asymmetrically distributed in their favour, they will practise no fraud, subject to some exceptions noted but not analysed by Mises.[29] Consumers make their own autonomous, rational choices. New prices emerge, and the market process continues. Its long-run outcome, governed by the consumer sovereignty, includes what is produced and whether exceptions to standardized, mass-produced goods will be produced; where it is produced; and how it is produced, including the choice of technology, and 'the conduct of the wrongly so-called "internal" affairs' of the firms.[30]

In factor markets, consumer sovereignty rules amid three harmonies. First, the interests of the consumers and their virtual mandataries, the entrepreneurs, are in harmony. Second, so are those of the consumers and the factor owners, for the latter, seeking income-maximization, will allocate their resources towards the uses yielding the highest possible factor prices. And the higher the factor prices, Mises assumes, the greater the utility (renamed the more 'urgent' the wants being satisfied) of consumers in product markets. Third, since the interests of the consumers and the entrepreneurs are in harmony, as are those of the consumers and the factor owners, it follows that the interests of the entrepreneurs and the factor owners are in harmony. Conditions paralleling those existing in product markets enforce this third harmony. The factor owners are rational, well-informed and mobile, and competition in the structural and behavioural senses exists. Thus entrepreneurs dare not pursue their profit interest in a way conflicting with the factor owners' interest.

In the setting of these harmonies demand and supply interact, creating a market process. The consumer sovereignty, having already determined product market prices and the choices of technology, ultimately determines factor market demands. The entrepreneurs transmit these demands to the factor owners. Competitive, initial factor prices come about, ultimately determined by the consumer sovereignty. Upon these initial but now just past prices entrepreneurs form expectations ('appraisements') about future prices, rationally calculate and issue demands. The factor owners rationally respond, and so occurs a rational resource allocation best satisfying the consumer sovereignty.

To illustrate for the particular case of factor markets for labour, consumer sovereignty rules over all. In any given labour market it ultimately determines the demands for labour, the entrepreneurs being intermediaries who, via their own expectations, transmit these demands. For labour markets as a whole, consumer sovereignty in the long run always creates enough aggregate labour demand to assure full employment opportunities.[31]

Consumer sovereignty also ultimately determines the market supply of labour, and in seeking to prove this Mises draws several more distinctions. Individuals who supply labour, he begins, are at once both consumers and labourers.[32] Their interest *qua* consumers is in consumption and leisure. Their consumer interest impels them to supply their labour to obtain purchasing power to be able to consume goods and services and leisure. Their interest *qua* consumers causes them *qua* workers to look upon their own labour as something that has no intrinsic value and yields no immediate satisfaction (or to be what Mises distinguishes as 'extroversive' labour),[33] and that will be supplied in all labour markets only at the cost of disutility. (Exceptions exist. Certain work is 'introversive', but it 'is to be qualified as consumption'. It is not labour at all. It is not 'a topic of catallactic disquisition'.)[34] Thus by nature labour supply in all labour markets in general comes at a cost of disutility. However, consumer sovereignty influences the relative cost of labour supply in particular labour markets, and in two ways. It ultimately determines the demands in all labour markets, and these in the form of opportunity costs affect the cost of labour supply in any particular labour market. Moreover, an individual worker's interest *qua* consumer will see that the labour to be done has 'attendant phenomena' that may elicit feelings of 'joy or tedium', and although these 'are in a domain other than the disutility of labour', still they may cause the labourer *qua* consumer to accept a lower wage in case of 'joy' or to demand a higher one in case of 'tedium'.[35] But such effects average out in any given labour market and so do not affect the labour supply cost for the market as a whole.[36]

Wage formation and labour allocation are aspects of the market process. The consumer sovereignty ultimately determines the set of initial, 'gross' wage rates, although customs and juristic law may impose costs that will transform these into 'net' wage rates.[37] Based on expectations about future wage rates and finished goods prices, entrepreneurs make wage offers. Labourers respond to these and, in quest of their own self-interest, they freely – although subject to the 'harsh social pressure' of monetary wage rates[38] – allocate their labour among job opportunities, thereby best serving their own and the consumers' interest.

Consumer sovereignty governs labour relations within the firm.[39] The stony-hearted consumer sovereignty compels the entrepreneurs, its virtual mandataries, to pursue efficiency, and to treat labour in a 'stony-hearted' way as a commodity.[40] However, labourers are knowledgeable and rational and mobile, full employment opportunities exist, and competition in the structural and catallactic behavioural senses exists, and so entrepreneurs dare not pursue their profit interest at the expense of the workers' interest, for such conduct will bring its own punishment.[41]

Rising to the level of the national economy as a whole, Mises distinguishes between kinds of ownership, and asserts that the consumer sovereignty has 'catallactic' ownership (or 'indirect' power of disposal) over all wealth, and governs the distribution of 'legal' ownership (or 'immediate' power of disposal) over it among individuals.[42] By 'an election daily repeated', it tests all entrepreneurs and factor owners, eliminating the inefficient and respecting no vested interests; only those successfully serving the consumer sovereignty preserve their legal ownership over wealth.[43] While legal ownership exists, the more fundamental kind is catallactic ownership, and this the consumer sovereignty possesses. Failure to appreciate this, Mises believes, can lead logically to socialist doctrines.[44]

A crude theory of personal income distribution emerges from the foregoing. In the pure case of capitalism where individuals by nature are unequal in their abilities, where unhampered praxeological freedom exists, and where consumer sovereignty governs both the distribution of ownership over resources and also the rate of remuneration for the use of each resource, it follows that by nature, by freedom, and by consumer sovereignty will come about an unequal distribution of personal income.[45] Thus, Mises reasons, consumer sovereignty ultimately determines today's distribution of purchasing power that will underlie tomorrow's consumer sovereignty.[46]

The restoration of economic growth brings about his next stage of theory construction. Now consumer demand, technology and the stock of capital goods can grow. In all cases consumer sovereignty rules. To begin, consumer demand is limitlessly expansionary. Entrepreneurs seek to anticipate new consumer wants, develop new goods and services, and offer them along with selling efforts 'to rouse latent wishes'.[47] The consumer sovereignty makes its own rational, autonomous choices. Due to the inequality in the distribution of income, some consumers are able to buy expensive luxury goods; they are entrepreneurs in consumption; and they contribute to progress, for their example 'awakens in the multitude a consciousness of new needs and gives industry the incentive to fulfill them'.[48]

Technological change can occur. Entrepreneurs often must decide either to keep their existing capital goods and products or to scrap them and to innovate. The consumer sovereignty will dictate the more profitable choice. Entrepreneurs, prompted by the motive of rational, long-run profit maximization (and in abstraction from the influence of risk-aversion, bureaucracy within their firms, and other than competitive structural conditions) respond.[49] Thus consumer sovereignty controls all technological change.

Consumer sovereignty regulates the capital accumulation process. It determines the degree of time-preference. And this controls the rate of 'originary' interest,[50] which 'determines both the demand for and the supply of capital and capital goods',[51] and the length of 'the period of production in every branch of industry'.[52] Recurrent cycles of enduring unemployment spelling loss of purchasing power (hardly desired by the consumer interest) do not occur.[53] And so the interests of consumers and savers and investors are in harmony, for 'selfishness impels a man to save and always to invest his savings in such a way as to fill best the most urgent needs of the consumers'.[54]

The restoration of money based on the Gold Standard, money being held to be purely a medium of exchange, brings about another stage of theoretical construction, as does the restoration of international trade. In both, consumer sovereignty's rule remains perfect.

Summing up thus far, the praxeological laws left unhampered in the case of strict *laissez-faire* capitalism establish consumer sovereignty and harmonize all other interests with it. Without coercion or any suppression of external freedom, consumer sovereignty governs all economic phenomena and optimally satisfies itself.

Yet what verges on being a contradiction resides in Mises's work. While consumer sovereignty governs all, entrepreneurs and not consumers are the 'driving force' of the market process, and the leaders on the way to 'unceasing innovation and improvement' and to 'material progress'.[55]

His persistent emphasis remains clear despite such commentaries about the entrepreneurs' importance, however. Consumer sovereignty, assured by the harmony of rational interests in the long run, governs all economic phenomena and optimally satisfies itself. This is the overarching doctrine identifying his version of substantive Austrian economic theory. Beneath it lie all of his ideas, including those concerning the entrepreneur, information and expectations, the market process of price formation and resource allocation, economic growth, money, and international trade.

## IV

As a response to events destroying external freedom in Europe and seeming to menace it in America during his lifetime, Mises's effort to prove the consumer sovereignty doctrine is a brilliant polemical accomplishment. As an example of results produced by the method of laying down axioms and proceeding by ratiocination, it is ingenious and admirable. As a contribution to technical economic theory, however, it is less impressive: focusing on the case of pure capitalism and the long-run time period, it draws on existing economic theory, but sets up a series of definitions, distinctions and assumptions, and on them mounts arguments that pass over or eliminate any considerations that might compromise consumer sovereignty, harmony of interest, and optimality of consumer satisfaction.

The greatest value of his contribution lies in its provocativeness. To those who wish critically to examine his work, his arguments can incite them to theoretical and empirical inquiry. To those who believe that socialists and Marxists are heinously wrong when they reason that private ownership over production equipment gives capitalists the power to rule the social order and to suppress the external freedom of others, it can reveal a magnificent system of thought held to be true *a priori*[56] that can give them a reassuring vision of how under strict *laissez-faire* perfect freedom, consumer sovereignty, and harmony will reign, and it can inspire in their hearts ideological ardor.

## Notes

1. I thank J. E. Elliott and P. Sicilian for discussions. Any errors are mine alone.
2. Rothenberg (1968, p. 326).
3. Fetter (1911, pp. 410, 392, 393); Mises (1922, p. 436; 1951, p. 443) refer to Fetter on this point.
4. Mises (1922, p. 437).
5. Mises's ideas 'strongly influenced' Benham and Hutt (Rothbard, 1968, p. 380; see also Rothbard, 1984, pp. 293–4). Hutt (1934a, p. 1; 1934b, p. 2) introduced the term 'consumer sovereignty'; Hayek (1935, p. 214) used it; Hutt (1936) discussed it at length.
6. Mises created a 'new "neo-Austrian" school of economic thought' (Rothbard, 1988, p. 24). '*Consumer sovereignty*' is one of the 'important tenets held by the Mises branch of Austrian economics' (Machlup, 1981, p. 22).
7. Mises (1966, p. 649; see also pp. 271, 275, 311, 357, 729).
8. Mises (1966, pp. 705, 743–4). At no point in his work does Mises explain how this aggregate phenomenon can be comprehended by aggregating gains and losses in utility across individuals.
9. Mises (1966, pp. 237, 264, 267).
10. Mises (1951, p. 192; 1966, pp. 280, 281, 648, 761).
11. Mises (1966, pp. 654–61).
12. Mises (1951, pp. 64, 329; 1966, pp. 176, 239n, 673–82).
13. Mises (1966, pp. 270, 271).
14. See text at notes 32–6 below.
15. Mises (1966, pp. 287, 840).
16. Ibid., p. 649.
17. Ibid., pp. 283, 286, 288, 600.
18. Ibid., p. 257.

19. Ibid., p. 613.
20. Ibid., pp. 299, 809–11.
21. Ibid., pp. 303–11. Mises (1944) elaborates.
22. Ibid., pp. 271, 272, 371.
23. Ibid., pp. 387, 681.
24. Ibid., pp. 116, 117, 273–9.
25. Ibid., pp. 269–71, 310, 649.
26. Ibid., p. 391.
27. The entrepreneurs' 'specific anticipative understanding of the conditions of the uncertain future defies any rules or systematization' (Ibid., p. 585).
28. Ibid., p. 214.
29. Ibid., pp. 320–2, 379–83.
30. Ibid., p. 649.
31. Ibid., p. 394.
32. Ibid., p. 626.
33. Ibid., pp. 587, 588.
34. Ibid., pp. 587, 588.
35. Ibid., pp. 588–92.
36. Ibid., p. 592.
37. Ibid., pp. 600–2.
38. Ibid., pp. 599, 600.
39. 'The workers are subject only to the supremacy of the consumers as their employers are too' (ibid., p. 634).
40. Ibid., pp 270, 271, 610.
41. Ibid., p. 634.
42. Mises (1951, pp. 37–50; 1966, pp. 682–4).
43. Mises (1966, pp. 225, 226, 271, 621).
44. Mises (1951, p. 50).
45. 'The inequality of incomes and wealth is an inherent feature of the market economy. Its elimination would entirely destroy the market economy' (Mises, 1966, p. 840).
46. Ibid., p. 271.
47. Ibid., p. 320; see also p. 542.
48. Mises (1927, pp. 30–3).
49. Mises (1966, pp. 503–14).
50. Ibid., p. 524.
51. Ibid., p. 527; see also pp. 522 and 845 on the coincidence of saving and investment. See also Mises (1950).
52. Mises (1966, p. 532).
53. Ibid., pp. 444, 565.
54. Ibid., p. 849.
55. Ibid., pp. 328, 255, 336.
56. The ' "fundamentalists" ' among Mises's disciples 'wanted to insist on the infallibility of the theory of consumer sovereignty on a priori grounds' (Machlup, 1981, p. 25).

## References

Benham, F. C. 1938, *Economics*, Pitman, London.

Fetter, F. A. 1911, *The Principles of Economics* (3rd edn), Century, New York.

Fraser, L. M. 1939, 'The doctrine of consumers' sovereignty', *Economic Journal* 49 (3), September, pp. 544–8.

Hutt, W. H. 1934a, 'Economic method and the concept of competition', *South African Journal of Economics* 2 (1), March, pp. 3–23.

——1934b, 'Co-ordination and the size of firm', *South African Journal of Economics* 2 (4), December, pp. 383–402.

———1936, *Economists and the Public*, Jonathan Cape, London.

Machlup, F. 1981, 'Ludwig von Mises: A scholar who would not compromise', in J. K. Andrews, Jr (ed.), *Homage to Mises: The first hundred years*, Hillsdale College Press, Hillsdale, Michigan, pp. 19–27.

Rothbard, M. N. 1968, 'Ludwig von Mises', in D. L. Sills (ed.), *International Encyclopedia of the Social Sciences*, vol. 16, Macmillan and Free Press, London and New York, pp. 379–82.

———1984, 'Ludwig von Mises', in H. W. Spiegel and W. J. Samuels (eds), *Contemporary Economists in Perspective*, vol. 1, JAI Press, Greenwich, Connecticut, pp. 286–96.

———1988, *Ludwig von Mises: Scholar, creator, hero*, Ludwig von Mises Institute of Auburn University, Auburn, Alabama.

Rothenberg, J. 1968, 'Consumer sovereignty', in D. L. Sills (ed.), *International Encyclopedia of the Social Sciences*, vol. 3 Macmillan and Free Press, London and New York, pp. 326–35.

Viner, J. 1938, 'Review: W. H. Hutt, *Economists and the Public*', *Journal of Political Economy* 46 (3) August, pp. 571–5.

von Hayek, F. A. 1935, 'The present state of the debate', in F. A. von Hayek (ed.), *Collectivist Economic Planning*, Routledge, London, pp. 201–43.

von Mises, L. E. 1922, *Die Gemeinwirtschaft*, Gustav Fisher, Jena.

———1927, *Liberalism in the Classical Tradition* (3rd edn, 1985), trans. R. Raico, Foundation for Economic Education, Irvington-on-Hudson, New York.

———1940 (reprinted 1980), *Nationalökonomie: Theorie des Handelns und Wirtschaftens*, Philosophia Verlag, München.

———1944, *Bureaucracy*, Yale University Press, London and New Haven, Connecticut.

———1949, *Human Action: A treatise on economics*, Yale University Press, New Haven, Connecticut.

———1950 (reprinted 1980), 'Lord Keynes and Say's Law', in L. E. von Mises, *Planning for Freedom and Sixteen other Essays and Addresses*, Libertarian Press, South Holland, Illinois, pp. 64–71.

———1951, *Socialism* (new edn enlarged with an epilogue), trans. J. Kahane, Yale University Press, London and New Haven, Connecticut.

———1963, *Human Action: A treatise on economics* (rev. edn), Yale University Press, New Haven, Connecticut.

———1966, *Human Action: A treatise on economics* (3rd rev. edn), Henry Regnery, Chicago.

# 12 The economic thought of J. B. Clark: an interpretation of 'The Clark Problem'

*Toshihiro Tanaka*

## Introduction

The purpose of this paper is to shed light on the characteristics of John Bates Clark's economic thought through the re-examination of the so-called 'The J. B. Clark Problem'. By 'the Clark Problem' is meant the transformation from the early Clark who had repudiated the competitive system to the support and defence of it in his later period.

There are at least two questions that arise in the interpretation of this transformation. One is whether it is to be taken as only 'a change of emphasis' or 'a radical transformation' in his basic social view. The other is what are the important forces which brought on this transformation.

P. T. Homan, J. M. Clark and J. Dorfman,[1] for example, interpreted it as 'a change of emphasis' or 'a drift in the point of view', although with different explanations. But J. Jalladeau[2] and the present writer have pointed out that it was a radical change of view. Jalladeau put emphasis on 'a conjunction of two profound motivations'.[3] We might call it a conjunction of a purely theoretical approach which is the theory of final (specific) productivity, and an ethical approach to income distribution, or consideration of social justice. The real problem, however, is not just a conjunction of two approaches, but the structure of the conjunction, because even in the early Clark we easily find a different form of conjunction.

Lately, J. F. Henry[4] denied that it was a radical transformation. He sees the conversion as one from the support of small farmers and small businesses who struggled against monopoly to support of monopoly capitalists, and that, he claimed, was a transformation always within a capitalist framework.

Henry, however, regarded the early Clark's 'socialism' or Christian socialism as essentially taken as backward-looking Populism. He stressed the aspect that Clark did not propose 'a change in the production relations in society'.[5] This under-evaluation of the early Clark's socialism seems to be the essential feature of his interpretation.

## The early Clark

The early Clark's economic thought can be seen in his *Philosophy of Wealth* (1886) which is based on the articles published in *The New Englander* from 1877 to 1883. We might call the time from 1877 through the publication of *Philosophy of Wealth* to the definitive article, 'Capital and its Earnings' in 1888 his early period.

The central theme of the early Clark's economics was social justice, especially justice in distribution. He was groping for a new industrial system and a new political economy that were different from the existing economic system and the old traditional *laissez-faire* economics. His greatest interest was to resolve the new economic problems resulting from the rise of business combinations and monopolies in the 1870s. He re-examined the theoretical assumptions of classical political economy, such as the conceptions of wealth, labour, economic man, the atomistic view of society and especially the concept of competition. He pointed out their defects and their inconsistencies with the contemporary industrial facts. In particular as to the concept of competition, he questioned the traditional economists' view that competition is an essential principle to the coordination of economic activities.

He distinguished 'true competition' or 'rivalry in giving'[6] from 'destructive competition' or 'predatory competition', and repudiated the latter, while he did not generally lose hope for the working of the former. He claimed that the progress of moral force was necessary to attain the equity of exchange and distributive justice:

> Individual competition, the great regulator of the former era, has, in important fields, practically disappeared. It ought to disappear; it was, in its latter days, incapable of working justice. The alternative regulator is moral force, and this was already in action. (*Philosophy of Wealth*, p. 148)

Thus he repudiated the principle of competition and emphasized a moral force in place of it. Although he was not necessarily consistent in his judgement of the practical working of the competitive principle,[7] his fundamental approach to the 'transitional and chaotic state of industrial society' (ibid., p. 148) could be found in his denial that competition was a regulator that could secure justice in distribution, and his expectation that moral force would work more effectively in the different forms.

In the process of abandoning the competitive principle and groping towards a new economic system based on moral force, Clark went on with the examination of arbitration, profit-sharing and economic systems based on the principle of a cooperative production system (not the Rochdale form of the cooperative store) as an ideal economic system, which could remove the fundamental causes of conflict between capitalists and labourers, regarding arbitration and profit-sharing as 'partial cooperation'. He wrote: 'Cooperation works in an opposite way in both respects. It concentrates the thought and energy of all on production, the process in which the interests of different classes are identical; and it develops harmony of feeling, while securing a large product for distribution' (ibid., p. 178).

Insisting on the survival of these four systems (competition, arbitration, profit-sharing and cooperative production system), Clark expected that the cooperative system would be the ultimate survivor. He stressed that 'Cooperation will, by this process, have a fair chance in the industrial world. If, in the comparison with other systems, it is shown that it ought to survive, it will do so, and that regardless of initial failures' (ibid., p. 189).

His support of a cooperative system in place of a competitive system was 'the Christian socialism of Maurice, Kingsley, Hughes, and their worthy co-labourers' (ibid., p. 198).[8] He had great expectation for the development of Christian socialism: 'It meets an imperative human need, and must grow surely, though not, as reformers are wont to estimate progress, rapidly' (ibid., p. 198).

He also highly evaluated the thought and opinions of Christian socialists in the United States such as W. Gladden,[9] R. T. Ely[10] and others, and wrote book reviews of J. Cook, J. P. Thompson and T. D. Woolsey.[11]

Clark's position on Christian socialism cannot be reconciled with the acceptance of capitalism. It pointed to an economic system beyond the capitalist system. We might say that Clark was in the process of groping for an ideal economic system beyond the capitalist system. On this point Henry's interpretation that Clark's Christian socialism was essentially identical with the backward-looking Populism which supported small farmers and small businesses struggling against monopolies, and that it did not go beyond the capitalist system, cannot be accepted. It is true that Clark criticized monopoly and supported small farmers and small businesses to bring back justice in distribution, and evaluated the movement of Farmers' Alliance as a progressive political activity for democracy.[12] However, he clearly recognized that the competitive system of small businesses was past. He did seek a new industrial system in place of the old competitive system. It is almost impossible to find in his early thought any backward-looking search with a view to the revival of the competitive system of small businesses of former times.[13]

**The later Clark**
Against the background of the stagnancy of the cooperative movement in the United States after the publication of *Philosophy of Wealth*, Clark shifted his stress from the cooperative system to arbitration and profit-sharing. He wrote in support of compulsory arbitration[14] in 1889 and claimed the necessity of arbitration frequently from 1896 to 1908.[15] On the other hand, Christian socialism in the United States (Social Gospel) itself changed partly and produced in a group who supported the American Socialist Party representing political (Marxian) socialism. Clark was critical of this, and his Christian socialist stand gradually faded.[16]

As Clark came to regard Marxian socialism and agrarian socialism of Henry George as more threatening, his criticism of these gradually strengthened and came to the front in contrast with the early Clark. Corresponding to this, Clark's social reformist thought with expectations of a new economic system weakened by degrees, and his emphasis on Christian socialism centred on the cooperative system gradually faded. Distinct references to it disappeared from his writings.

In this situation, recognizing distributive justice as the rule that a labourer gets what he creates, Clark began to seek for the proof that the distributive justice in this sense was secured in the existing economic system. This pursuit of 'a natural law' in distribution became his primary interest.

Introducing the concepts of competition and economic man as the assumptions of theory, he constructed the final productivity theory of distribution as a static law of distribution under the condition of perfect competition. It was basically formulated first in his 1888 article 'Capital and its Earnings',[17] then developed in 'Possibility of a Scientific Law of Wages' (March 1889),[18] 'The Law of Wages and Interest' (1890),[19] and 'Distribution as Determined by a Law of Rent' (April 1891).[20, 21] These articles and others, needless to say, resulted in the *Distribution of Wealth* (1899).[22]

In the formulation process of Clark's distribution theory, we find three most important points. They are the confusion of a descriptive approach and ethical approach at three levels: the statement of a problem, construction process of the theory itself, and a consideration of its social implications.

First, the formulation process by Clark was led by his distinctive

ideology, the criticism of 'agrarianism and state socialism'.[23] His way
of stating a problem is most clearly shown: 'Does society, under
natural law, take from labour a product that is distinctly attributable
to it? This is one of the most important questions in economics.'[24] He
wanted to refute the socialist position which had emphasized institutional injustice in distribution in the capitalist system, that is exploitation. We find here his basic position in the later period, the moral
justification of private property and free competition. In the case of
Clark the combination of marginalism and anti-socialistic ideology was
his characteristic feature.

Secondly, led by anti-socialistic ideology, Clark was not satisfied
with the final productivity theory such as Von Thünen's theory of
wages, which allowed the logical possibility of exploitation. Clark felt
he had to criticize it as an imperfect final productivity theory, and
tried to construct a perfect theory which could rebut the socialist
position on exploitation. His way of stating the problem naturally led
him to the next question: 'What needs to be known is what part of
the composite result of industry is distinctly due to labour itself.'[25] To
Clark who wants to deny exploitation, final productivity theory 'needs
to become, in addition, *a specific productivity* theory, which makes
the pay of each unit of labour conform to its own specific product'
(*Distribution of Wealth*, p. 324). Specific productivity theory was the
conceptual contrivance constructed to distinguish what capital created
and what labour created in the joint product of capital and labour.
Final productivity should have been specific productivity.

Thirdly, after establishing the specific productivity theory, Clark
drew his ethical and ideological implications from its conclusion.
According to him, it was proved scientifically that 'free competition
tends to give to labor what labor creates, to capitalists what capital
creates, and to *entrepreneurs* what the coordinating function creates'
(ibid., p. 3). Since the rule 'to each what he creates' (ibid., p. 9) is
observed in capitalist society, it is an honest society and had the right
to exist in its current form. And also it was probable that the current
system would continue to exist, he insisted, because it promoted economic progress. Socialism then, which insists on the existence of the
exploitation of labour and seeks to revolutionize society, should be
resisted. This social criticism drawn from his specific productivity
theory was most plainly stated in his articles on the law and ethics of
distribution in Palgrave's *Dictionary of Political Economy* (1894). This
specific productivity theory and its social implications were the most
important aspects to Clark himself, as J. M. Clark pointed out.[26]

Clark's *Distribution* contained both his argument that the capitalism was efficient and just and his criticism of socialism. It can hardly be said that *Distribution* is a book on the marginal productivity theory of distribution as a 'pure theory'.

The transformation, therefore, from the early Clark to the later Clark was nothing but a radical transformation in his basic social view from Christian socialism, which repudiated the competitive system and supported a cooperative system as an ideal system, to the sophisticated justification and defence of the competitive capitalist system.

**Clark as an advocate of anti-monopoly policy**
After concluding that a competitive system has the right to exist from the viewpoints of justice and productive efficiency, Clark shifted the emphasis of his early social reform mainly to anti-monopoly policy and competition maintaining policy. In 1870s and 1880s Clark showed his great interest in monopoly, but the monopoly problem in the United States entered into a new stage in the 1890s. At this stage in his later period, Clark proposed the prevention and elimination of the evils of monopoly, with a view to achieving both distributive justice and productive efficiency within the capitalist system. After March 1890, when he wrote his first essay on trusts, he developed his anti-monopoly policy through the publication of the *Control of Trusts* (1901), *The Problem of Monopoly* (1904),[27] and the second edition of the *Control of Trusts* (1912 with J. M. Clark).

In *The Control of Trusts* (1901), Clark distinguished three things: 'first, capital as such; secondly, centralization; and thirdly, monopoly' (p. 6). He criticized the attack on capital as such. And here he stressed the attainment of the economies of scale by large trusts on the one hand. On the other hand, he criticized monopoly on the ground that its monopolistic power excludes competition, reduces production, raises price and yields monopoly profits. He proposed anti-monopoly policy to remove monopolistic power from trusts. His policy is 'the policy which welcomes centralization, but represses monopoly' (ibid., p. 81). He wanted to have 'concentration without having monopoly' (ibid., p. 8).[28] He claimed that its purpose is to blend efficiency in production with equity in distribution (ibid., p. 81). This coordination between efficiency and equity was, he thought, secured by competition: 'It is the policy that relies wholly on competition as the regulator of prices and wages and as the general protector of the interests of the public (ibid., p. v). According to him, through the policy to remove monopolistic action, 'residual' and 'latent' competition are secured, and this secures the increase of production, and improves the wages of labourers. In any case Clark's anti-monopoly policy was based on the revival of the competitive principle, and therefore it was a policy of reform within the capitalist system. His anti-monopoly policy was not intended to 'crush the trusts' (ibid., p. 5), nor to destroy the productive efficiency of them. In relation to this point, he criticized the Populists in the South and West, because they 'undervalued the productive power' of trusts (ibid., p. 3), although he praised their zeal against monopoly. He was also against the 'letting them alone' policy (ibid., p. 5),[29] which could not prevent the evils of monopoly. He aimed at a policy of monopoly *regulation*. He pointed out:

> There are two small classes of people who are predisposed to favor trusts, even though they shall prove to be real monopolies. These are, first, the revolutionary classes – socialists, anarchists, communists and the like; and secondly, the workmen in a few highly organized trades. (ibid., pp. 4–5)

Clark understood socialism and anarchism as a sort of let-alone policy with respect to monopoly, because he thought that they welcomed monopolization, since it would eventually facilitate nationalization of whole industries.

Seen from the point of view of the formulation of his anti-monopoly policy, the radical transformation in Clark's attitude towards the competitive system and the principle of competition, corresponds to the beginning of the formulation of his specific productivity theory, say in 1887–8.

In the article 'The Limits of Competition' (1887),[30] we find the later Clark's basic views of trusts and monopolies. Here he clearly relies on the principle of competition and proposes to preserve residual and latent competition and to remove monopolistic action with trusts. We find the distinct revival of the competitive principle as a regulating force.

With the background of the new development of trusts and monopolies on the one hand, and the corresponding active movement of 'the revolutionary classes' on the other hand, he justified and defended justice and efficiency in the competitive capitalist system, and at the same time proposed anti-monopoly policy guided by the theory of distribution in a system of large industrial combinations. The gradual reformism centering on the anti-monopoly policy within the capitalistic framework was a feature of his fundamental ideas.

The point that the later Clark finally reached was his small book, *Social Justice without Socialism* (1914) in which we find the essentials of his final position with regard to socialism and social reforms. They are the following:

1. Criticism of state socialism, agrarian socialism, anarchism, communism and so on, because they impaired economic growth;
2. The ethical justification of distribution in the capitalist system drawn from the theoretical conclusion of the specific productivity theory, and the defence of competition, economic progress based on the ground that it provides economic progress;
3. Removal of defects and evils from the capitalist system centred on the anti-monopoly policy;
4. Gradual social reformism with an optimistic religious perspective.

**Summary**
In this paper the following four points have been claimed:

1. Clark's 'transformation' in his basic social view was not 'a mere change of emphasis', but a radical change or conversion;
2. As a Christian socialist the early Clark regarded the cooperative system as an ideal economic system, not necessarily within the capitalist framework, and in fact repudiated the competitive system from the viewpoint of social justice;
3. The later Clark's 'transformation' to the justification and defence of the capitalist competitive system was brought about by the establishment of his specific productivity theory of distribution as a natural law. The construction process of this theory involves the confusion of the ethical approach and the theoretical approach on three levels: the statement of a problem, construction of the theory itself, and a consideration of its implications;
4. The later Clark as an anti-monopoly policy proposer approved trusts without monopolistic power in order to harmonize productive efficiency and social justice. His gradual and optimistic reformist position centering on this anti-monopoly policy was finally clearly revealed in his *Social Justice without Socialism*.

**Acknowledgement**
An earlier draft of this article was read and commented on by Professors Eugenne Rotwein and Donald Dewey. I would like to thank them, and especially for improvement of English by the former. The responsibility for any errors is, of course, my own.

## Notes

This paper is based on the following six papers published in Japanese by the author: 'The economic doctrines of J. B. Clark. In particular on his *Philosophy of Wealth'*, *Keizaigaku Ronkyu* (Journal of Economics of Kwansei Gakuin University, abbreviated *JEKGU*) XX (3) October 1966: 'The formation of J. B. Clark's views on marginal utility. Social utility theory of Value', *JEKGU*,, XXII (4) January 1969; 'J. B. Clark's theory of marginal productivity and its ethical implication', *JEKGU*, XXIV (2) July 1970; 'John Bates Clark and marginalism: The formation of marginal productivity theory of distribution', *Konan Keizaigaku Ronshu* (Konan Economic Papers) XIV (2) September 1973; 'John Bates Clark on competition and monopoly with regard to "The J. B. Clark Problem" ', *JEKGU* XXX (3) September 1979; 'J. B. Clark on the anti-monopoly policy: a theory of effective competition', *JEKGU* XXXIV (1) June 1980.

1.  Paul T. Homan 1928, *Contemporary Economic Thought* New York and London; J. M. Clark 1952, 'On J. B. Clark', H. W. Spiegel (ed.), *The Development of Economic Thought. Great Economists in Perspective*, New York and London; idem, 1968, 'Clark, John Bates' *International Encyclopedia of the Social Sciences*, ed. D. L. Sills, vol. 2. Joseph Dorfman 1949, *The Economic Mind in American Civilization*, vol. III, New York, idem, 1971, 'John Bates and John Maurice Clark on monopoly and competition', Introductory Essay to J. B. Clark and J. M. Clark, *The Control of Trusts* (1912), Kelley's reprint edition New York.
2.  Jöel Jalladeau 1975, 'The methodological conversion of John Bates Clark', *History of Political Economy* VII (2).
3.  Ibid., p. 223.
4.  John F. Henry (1982), 'The transformation of John Bates Clark: an essay in interpretation', *History of Political Economy* XIV (2).
5.  Ibid., p. 177.
6.  J. B. Clark 1886, *The Philosophy of Wealth. Economic Principles Newly Formulated*, Boston; 2nd edition, 1887, p. 155.
7.  He wrote in the other chapter: 'Society does not and will not completely abandon the competitive principle; it is still needed as an agent of distribution, and it is the sole means on which we can rely for the securing of a large product to distribute' (ibid., p. 207).
8.  The names of the Christian socialists were not in the article of 1879, but added in the first edition of *Philosophy of Wealth*.
9.  Clark supported Christian socialist, Washington Gladden's thought in the essay 'Christianity and modern economics', *The New Englander and Yale Review* 47, July 1887.
10. Book review of *The Labor Movement in America* (1886), by Richard T. Ely, *The New Englander*, December 1886.
11. Reviewed by Clark in *The New Englander. Socialism. With preludes on current events*, Boston, 1889, by Joseph Cook, September 1880; *The Workingman: His False Friends and his True Friends*, New Haven, 1880, by Rev. Joseph P. Thompson, May 1880; *Communism and Socialism in their History and Theory. A Sketch*, New York, 1880, by Theodore D. Woolsey, May 1880.
12. 'The present aspect of the Farmers' Movement', *The Congregationalist*, 16 March 1893. He says: 'It is the protection of the growing American democracy from really dangerous encroachments.' 'The Farmers' Alliance is the best organization now existing for asserting the people's right to dictate legislation.' But in this essay he criticized the free silver movement of the Populists.
13. Even if Clark's Christian socialism could be regarded as Populism, as Henry claims, its backward-looking character stressed by him seems to be doubtful. Henry's interpretation of Populism is based on Richard Hofstadter's *The Age of Reform*, New York, 1955. But this understanding has been revised in recent studies. According to Norman Pollack, for example, it is denied that Populism did not adjust itself to industrialism and had only unrealistic measures. He says:

Populism accepted industrialism but opposed its capitalistic form, seeking instead a more equitable distribution of wealth . . . it was far more radical than is generally assumed. Had Populism succeeded, it would have fundamentally altered American society in a socialist direction. (*The Populist Response to Industrial America. Midwestern Populist Thought*, Cambridge, Mass., 1962, pp. 11–12).

14.  'Arbitration and how to prevent strikes', *The Christian Union*, 21 February, 1989.
15.  See the essays in *The Century Magazine*, August 1896; *The Independent*, 13 November 1902; *Political Science Quarterly*, December 1902; *The National Magazine*, December 1902; *Public Policy*, 10 January 1903; *Public Opinion*, 14 January 1904; and *The Report of the Lake Mohonk Conference on Arbitration*, 1908.
16.  In May 1910, Clark criticized J. Spargo, a leader of Christian Socialist Fellowship, and developed his criticism of political socialism. See *The Christian Endeavour World*, 5 May 1910.
17.  *Publications of the American Economic Association* III(2), May 1888.
18.  *Publications of the American Economic Association* IV(1), March 1889.
19.  *Annals of the American Academy of Political and Social Science* I(1), 1890.
20.  *The Quarterly Journal of Economics* V(3), April 1891.
21.  As an excellent analysis of the formation of Clark's final productivity theory written in English, see John F. Henry 'John Bates Clark and the marginal product: an historical inquiry into the origins of value-free economical theory', *History of Political Economy* XV (3), 1983.
22.  J. B. Clark 1899, *The Distribution of Wealth. A Theory of Wages, Interest and Profits*, New York.
23.  'Capital and its earnings', op. cit., p. 12.
24.  'Distribution, ethics of', Palgrave's *Dictionary of Political Economy*, p. 599.
25.  Ibid.
26.  Spiegel (ed.), op. cit., p. 610.
27.  *The Control of Trusts. An Argument in favor of curbing the power of monopoly by a natural method*, New York, 1901. *The Problem of Monopoly. A study of a grave danger and of the natural mode of averting it*, New York and London, 1904.
28.  Clark maintained: 'Monopoly is that monopoly does' (*The Control of Trusts*, p. 73).
29.  This position was represented by economists such as Von Halle and J. W. Jenks.
30.  *Political Science Quarterly* II(1), March 1887.

# 13  The social economics of Frank H. Knight

*J. Patrick Raines*

## Introduction

Frank Hyneman Knight is well known for his 1924 critique of Pigou-vian welfare economics and his subsequent rehabilitation of neoclassical economics. During his thirty years at the University of Chicago, Knight thoroughly developed the theory that economic freedom and market competition are essential to maximize society's welfare. However, Knight's fervent belief in the superiority of the market mechanism did not preclude a serious concern about issues of social justice, ethics and values. In his search for possible ethical principles in economics, Knight developed a view of social economics uniquely his own. Specifically, it was his concern for ethics that provided the link between the application of pure theory and the reality of social economics (Schweitzer, 1975, p. 290).

The purpose of this study is to set forth clearly Frank Knight's system of social economics. A 1975 attempt to isolate Knight's social economics by Arthur Schweitzer, although insightful, suffers from an inadequate conceptual framework for the field of social economics. The scope herein is to extricate Knight's social thought and to bring it into focus in the light of recently articulated characteristics of social economists (Angresano, 1986, p. 146; Gruchy, 1981, p. 243; Jensen, 1987, p. 15). Unquestionably, Knight's prominence and influence in economics warrants this investigation of his contribution to the intellectual history of social economics.

A general framework for identifying and evaluating contributions to the field of social economics is presented in the next section. Then the specific elements of Knight's social economics are considered in each category.

## A framework for social economics

Some consensus is evolving with regard to the characteristics of a practitioner of social economics; if it is not a consensus, at least it is a well-defined group of traits which provides a framework for analysing one's qualifications as a social economist. Thus, Knight's contributions to the field of social economics will be demonstrated by focusing on the following characteristics found in his substantially important work in economics:

1.  his articulation of social goals for modern American capitalism;
2.  his multidisciplinary approach to social issues which emphasizes non-economic factors;
3.  his utilization of inductive reasoning and refutation of dogmatic, static equilibrium analysis;
4.  his willingness to recommend policy and institutional reforms where social conditions can be improved.

The next section identifies and shows how Knight's work is compatible with these characteristics of a social economist.

## Elements of Knight's social economics

### Social goals

The major contribution Frank Knight made to social economics is his concept of a social standard (Schweitzer, 1975, p. 291). In the view of the author, Knight advocated the highest ideals to which a society can aspire, namely, freedom and intelligent democratic initiative. Knight did not believe individual freedom would solve social problems (1960, p. 112). Actually, he recognized that some limitations on the exercise of freedom may be necessary. Unlimited social freedom would mean the right to use great economic power at will; to be able to use it indefinitely to get even more power. Thus freedom, particularly economic freedom, has to be supervized by rules that are made and enforced by social institutions acting in the general interest of society. Without such rules, collusion and coercion will be perpetuated by individuals and the government and freedom will be precluded.

In a metaphysical sense, one choice is just as free as any other. It is the reality of choices with which society must be concerned. In a market organization of economic cooperation, individuals effectuate freedom by their choices of alternatives offered to them and in what they offer to others. Freedom to make such choices with regard to production, employment and consumption is the ultimate economic freedom. Freedom in economic choices requires – in fact, inculcates – responsibility of critical analysis – sizing up what's best for oneself. This characteristic serves citizens well who participate in political systems that require decisions as to what is best for society.

Knight's view is that 'progress is to be achieved by freedom' (1960,

p. 118). In a liberal dynamic society individuals must possess the requisite reasoning skills for carrying the social responsibilities of membership in such a society. Having been freed from rulership by the whip and custom or tradition, individuals are required to accept new economic, political and cultural responsibilities. Order and cultural inheritance must be preserved and progress achieved. In this sense, social change and progress is predicated upon freedom – the condition which inspires and allows change. Ultimately, knowledge of social ideals achieved through free discussion is imperative for social progress.

At times, it appears that Knight does not contribute much to the definition of an ideal organization of society beyond recommending 'playing the competitive game', being a good sport and trying to improve the rules of the game (Raines and Jung, 1986, p. 438). However, Knight makes a very important contribution to the definition of a social ideal. His legacy is the true meaning of a liberal democracy, namely, democratic policy in a free society must be guided by a cooperative quest for truth, intelligent initiative and critical intelligence. His steadfast refusal to accept or promote dogmatic philosophical or scientific guidance for individual action advances the fundamental proposition of liberal democracies; choices are complex, they must be made responsibly, and simple rules or formulae are inadequate for making reliable decisions. He insists that there should not be any such thing as a sacred truth or set of values which is not open to question or change in a free society (1960, p. 129). Knight worries considerably about the effects of social change enacted on the basis of religious ethical principles. He argues that the greatest danger to social order is the enactment of economic legislation inspired by the clamour of self-interested and/or naive preachers. He views a moralistic approach to public policy as especially hazardous because it is 'the natural consequence of exhortation without knowledge and understanding of well meaning people attempting to meddle with the workings of extremely complicated and sensitive machinery which they do not understand' (1939, p. 418).

Many of the problems having to do with economic justice Knight attributes to ill-informed legislative action and the inherent difficulties of democratic politics. The main problems stem from the difficulty of intercommunication necessitated by a government of discussion and from society's aversion to the mental effort required for critical intelligence. Knight urges intelligent social action through acquiring 'knowledge, particularly knowledge of the good, or ethical knowledge, the meaning of progress – and then knowledge of what is possible and how to achieve possible improvement' (1960, p. 119).

Knight's view of social ideals reflects his commitment to free choice and critical intelligence. He is wary of social reformers and doubts the efficacy of economic legislation. Ultimately he holds that society and policy-makers in a capitalist economy must understand the fundamental laws of a free market system and seek to find 'the best way to integrate tendencies of the free market system with political action' (1960, p. 111). Knight believes such enlightened policy would ensure efficiency in industry, freedom in democracy, and prosperous social and economic conditions.

*Interdisciplinary approach*
Frank Knight begins his classic work *The Economic Organization* by stating:

> It is somewhat unusual to begin the treatment of a subject with a warning against attaching too much importance to it; but in the case of economics, such an injunction is quite as much needed as an explanation and emphasis of the importance it really has. It is characteristic of the age in which we live to think too much in terms of economics, to see things too predominantly in their economic aspect; and this is especially true of the American people. There is no more important prerequisite to clear thinking in regard to economics itself than the recognition of its limited place among human interests at large. (1967, p. 3)

The refusal to accept doctrinal statements of religion, philosophy and economics is inextricably linked to Knight's Midwestern rearing, his early evangelical-based education and his formal training in philosophy and economics at Cornell. In fact, the philosophy department concluded that his ingrained scepticism interfered with his study of philosophic doctrine to such an extent that they gladly accepted his transfer to the economics department. Under the direction of Allyn Young, Knight completed his prize-winning dissertation *Risk, Uncertainty and Profit*, and took his PhD in economics in 1916 (Buchanan, 1964, p. 424).

Generally, the view that individuals know what gives them satisfaction and order their conduct with a view toward getting such things is acceptable to Knight. However, he also recognizes that the romantic, the social animal, the prejudiced ignoramus exist alongside the calculating, self-interested individual. Thus, in economics, and in other areas of scientific inquiry, Knight attempts to expose the fallacies, nonsense and absurdities in what is passed off as sophisticated-scientific discourse.

It is ironic that Knight's neoclassical link to modern positivist economics is the reconstructed, rational economic man. The view Knight holds of the economic man is that it is unrealistic but a necessary evil for model building. He recognizes that in order to build a rigorous and useful model of economic maximization, man must be described as purposely and consciously utilizing means to attain predefined ends, i.e., the rational economic man. However, he is also aware no such man exists because human beings do not know what they want – not to mention what is 'good' for them – and do not act very intelligently to get the things which they have decided to acquire. Besides, to act completely rationally would require totally impersonal and non-romantic behaviour which is not only irrational but impossible. Specifically, he notes: 'Living intelligently includes more than the intelligent use of means in realizing ends; it is fully as important to select the ends intelligently' and 'Living is an art; and art is more than a matter of scientific technique and the richness and value of life are largely bound up in the "more" ' (1967, pp. 3–4). Knight points out that an exact science of conduct is an impossibility because the data of conduct are provisional, shifting, and individual-specific to such a high degree that generalization is relatively fruitless (1935, p. 35). He holds:

> Man is certainly not the rational animal that he pretends to be. . . . He is very superior to other animals in reasoning power, but reason is not distinctive of man and is hardly his predominant trait; it is often used for irrational ends. (1960, p. 52)

Further, he rejects the view that economic theory can 'be operational in the modern methodological sense' because economic theory can only be useful in predicting real-world events to the extent that agents act in conformity with idealized behaviour. Thus, theories of economic action which are based upon the rationally calculating economic man should not be extended too far. Knight suggests the study of individuals' tastes and preferences may be better analysed by using assumptions and methodologies of other social sciences (Breit, 1971, p. 199). In his study of 'The Limitations of Scientific Method In Economics', Knight states: 'Wants are in the province of psychology, sociology, and ethics' (1939, p. 141). Clearly, Knight recognized and accepted a place for social sciences and disciplines other than economics in the analysis of individual action.

The unequivocal 'economic' explanation of human behaviour as well as predictions of future economic events from idealized theoretical economic models is particularly condemnable to Knight. He finds Marshallian definitions of economics, viz., 'the ordinary business of life' or the 'science of rational activity' to be useless and misleading. These definitions suggest that economics is the science of everything that generally concerns mankind. He points out that the scope of economics is not so broad and that life is much more than rational conduct or intelligent use of resources to achieve predetermined results. Ultimately, Knight cautions against the overzealous application of economic theory to sociological phenomena. He recommends: 'If one wishes to study the concrete content of motives and conduct, he must turn from economic theory to biology, social psychology, and especially culture history. . . . [The latter] gives a genetic, and not scientific account of its subject-matter' (1935, pp. 36–37).

*Epistemological system*
Frank Knight clearly favours a heterogeneous approach to the study of knowledge and society. He emphatically demonstrates dissatisfaction with the methodology of static equilibrium analysis in his essay 'Statics and Dynamics' (1935, p. 161). In this work, he points out that even the terms, 'static' and 'dynamic', are poorly defined in economics and argues against using static models for public policy guidelines due to the evolutionary character of capitalistic enterprises.

Knight advocates de-emphasizing mechanical equilibrium analysis in economics by increasing the importance of force, resistance and movement in economic analysis. Instead of constantly assuming perfect knowledge in analysing market prices, he suggests it is conceivable to study the role of resistance, ignorance, and prejudice in economic outcomes. This view is parallel to the Swedish social economist Gunnar Myrdal's notion that static models of price determination overlook the role of fundamental social changes in the economic process. Myrdal emphasizes the inadequacy of static equilibrium analysis in explaining social change and popularized the view: Everything is cause to everything else (Angresano, 1986, p. 153). Similarly, Knight discredits the traditional assumptions of static equilibrium analysis. He notes the interconnectedness of all growth elements involved in economic progress and specifically describes as misleading the assumption in models of price determination that population growth can be described as tending toward any discernible state of equilibrium. He states: 'Each changing economic element is a condition affecting the change of any other element or its ultimate stability of position, just as the features of the non-economic environment are conditions; but the former cannot be assumed equal' (1935, p. 179). The essential point is that equilibrium must relate to economic progress as a whole and this must include elements of the social condition.

Knight also emphasizes the importance of psychological traits in explaining economic outcomes. Knowledge, skills, aptitudes, personal energy and morale affect production, and, in fact, are responsible for the development of most technology as well as entrepreneurial activity in business endeavours. Consumption is also affected by psychic traits. Knight suggests that individual wants may stem more from the social implications of goods than the goods themselves, or their direct physical effect on an individual. The implication is that since psychological traits are both innate and social products they are difficult to discover empirically and, thus, theoretical economic models of behaviour should be careful not to claim to definitively explain consumer behaviour.

With regard to the distribution of ownership of productive resources, which are specified as a constant in a static economy, Knight points out the cumulative rather than equilibrating effects of economic forces over time. Knight theorizes that ordinary economic forces tend towards a progressive concentration; wealth does breed: 'to him that hath shall be given, and from him that hath not shall be taken away' (1935, p. 184). He recognizes that the trend would be more empirically prominent if not for social action, accidents and other factors which make any large mass unstable. This process of income distribution tends over time to negate the proposition that 'other things remain equal' as possessors of vast fortunes cannot be expected to have the same motives and interests as the less fortunate. Similarly, he notes that the workings of competition educate men progressively to monopoly (1939, p. 52).

The self-important, often condescending, nature of practitioners of positive economics particularly disturbs Knight (1956, p. 151). He warns society about the dangers of those who speak of the omnipotence of scientific methodology in awe-inspiring tones similar to those common in public prayer. He contends that attempts to build a social science on a scientific foundation which deletes emotion and value-judgements infer that human beings can be studied like natural objects and, therefore, are not actuated by love, hate, capriciousness and contrariness. Policies that are founded upon such an incomplete methodology are likely to be too rigid or inflexible to serve society as it really exists.

In a review of T. W. Hutchinson's treatise on methodology, *The Significance and Basic Postulates of Economic Theory*, Knight points out the 'superficiality and dogmatic oversimplification' of economic theory which ignores broad-based human or social data. Specifically, he points out: 'Concrete and positive answers in the field of economic science or policy depend in the first place on judgements of value and procedures, based on a broad general education in the cultural sense, and on "insight" into human nature and social values rather than on the findings of any possible social science' (1956, p. 177). The significance of Knight's view is that social action to ameliorate economic problems should only be taken after a full consideration of the principles of relevant social disciplines. This approach is warranted because no problem which affects society is purely economic except by abstraction and only an extremely limited part of human problems can be treated by positive science.

This view of scientific methodology influenced Knight's model of effectuating social reform. The logical process for social change which Knight develops is not formulated to bring about a transformation of capitalism. Rather, his system for social reorganization is primarily intended for moralistic social reformers and positivist scientists whom he contends are largely responsible for much of the extant confusion about the nature of and remedies for social problems.

*The process of social reform – the role of experts*
In Knight's system, the first step to 'scientifically' solving socioeconomic problems is to acquire knowledge about current socioeconomic conditions. Naturally, this has to be undertaken prior to action, and necessitates an understanding of both economic theory and the features of contemporary social and economic systems. Only after such information is assimilated, is it possible to speculate on the difference between reality and the theoretically ideal.

The next step of the analytical process of social reform is to formulate a sense of direction toward a desired end. Knight submits it is not necessary to have a detailed view of the ideal society before action is undertaken because elements of uncertainty are present in all action, and ends are never completely foreseen prior to action. However, social ideals must come from criticism of what is and rational discussion on the possibilities of improvement (1939, p. 412).

Finally, the appropriate means for social change must be determined. Knight avers that change can be induced by economic decisions of individuals and families or by politico-legal social organization. He warns against the latter as most political action aimed at improving economic conditions involves the transfer of responsibilities from families, the primary social unit, to the state. His influence on the modern ublic choice school is obvious in that he suggests legislative outcomes will tend to maximize the welfare of policy-makers and, perhaps, a narrow political constituency rather than society in general.

The disdain for righteous social reformers which Knight holds is clearly and famously articulated in his 1950 presidential address to the American Economic Association. He laments the tendency in society to legislate positive social action which is characterized by 'passing laws and employing policemen'. Knight states 'I mistrust reformers', and clarifies with one of his most well-known comments:

> When a man or group asks for power to do good, my impulse is to say, 'Oh, yeah, who ever wanted power for any other reason? and what have they done when they got it?' So, I instinctively want to cancel the last three words leaving simply, 'I want power'; that is easy to believe. And a further confession: I am reluctant to believe in doing good with power anyhow. (1951, p. 29)

According to Knight, capitalistic monopolies and business-cycles are the 'chief mechanical defects' in a market economy. He considers business-cycles to be the more serious of the two defects and declares that the public grossly exaggerates the extent and power of business monopolies. He argues that the economic power which may result from the freedom to use one's resources to achieve desired ends is generally beneficial to society; a stimulus to devising and introducing new products and technologies. Knight does not see a lack of competition as the cause of economic injustice in American capitalism. In fact, he holds that if modern capitalism performs near to the competitive ideal it would be 'socially quite intolerable'. Further, he reminds society that the enormous increase in economic efficiency resulting from large-scale production has created economic conditions that have led to the liberal revolution in the political system.

Knight recognizes the likelihood of 'treatment' for conditions popularly considered to be social problems, but is sceptical of the prescriptions of 'social doctors'. In the case of monopolies, he points out the difficulties of measuring the short-run costs and potential long-run benefits of monopoly power. Thus, he recommends against using simple legal formulas or definitions to remedy the complex situation of economic power and argues, instead, for carefully considered and enforced legislation to achieve a socially beneficial competitive balance (Raines and Jung, 1988). In the case of business-cycles, Knight urges monetary control employing deliberate action, based on constant attention to correct incipient tendencies in a market economy to expand or contract. The rationalization for Knight's advocacy of proactive monetary policy is that he contends monetary stabilization policy is simply a matter of economic understanding, political intelligence and administrative competence in matters of an essentially technical nature (1956, p. 225). In other words, if positive monetary control is exercised, Knight suggests the serious economic loss from business cycles, which affects virtually all of society in a capitalistic economy, could be avoided. This view of monetary policy is indeed an interesting one in light of Knight's role in developing the Chicago School and its monetarist philosophy.

### Summary and conclusions

Frank Knight urges society to develop and exercise the capacity for truth seeking. A free society must seek ethical knowledge and work to promote social justice through informed economic and political action. Critical intelligence, the requisite for Knight's intelligent democratic initiative, is attainable only by a multidisciplinary understanding of society. All conduct is not economic in nature, and action to correct socioeconomic problems should consider broad-based human and social information, namely, cultural considerations, human nature and social values. Since Knight doubted the ability of a benevolent and powerful government to optimally order economic affairs, he encouraged individuals through the family unit to help find solutions to social problems by looking to combine the characteristics of a free market system with intelligent democratic action. Knight's consistent advocacy of an informed, multidisciplinary approach to socioeconomic problems is certainly worthy of consideration for contemporary societies.

### References

Angresano, James 1986, 'Gunnar Myrdal as a social economist', *Review of Social Economy* 44, pp. 146–58.

Breit, William 1971, 'Frank H. Knight – philosopher of the counter-revolution in economics', *The Academic Scribblers*, Dryden Press, Hinsdale, Illinois.

Bruyn, Severyn T. 1982, 'Social economy: a note on its theoretical foundations', *Review of Social Economy* 39(1), pp. 81–4.

Buchanan, James M. 1964, 'Frank H. Knight', *International Encyclopedia of Social Sciences*, New York, pp. 424–8.

Gruchy, Allan G. 1981, 'Theory and policy in John M. Clark's social economics', *Review of Social Economy* 39(3), pp. 241–56.

Jensen, Hans E. 1987, 'Alfred Marshall as a social economist', *Review of Social Economy* 45(1), pp. 14–35.

Knight, Frank H. 1924, 'Fallacies in the interpretation of social cost', *Quarterly Journal of Economics* 38 (May) pp. 582–606.

——1933, *The Economic Organization*, privately published; Reprint, Kelley, New York, 1967.

——1935, *The Ethics of Competition*, Kelley, New York.

——1939, 'Ethics and economic reform, III. Christianity', *Economica* 6, November, pp. 398–422.

——and Merriam T. W. 1945, *The Economic Order and Religion*, Routledge, London.

——1951, 'The role of principles in economics and politics', *American Economic Review* 41, March, pp. 1–29.

———1956, *On the History and Method of Economics*, University of Chicago Press, Chicago.

———1960, *Intelligence and Democratic Action*, Harvard University Press, Cambridge, Mass.

×———1982, *Freedom and Reform*, Liberty Press, Indianapolis.

Raines, J. P. and Jung, C. R. 1986, 'Knight on religion and ethics as agents of social change', *The American Journal of Economics and Sociology* 45(4), pp. 429–39.

———1988, 'Monopolies as mechanical defects: Frank Knight on market power', *History of Economics Society Bulletin* 10(2), pp. 135–43.

Schweitzer, A. 1975, 'Frank Knight's social economics', *History of Political Economy* 7(3), pp. 279–92.

# 14 The Stolper-Samuelson Theorem revisited

*John T. Harvey*

## Introduction

The empirical applicability of theory is extremely important if economics is to offer viable policy recommendations. An issue of importance addressed by Magee is the effect of trade liberalization on the distribution of income (Magee, 1980). In examining this question, Magee tests the Stolper-Samuelson theorem and its 'extreme theoretical alternative' (Magee, 1980, p. 138) the Cairnes's theory of non-competing groups (Stolper and Samuelson, 1941; Cairnes, 1874). He concludes that the latter is a superior explanation of the real world.

Cairnes's theory predicts that, with factors of production assumed to be constant through the long run, trade liberalization will give rise to an increase in the real income of all factors in the export industries and a fall in the real income of all factors in the import-competing industries. Stolper-Samuelson holds that the factor used intensively in the protected industry (the relatively scarce factor overall, else it would not have required protection) loses from trade liberalization, while the factor not intensive in that protected industry gains. Furthermore, these gains and losses are economy-wide, not only in the particular industries; that is, if labour is the relatively scarce factor in an economy, then all labour loses from liberalization and all capital gains.

It is this author's contention that the two theories are not mutually exclusive, as Magee asserts his data indicate. Rather, the observed contradictions arise from the factor definitions used by each theory, from Magee's (and most textbooks') preoccupation with the simple version of the Stolper-Samuelson Theorem, and from Magee's assumption that factors of production lobby on the basis of 'rational present-value calculations of their self-interest' (Magee, 1980, p. 139). Each of these issues will be addressed in the order listed.

## Factor definitions

The simple version of the Stolper-Samuelson Theorem envisages a two-good, two-factor world where those factors are labour and capital (Stolper and Samuelson, 1941 p. 63). Cairnes's model instead envisages a multi-good, multi-factor world. Cairnes's factor definitions must be very narrow, so much so that one can imagine possible factors as being 'labour trained in the production of televisons' or 'capital designed to produce automobiles'. When viewed in this light it is clear why, since 'labour trained in' or 'capital designed for' the aircraft industry could hardly be used for agriculture, factors must be held specific in the long run and that removing tariffs from automobiles is bound to hurt both auto workers and General Motors's plant capital.

Stolper-Samuelson, with its broad definitions of factors as capital and labour, allows shifting of those factors among industries:

> Throughout we follow the conventional method of comparative statics, disregarding the process of transition from the old to the new equilibrium. Full employment of both factors is assumed to be realised before and after the change, and *each factor is assumed to have perfectly complete physical mobility*. (Stolper and Samuelson 1941, p. 63; emphasis added)

Since it does not confine a factor to a particular industry or skill, capital, for instance, can move from the industry where the tariff has been removed to one more 'naturally' competitive. So in the instance that capital was the non-intensive factor in the liberalized industry (the abundant factor in the economy) then even capital gains from the lost protection once it has been retooled. And if a higher return were available to capital elsewhere, Stolper-Samuelson's assumptions of perfect factor mobility and pure competition would solve that (Stolper and Samuelson, 1941, p. 63). In the example in the previous paragraph, but in Stolper-Samuelson terms, General Motors could sell its plant capital and reinvest elsewhere and the autoworkers could retrain for another trade. Therefore, Cairnes uses narrow factor definitions while Stolper-Samuelson uses broad ones.

In his test, Magee divides factors into labour and capital alone in his contingency tables, but then collects data on group positions on United States trade policy by industry. Thus he tests the Stolper-Samuelson theorem while implicitly using Cairnes's factor definitions. Magee rejects Stolper-Samuelson because he expects it to predict results it was not designed to foresee.

**Magee's tests: interpretations of Stolper-Samuelson**
The tables mentioned above are used in the three tests Magee designed for Stolper-Samuelson. His test 1 of the Stolper-Samuelson theorem states that, for Stolper-Samuelson to hold true, capital and labour must always oppose each other in questions of trade policy, even in the same industry. To test this, Magee must assume that 'factors of

production base their lobbying on rational present-value calculations of their self-interest' (Magee, 1980, p. 139). Magee implies then that Stolper-Samuelson claims to predict the gains and losses to each factor in the face of protection or liberalization and that, since when labour wins capital loses, labour should always oppose capital in its stance on trade policy (protectionist or free).

Crucial to this interpretation is that Stolper-Samuelson must indicate that when protection is removed each and every labour force in the United States will gain, for instance, while all capital owners lose. This is the view of Stolper-Samuelson echoed by economics textbooks. In the popular book by Wilfred Ethier, *Modern International Economics*, it is described:

> An increase [or decrease, as in the case of trade liberalization where labor is the scarce factor overall] in the price of the labor-intensive good will increase [decrease] the wage rate relative to both commodity prices and reduce [raise] the rent [the return to capital] relative [sic] to both commodity prices. (Ethier, 1988, p. 111)

And in the brand new Yarbrough and Yarbrough

> This is called the *Stolper-Samuelson theorem* after Wolfgang Stolper and Paul Samuelson who coauthored the 1941 paper that first demonstrated it. In its most general form, the theorem states that under the assumptions of our model, a rise in the relative price of a *good* raises the relative price of the *factor* used intensively in its production. When the assumptions of the Heckscher-Ohlin model are added (that a country has an advantage in the good that utilizes the abundant factor intensively), the Stolper-Samuelson theory implies that opening trade will increase the reward to the abundant factor and lower the reward to the scarce factor. (Yarbrough and Yarbrough, 1988, p. 96)

While these are relatively accurate descriptions of the simple, two-good, two-factor version of Stolper and Samuelson, the original article does not leave matters so cut and dry:

> However, we must admit that three or more factors of production within a single country do seriously modify the inevitability of our conclusions. It is not only that the relatively scarce factor can be defined only circularly as the one whose price falls the most after trade, but even if we do know the behavior of relative factor prices, i.e., relative shares in the national income, it seems that we cannot infer unambiguously that the physical marginal productivities move in the same direction. Even though these continue to depend only upon the proportions of the factors in the respective industry, diverse patterns of complementarity and competitiveness emerge as possibilities. It is outside the scope of the present paper to

attempt a catalogue of the various conceivable permutations and combinations. (Stolper and Samuelson, 1941, pp. 72–3).

Nor is the view so simple in Richard Caves' *Trade and Economic Structure*: 'By *strategic choice* of assumptions, W. F. Stolper and P. A. Samuelson succeeded in showing that under very general circumstances a change in import duties can raise the real wage of labor' (Caves, 1960, p. 68), and 'In the light of Metzler's paper, it grows clear that the Stolper-Samuelson results are fairly vulnerable to additional complexities' (ibid., p. 72).

So the situation with respect to empirical applicability has never been clear. And surely Stolper and Samuelson would grant that the more-than-two-factor version of their model is the more accurate one in terms of empirical testing. Further, if Stolper and Samuelson were not adverse to relaxing their assumptions, as the sections on 'Three or More Commodities' and 'More Than Two Factors' indicate, then it may not be too much to say that the Stolper-Samuelson Theorem can, for empirical purposes, be interpreted in an aggregate, less-than-full-employment sense. Capital need only gain more than some units lose if it is the abundant factor under liberalization. This is purely speculative, of course, but Magee's test 1 is not designed to allow for this contingency.

Magee's test 2 contends that under Stolper-Samuelson all labour, if the scarce factor, will favour protection, and all capital, if relatively abundant, will favour free trade. The third test holds that factors will take a stand on trade independent of whether their industry is import-competing or export-oriented if Stolper-Samuelson is correct. Both of these tests falter when one considers either the problem of factor definitions or the aggregate interpretation of Stolper-Samuelson.

### Present-value calculations

All the previous discussion centres on the niceties of model specification and interpretation and are, in the long run, irrelevant if the overall purpose is empirical applicability. Here the present author sympathizes with Magee in his belief that the 'as is' version of Cairnes is more useful. On the other hand, the proxy used for the agents' perceived change in future income seems inappropriate.

The problem with Magee's approach is the assumption not so much that economic agents base their actions on rational present-value calculations (not that there may not be problems with this), but that those calculations necessarily add up to the same thing as their future changes in real income. For indeed, this must be what he implies as monetary reward is the benefit which accrues to the 'winner' in either Stolper-Samuelson or Cairnes. Magee himself states:

> The Stolper and Samuelson (1941) theorem asserts that in a two-factor world with complete mobility of factors within a country, liberalization of international trade will lower the *real income* of one factor of production and increase the *real income* of the other. (Magee, 1980, p. 138; emphasis added)

His reference to Cairnes is less clear, but if we are to compare the two, one would imagine that 'benefit' and 'hurt' must again refer to monetary gain or loss:

> It [Cairnes's theory] suggests that factors of production are industry-specific even in the long run so that trade liberalization would *benefit* all factors in the export industry (which enjoys increased demand) but *hurt* all factors in the import-competing industry (which faces increased import competition). (ibid., p. 138; emphasis added)

Magee's assumption is worded:

> We assume that the factors of production base their lobbying on rational present-value calculations of their self interest. If the present value of their income streams (inclusive of non-pecuniary considerations and taking lobbying costs into account) would be increased by free trade, we can expect them to lobby for free trade (and vice versa). This 'revealed-preference' approach to testing for the redistributive effects of tariffs shifts the voluminous amount of information required for an empirical test from the researcher to the representatives of the factors of production. (ibid., p. 139)

and,

> Tariffs are set by politicians. Recent work on the economics of special-interest politics indicates that tariffs can be thought of as prices which clear political markets. (ibid., p. 139)

Magee's parenthetical reference to 'non-pecuniary considerations' both plays down their importance and ignores that Stolper-Samuelson and Cairnes are clearly dealing with pecuniary gain.

Pursuing the subject of the last two quotations, economists seem to have an overwhelming tendency to associate well-being with high levels of per capita income. But becoming unemployed because the industry in which one works loses protection entails more than a simple trip to the local Walrasian auctioneer to find new employment. The loss of sense of self-worth, the fear for the future of self and family, and stigma applied in our society to those unemployed no doubt play a much larger role in the lobbying decisions of factors of production (especially labour) than do present-value calculations of future income. Thus, the monumental jump Magee makes when he links voting patterns (something he appears to recognize includes non-pecuniary matters) to expected changes in future income streams (which he must assume to test Stolper-Samuelson and Cairnes) treads on very thin ice indeed.

### Conclusions

This author sympathizes with Magee that the Stolper-Samuelson Theorem is not very useful in predicting or explaining the actions of factors of production, at least in the short run. However, to submit the theorem to tests for which it was not designed proves nothing of worth. Magee's attack, though in many respects justified, would be bolstered if he simply acknowledged the differences in approach of Stolper-Samuelson and Cairnes, ceased to dwell exclusively on the simple version of the Stolper-Samuelson Theorem, and, rather than claim the superiority of one over the other, suggest a third approach (perhaps based more closely on Cairnes) in which trade liberalization led to a decline in income – both pecuniary and psychic – of the protected factors in the short run. Only then can the empirical applicability he seeks be found.

### References

Cairnes, J. E. 1874, *Some Leading Principles of Political Economy*, Macmillan, London.

Caves, Richard E. 1960, *Trade and Economic Structure: Models and Methods*, Harvard University Press, Cambridge, Massachusetts.

Ethier, W. 1988, *Modern International Economics*, W. W. Norton, New York.

Magee, S. 1980, 'Three simple tests of the Stolper-Samuelson Theorem', in P. Oppenheimer (ed.), *Issues in International Economics*, Oriel Press, London.

Metzler, Lloyd A. 1949, 'Three simple tests of the trade, and the distribution of national income', *Journal of Political Economy*, 57, February, pp. 1–29.

Stolper, W. F. and Samuelson, P. 1941, 'Protection and real wages', *Review of Economic Studies*, November, pp. 58–73.

Yarbrough, B. V. and Yarbrough, R. M. 1988, *The World Economy: Trade and Finance*, The Dryden Press, Chicago.

## 15 American economic history and the European connection

### Jonathan Hughes

> It is worth while also to notice another class of small . . . mostly independent communities which have supported and enriched themselves almost without any productions of their own (except ships and marine equipments,) by a mere carrying trade, and commerce of *entrepot*; by buying the produce of one country, to sell it at a profit in another. Such were Venice and the Hanse towns.
>
> J. S. Mill, *Principles of Political Economy*
> (Longmans, Green, London, 7th edition, 1911), Book III, ch.
> XXV, p. 415.

**I**

The purpose of the epigraph to this paper, taken from Mill's *Principles*, is to illustrate a simple fact about the history of economics: that is, that economists from Adam Smith to the present day have made use of economic history for their own purposes. This is not true of all, to be sure. Ricardo relied little, indeed, upon overt use of historical material. But others, like Marshall, Taussig, Keynes, Schumpeter and Hayek – not to mention Karl Marx and his followers – have found economic history an indispensable aid to their own thinking. Sir John Hicks, not only a skilled user of economic history as background information for his theoretical work, even wrote a book about economic history itself.[1]

On the North American continent economic history is at ease with economics, and where if it is taught separately at all, tends to be taught within departments of economics by people with PhDs in economics. Such is the present situation, and such has long been a *desideratum* of practising economic historians.[2] It is agreed among leading economists that economic history has much to offer and economic historians are no source of resistance (as they once were) to the centrality of theory and econometrics in the education of the well-rounded economist.[3] Congenially, we all believe more of everything should be known.

174

But time and resources are limited. So economic history is a minor field within the entire spectrum of economics studies. Such has always been true in the United States and will no doubt continue so to be. The proliferation of new special subjects (e.g. medical economics, environmental economics, economic development) in the field, the expansion of the time required to learn modern theory and econometrics, together with the recent vogue to reduce the number of required courses in PhD programmes (and the number of years to completion) have given economic history, the history of economic thought, fiscal policy and other special disciplines a common experience – the prospect of zero growth. There has also been some crowding out. At the present time one can see no remedy for it. If required course loads returned to the three and four years that once were common, demand for offerings of economic history and other special field courses would no doubt increase.

Even with such bleak prospects, one does not hear proposals that economic history should become established independently. Once, of course, in the nineteenth century, the German Historical School did just that: it proposed to develop economics by strict historical induction, abandoning the deductive traditions of Ricardo and the followers of Quesnay as excessively and artificially abstract.[4] The effort was doomed from the beginning, but there was some long-term fallout: the (still) independent economic history departments in Britain, and the existence of economic and social history in Europe with no departmental ties to formal economics.[5] This phenomenon is no doubt in part due to modern Marxist scholarship with its emphasis on economic determinism in history.

Economic history has had its own strictly internal problems, of course. Where economic history in North America has been weakened to some extent in recent decades it has been due to one of its own major achievements: the 're-unification' with economics. Practitioners in history departments and elsewhere have been alienated by the ever-growing load of mathematical technique and jargon being pumped into the field in the wake of advances in economic theory. Frankly, I can see no way out of this problem except to hope for toleration and common sense. If we can all gain from advances in knowledge, then it makes little sense to restrict and legislate the language and techniques used.

As a practical matter, then, if you are an economist who writes and teaches economic history you should not feel alien to be lodged in an economics department. I am not saying, though, that you should feel totally at one with your colleagues who have (most likely) never studied economic history. You are likely to regret their lack of participation in one dimension of your own training, the 'feel' for history and its importance. That remains a special flavour, a 'twist' to economics research done in the realm of history that is powerful. It needs to be explained a bit.

## II

Was the October 1987 stock market crash mainly a re-run of the one in 1929? You must know some economic history to give an informed answer to that question. I guarantee you that deductive methods will not provide you with a sensible answer. There must be some carefully selected facts to find the answer. The crash of 1929 was never explained by economists. That is embarrassing. Economic historians can describe the crash of 1929, but an explanation of it must lie in the realm of theory. The facts do not speak for themselves. You have to choose the relevant facts. However, that theory must concern the real world of 1929, and that cannot be deduced from any general principles. What is known of that real world lies within the realm of economic history, the (still) special world of economic historians.

It is still true of economic historians that they are not merely 'historical economists', as Edwin Gay pointed out in 1941.[6] In the education of an economic historian there is still an additional twist, even if you begin life as a 'straight' economist. That special twist comes from the realization that any real phenomenon located at any point in time must have been determined by forces that occurred prior to that point in time.[7] If you want to know why the phenomenon in question came into existence you must engage in historical research. You are not satisfied with comparative statics; you do not accept as reasonable, a timeless, personless, institution-free world.

The total immersion in a different time (and perhaps also a different culture) that comes from research and writing necessarily makes one at least partially an historian: one who becomes accustomed to working with time as an explicit explanatory variable in the study of economic and social change. In modern American economics PhD programmes those who will ultimately become economic historians are mainly trained in tandem with others, those destined for pure theory, and also for less stratospheric pursuits. The uniform mould is broken for the future economic historian when the student first accepts the fact that the past (whatever past he is dealing with) was different from now, and that past needs to be studied for its own sake as well as merely looted for available antecedents of the present.

Accepting the impact of the past on the search for background and initial conditions of his analyses is the necessary first step into the world of the economic historian. Otherwise, the modern economist-economic historian is an economist, pure and simple, and if he be ignorant enough, why then 1987 was in fact just a re-run of 1929. It would have to be, after all, since only historical differences could make it not so.

## III

Every economy has a history. So every country has an economic history. How well developed it is, as written history (historiography), depends upon both its writers and the uses to which such information is put in each economy. The former may account for the eloquence of an historiography,[8] but the resources dedicated to development of any historiography largely depend upon the latter. If economic history is seen as useless, as the Thatcher government allegedly views knowledge of Greek and Latin, then the subject will be stunted for lack of dedicated resources. There must be expenditures to find history, any history. It is, after all, what the historians say it is, and so there must be historians, trained, paid, encouraged, housed and fed to write historiography.

North American economic history has been written by people of diverse professional background and affiliation.[9] But the bulk of it has come from departments of History, Economics, and from business schools. It was only during World War II, when Britain's Economic History Society had nearly to abandon publication of its journal, *The Economic History Review*, that North Americans bestirred themselves, organized the Economic History Association, and launched their journal, *The Journal of Economic History*. That was the first specific economic history journal on that continent since the old *Journal of Economic and Business History* ceased publication in 1932. The new journal and organization showed a European influence from the beginning, purposely to some extent. Arthur Cole stated it flatly: 'The ideas that conditioned the evolution of economic and business history came initially from Europe.'[10]

The European influence on American economic history, there from the beginning, proved to be a decisive extra dimension in the movement towards quantitative emphasis. Without the Europeans and their ideas American economic history might have been malnourished from its native sources of intellectual nutrition.

Economic history in the United States has struggled to some extent against three counterforces:

1.  the fact that mainstream historians have considered economic history to be largely a sideshow until quite recently;[11]
2.  the American educational system only feebly educates students in fields of history;
3.  in economics departments economic history, like other fields in the menu of economics, must fight for budget share after theory and econometrics have devoured perhaps the majority of the budget.[12]

The claim of economic history to its place is no different from those of other claimants: its practitioners believe in the transcendent value of its subject matter. The subject matter of economic history is mainly the study of economic structure, institutions, change, and their determinants over time.

If the subject of enquiry in any science is a developing entity (or one that did develop once), whether it be astrophysics, earth science, microbiology or anything in between, sound scientific practice necessarily includes the search for the subject's history, however obscure or difficult to discover. The developmental processes will contain keys to the future. Only in the (unknown?) case where development is totally instantaneous and *ab novo*, would the future be unrelated to the past. So economic history does no more or less for the study of the economic than does geology for the earth sciences, or the study of relics of ancient life forms for biology and zoology.

In so far as the science of economics is concerned with understanding existing economic structure so it ought to be concerned with that structure's evolution though time – with its history. That such elementary logic has escaped the designers of some economics department curricula (I can include here at least one major department, but scores of second-rate ones) is more a comment on the state of the discipline in those departments than on the utility of historical knowledge itself. The worst-case results are too common to require extensive comment.[13] It is a fortunate circumstance that economic history in North America, and especially in the United States, was spared from the worst consequences of our curious nativism by both the immigration of European ideas and European scholars at crucial points.

## IV

Thus for American economic history (as for American economics in general),[14] the European influence was vital: it helped to save us from ourselves. The Europeans, including the English, are drilled in their history from early school days, and their economists employed the historical dimension, sometimes to great effect. The first professor of economic history in North America, William Ashley, an Englishman, had come first to Toronto in 1888 as a professor of political science. Then in 1892 he was invited to Harvard to be professor of economic history.[15] The British economists, Marshall, Pigou, Keynes, Dennis Robertson, Alexander Cairncross, Sir John Hicks, Brinley Thomas, all used economic history with ease in their writings. In Britain, as in the rest of Europe, the use of history as part of normal intellectual furniture was routine. The problem was to bring that tradition into the new world, and especially the United States, where scholars in fields like the social sciences quite normally considered ignorance of history to be unimportant.

By 1940 the Economic History Association would try to establish its subject matter right in the middle of economics. The new association's first president was Edwin Gay, in 1941. By then he had already played a central role in the development of quantitative studies. He had been in Gustav Schmoller's seminar in Germany (he was in Germany for twelve years of post-doctoral study) and became a life-long advocate of the search for quantification in economics and economic history. As Arthur Cole and, more lately, Craver and Leijonhufvud have emphasized,[16] the influential Edwin Gay, the first Dean of the Harvard Business School and first President of the National Bureau of Economic Research (1920–33), played a powerful role in the systematic development of data-bases by piloting research funds and making pivotal appointments where they mattered. This emphasis on historical research in the interests of quantification, mixed with the neoclassical training of mainstream American economists and the native tradition of pragmatism had tempered the 'strict inductivism of the German Historical School'.[17] But the influence was still there. Gay had joined with William Beveridge to fund the search for historical prices that yielded a bonanza. At the NBER and in the Economic History Association and the associated Committee on Research in Economic History the quantification of economic knowledge produced a revolution in economic understanding.[18]

So when the EHA was formed in 1941 it was led by perhaps the leading exponent of quantification in the ranks of American economic historians. Through him, and other leading American economists and historians who had studied in Germany, the old German Historical School still weighed in with influence. Then, the young W. W. Rostow, partially educated at Oxford, began publishing work of unexampled influence. His brilliant 1941 paper on the Napoleonic Wars[19] was soon followed by the work which was published as a book, *British Economy in the Nineteenth Century*,[20] a book that arguably was the single most influential book published in economic history in the postwar period. Rostow became the intellectual role-model for a new generation, and he was equally at home with history, statistics and theory.

Of the immediate postwar generation of graduate students, the returning war veterans whose work began appearing in the late 1940s and early 1950s, several (Rondo Cameron, David Landes, William Parker and Henry Rosovsky) began as specialists in European economic history and their work brought recent European contributions into American seminar rooms. At Harvard, the influence of Alexander Gerschenkron, a great European scholar, was now being felt, and for years to come, his students would populate the Economic History Association with some of its brightest stars – and their work was all quantitative.

Another European scholar, Simon Kuznets, had begun his Nobel Prize career in the 1920s at the NBER with brilliant papers. Then in the 1930s his GNP estimates began to appear, and those changed the landscape of economics and economic history. His students, among whom notably were Lance Davis, Richard Easterlin, Robert Fogel, Stan Engerman and Robert Gallman, added another phalanx of brilliant and creative economic historians to the now-maturing EHA. They, in turn, have produced another generation.

## V

I do not mean to undervalue the work contributed by the pioneer generation of Canadians and Americans, men like Harold Innis, Arthur Cole, Harold Williamson, Carter Goodrich, Chester Wright, Earl Hamilton, M. M. Knight, A. P. Usher, John U. Nef and their students. But those achievements are well known and much celebrated. I simply want to give the emigré European scholars and the older European tradition their due. The sensational development of 'Cliometrics' (its early years lauded by Gerschenkron: 'Periods like this are the star hours in the history of a discipline')[21] was considered to have been a strictly North American show[22] at its beginning. But many currents fed into those first meetings of the Cliometricians, and in the early crucial years in the 1960s, the European influence had played a powerful if perhaps background role.[23] The Europeans and their ideas had contributed to the sturdy independence and developmental force of the Cliometric revolution when it got underway. In North America our hybrid vigour was always fed by immigrant labour. European intellectuals and their ideas contributed to that vigour. The best of it all remains.

## Notes

1. John Hicks 1969, *A Theory of Economic History*, Clarendon Press, Oxford.
2. In the nineteenth century, under the leadership of the German Historical School (below) economic history had developed separately from the rest of economics, but by the early decades of the present century the folly of the separation had become widely recognized. One of the most famous arguments for explicit use of formal economic theory in economic history research was made in 1928 by the Swedish scholar, Eli Heckscher in a speech 'A Plea for Theory in Economic History'. In 1941 Edwin Gay (below) argued for 'a more complete connection between the two disciplines'. Both the Heckscher and Gay papers were reprinted in Frederic C. Lane and Jelle C. Riemersma 1953, *Enterprise and Secular Change*, Richard D. Irwin, Homewood, Ill. With the appearance of Cliometrics (so-named in 1960) the separation of economic history from the whole field of economics become artificial and was seen as a barrier to further progress. As we put it in 1960: 'Our main point is that modern statistical techniques and computing equipment make possible the intensive exploitation of a vein of historical materials that was perforce little worked in the past; and that if even a few economic historians would take time to learn even a little of these new techniques, the 1960s could easily prove to be the most productive years in the history of the discipline' (Lance E. Davis, Jonathan R. T. Hughes and Stanley Reiter 1960, 'Aspects of quantitative research in economic history', *Journal of Economic History* 4, December, p. 547: reprinted in *Purdue Faculty Papers in Economic History*, Richard D. Irwin, Homewood, Ill. 1967). The term Cliometrics was coined by Stanley Reiter and was first published in this essay. By 1964 Robert W. Fogel was able to celebrate 'The Reunification of Economic History with Economic Theory' in a special session on economic history of the American Economic Association's annual convention. The Fogel paper, along with others on the subject is in *The American Economic Review: Papers and Proceedings* LV (2), May 1965.
3. See, e.g., papers by Arrow and Solow (1975) in *American Economic Review: Papers and Proceedings* 75 (2), May, pp. 320–3, 328–31. Solow, in fact, seems to wish that modern economic historians were more historian and less econometrician. Far from resisting the temptations of quantification, they are too easily drugged.
4. Theo Suranyi-Unger 1968, 'Economic thought: the Historical School', *International Encyclopedia of the Social Sciences*, ed, David L. Sills, Macmillan and Free Press, New York, vol. 4.
5. Professor Rolf Dumke believes that there is an independent German background that is relevent to the pursuit of Cliometrics, and that background is in part the tradition of the German Historical School itself. 'Clio's climacteric? Betrachtungen über Stand und Entwicklungstendenzen der Cliometrishcen Wirstschaftsgeschichte', *Vierteljahrschrift für Sozial-und Wirtschaftsgeschichte* 73 (4), 1986.
6. Edwin F. Gay, 'The tasks of economic history', in Lane and Riemersma, p. 407.
7. That problem, the problem of colligation, I describe in 'Fact and theory in economic history', *Explorations in Entrepreneurial History*, second series, vol. 3, no. 2. Reprinted in *Purdue Faculty Papers in Economic History, 1956–66*, Richard Irwin, Homewood, Ill, 1967.
8. Thus a region like the Rocky Mountains can have a considerable written economic history even though it is mainly due to the great talents of a single scholar, rather than to any considerable expenditure on the subject by attending academic or political institutions.
9. Matthew Josephson (1934), for example, the muckraking author of vastly influential book, *The Robber Barons* (Harcourt Brace, New York), was a freelance writer, not a professional historian. A fact which, hopefully, accounts for some of the near-plagiarism in his masterpiece.

10. Arthur H. Cole 1968, 'Economic history in the U.S.', *The Journal of Economic History*, XXVII (4), December p. 565.
11. The demand for 'relevance' in the 1960s produced an enlargement of enquiries by history department historians into social and economic history.
12. I do not mean to imply that economic history in the United States would be better than it is if it had been given larger budget shares over time. I am not certain that would have been true. The foolishness of some otherwise quite brilliant (and established) theoretical economists regarding ideas of historical causation make me doubt that a mere increase in numbers of economists doing economic history would improve the field.
13. It is not typical, but it is, alas, not uncommon for economists to be not only wholly ignorant of any economic history, but even of the basic facts of the *existing* economy. Indeed, it can be a point of perverse pride sometimes to *maintain* strict ignorance of present-day economic facts. It is argued that facts clutter the economist's mind. So ahistorical, and anti-historical attitudes, evident among some economists, are only part of a larger aversion to factual material. That is especially true of economic information that is not quantified. Such conditions can thrive in the United States where ignorance of history is factored into the structure of learning from childhood onwards. For the teacher of economic history these conditions pose a problem not unlike those facing a calculus teacher with a classroom full of students who have never studied algebra.
14. The intellectual and personal contributions of European economists to the development of the field on this continent are almost too numerous to mention. Raymond Goldsmith, Arthur Marget, Tjalling Koopmans, Leonid Hurwicz, Vassily Leontieff, Simon Kuznets, Fritz Machlup, Jacob Marshak, Evsey Domar, Oskar Lange, Gottfried Harberler, Joseph Schumpeter, Friedrick von Hayek, Ludwig von Mises, Jan Tinbergen, Tibor Scitovsky, Richard Musgrave, Ragnar Nurkse – these come to mind. A complete list would be an interesting one, especially if it included the Federal Reserve System, which at one point was studded with extraordinary European economists.
15. Arthur Cole, 'Economic history in the U.S.', p. 559. As Cole put it, Ashley, in 1892 'thus became the first academic person anywhere in the world who was technically supposed to devote his primary efforts to the teaching of economic history'.
16. Cole, 'Economic history in the U.S.', Erline Craver and Axel Leijonhufvud 1987, 'The Continental influence', *History of Political Economy* 19 (2).
17. Craver and Leijonhufvud, op. cit., pp. 178–9.
18. See the introductory matter, pp. ii, v-vii of *Historical Statistics of the United States*, USGPO, 1945 for some little-known justification of this assertion. The Harvard economic historian, Arthur Cole, as so often was true in his career, played a critical role in the development of this seminal volume.
19. 'Adjustments and maladjustments after the Napoleonic Wars', *American Economic Review: Papers and Proceedings*, vol. xxxii, no. 1, pt. 2, supplement, March 1942. The paper was read in the December 1941 meetings held in New York City.
20. Clarendon Press, Oxford, 1948.
21. Alexander Gerschenkron 1967, 'The discipline and I', *The Journal of Economic History*, xxvii (4), December, p. 458.
22. There were both Canadians and Americans at the first Purdue meetings in December 1960.
23. For the record, the present author modestly notes that he was partly educated in Oxford University, with Professor Sir John Habakkuk as his supervisor.

# 16 Economic and business history: one discipline or two?

## Louis P. Cain

Upon assuming Oxford's chair of economic history, G. N. Clark delivered his inaugural lecture in 1932 on 'The Study of Economic History'.[1] Among the topics he discussed was the relationship of economic and business history:

> It has become the fashion lately to talk about 'business history' as another specialised sectional study. The expression is ambiguous, and it seems to mean sometimes the history of separate firms or businesses, sometimes the history of business in a somewhat wider sense, of business methods and organisation.[2]

Clark was one of many who have addressed the relationship between economic and business history, and the issue is not much clearer more than a half-century later. While there exists a (by no means unanimous) consensus that business history is a proper subset of economic history, there is no agreement as to what is unique to each and what is common to both. Someone visiting a modern university is likely to encounter one group doing economic history and another doing business history, with relatively little communication between the two. Economic history is still largely defined as what economic historians do.[3] Clark, however, offered an operational definition of business history that should be considered from the outset of this exercise:

> The *differentia* of 'business history' is, in fact, to be sought not in its method or point of view so much as in its materials: it is history based on the records of business itself, as distinguished from the information about business collected by governments or tabulated by economists and statisticians.[4]

While many contemporary business historians will debate Clark's definition at length, it is significant in that it represents how events then transpiring at Harvard were being felt by the rest of the world.

In the early 1920s, Dean Wallace Donham of the Harvard Business School, successor in that position to the esteemed economic historian Edwin F. Gay, noted:

> For our purposes we need business history written not primarily from mass

data such as the census reports, but from the study of specific situations as they came to business men and their communities in the past, so that we may compare understandingly these situations with current conditions.[5]

Donham's conception of business history was quite broad, broader than that in Clark's definition, and to that end he hired Norman S. B. Gras, one of Gay's students, 'to do research, teaching, and writing in the field of Economic and Business History which [should] be so closely related to the problems of the business man that it will be effective socially'.[6] In fact, Gras had begun such work at the University of Minnesota and continued to work in this broad vein when he occupied the first American chair of business history at Harvard in 1927. At this juncture then, business history was intertwined with economic history, not estranged from it.

# I

Three events were soon to rend the two asunder. The first of these was the founding of the Business Historical Society in 1925. According to its charter from the Commonwealth of Massachusetts, the Society's primary purpose was 'to encourage and aid the study of the evolution of business in all periods of all countries'.[7] Members of the Society were largely American and Canadian businessmen who were friends of Dean Donham. The initial group included two Harvard academicians, Gay and Arthur H. Cole, but a year later the Society created an Associate status for those directly involved in research and writing. Among the Society's most important contributions was the gifts of books, papers and documents to Harvard's Baker Library. In its zeal, however, it unwittingly contributed to the separation of business and economic history. In spite of the broad conception of business history it adopted, academicians at large considered, and in many quarters continue to consider, business history to be what Fritz Redlich termed a 'narrow-minded newcomer' and an apologist for business. Indeed, another purpose of the Society was:

> to promote better understanding of the essential unity of financial, commercial and industrial activity throughout the world; its inseparable relation to the welfare of man and its power as an international, intersectional and interclass binding force; to cooperate in work to this end; and to aid in the advancement of the science and the profession of business.[8]

With the coming of the Great Depression and the New Deal's antipathy toward business, business history's critics became more credible.

The second event is the disagreement that developed between professors Gay and Gras, the two outstanding personalities of the 1920s.

The Business History Society sponsored the *Journal of Economic and Business History*. Both Professors Gay and Gras were involved with its editorial functions. As a result of the journal, some joint sessions were arranged at the annual meetings of both the American Economic Association and the American Historical Association. It was a journal that 'achieved a brilliance and authority still to be envied by publications that survived its lamentably short existence [1928–32]'.[9] As the controlling figure, Gay insisted that all papers be of the highest quality. While he was in no ways opposed to business history, most of the submissions from business historians were not of the same quality as other submissions. Gras, the managing editor, was more interested in using the journal as an outlet for business history regardless of its quality. In a letter dated 28 January 1931, Gras indicates his hope was to take over the journal for business history, but this was not to be.[10] In the attempt, the journal ceased publication. The business history faction, including control of the Society, retreated to the relative safety of the Harvard Business School under the leadership of Professor Gras.

The Great Depression itself was the final event that worked towards separation. As funding for business history broadly conceived evaporated, scholars turned to writing subsidized biographies of companies and their leaders. This activity became so prevalent that by 1950 company history had become synonymous with business history.

The economic historians retained an important outlet for publication in the English *Economic History Review*, but as the Depression gave way to World War II, it became important to develop an outlet in North America. The result was the Economic History Association, born in 1941 with Edwin F. Gay its first president. Its aims, defined in a 1941 membership circular, reflect a broad conception and a concern for what many consider its easily identifiable 'specialised sectional studies'.

> The Association will endeavor to encourage research and teaching in the history of economic activity (private and public) and of economic thought. It will seek to cooperate with the Societies devoted to the study of agricultural, industrial, and business history, and serve as a means for bringing together economists, statisticians, historians, geographers and others who find that the story of economic change throws light on their fields of interest or is enriched by their contributions. Its chief activities will be the arrangement of meetings and the publication of a journal.[11]

The inclusion of business history in the list of associations which the EHA pledged to leave undisturbed is attributable to Arthur Cole's involvement in the formation of the Economic History Association (he served in Harvard Business School's Baker Library) and to what Richard Wohl termed 'the steady attrition in the scope of business history as it is defined in his [Gras's] writings'.[12] In an article published in 1950, Gras commented:

> Perhaps it would be well to weigh the consequences of broadening the scope of business history . . . For instance, if economic historians write what is called business history, but which is in reality the economic history of business, then there will be repeated the time-honored neglect of administration and the business man. This means just one thing, which is at once subtle and potent, namely, the conclusion that the business man is in reality predatory and parasitic, that he does not administer nor produce, though he does take a profit.[13]

Gras had also developed a very strong view about who should write business history:

> In this process of orientation it is better to start with one who is either a general historian or not a historian at all. The economic or social historian has too much to unlearn. The general historian at least has the historical point of view.[14]

Such a view seems inconsistent with the work of other business historians active at that time such as Thomas Cochran, Richard Overton, Harold Williamson, and Gras's colleague at Harvard, Fritz Redlich.

## II

At this juncture, economic history and business history were as separate as they would become. Three events that took place during the decade of the 1950s facilitated a reconciliation, but business history did not revert to the broad agenda with which it began nor did its practitioners want to consider themselves part of a 'specialized sectional study'. Business historians, largely trained in history, implicitly began to narrow the definition of economic history to what was done by those trained in economics. Such definitional concerns did not plague the first of these events, the initial meeting of the Business History Conference.

In February 1954, Professor Joseph Franz of the University of Texas – Austin planned to visit Northwestern University to discuss with colleagues there the teaching of business history. The Northwestern University Committee on Business History decided to hold a 'Saturday Seminar on Business History' and invite colleagues from other schools. As Harold Williamson described them, these were individuals who were 'either ignorant of or indifferent to the fact that they lacked the proper qualifications', but who, nevertheless, had 'begun writing about business and businessmen'.[15] One exception to this was Ralph Hidy, then at New York University, who eventually replaced Gras at Harvard and sponsored two conferences to be discussed shortly.

The group that met was evenly divided between economists and historians, and Williamson believes most considered themselves to be economic historians whose research carried them into business history. During the morning session on 'The Teaching of Business History', it developed that the standard outline used for a course of that name fundamentally was identical with the outline used for courses entitled economic history. What was emphasized depended upon one's view of the nature of business history. The differences among the group were more clearly articulated during the afternoon session on 'The Writing of Business History', but even there the nature of the data led to a greater commonality of interests than many had suspected before the fact. The result was, after the fact, the group agreed to meet again, and has been meeting annually ever since. As Harold Williamson, one of the hosts of the first meeting at Northwestern, noted after two decades of meetings:

> The meetings over the years have continued to attract individuals from different disciplines who because of their varied backgrounds and training have tended to differ in respect to their research objectives, collection of data, and methodology. I am sure that I am not the only member of the Conference who gained a much greater understanding and appreciation of what various disciplinary approaches can contribute to the field as a result of these contacts.[16]

The second event during these years was also interdisciplinary in scope, the operation of the Harvard Research Center for Entrepreneurial History under the leadership of Arthur Cole from 1948 to 1958. Cole conscientiously sought to forge a tighter link between economic and business history.[17] The Center's great disappointment was its inability to discover a general theory of entrepreneurship.[18] In fact, many of the economics-trained practitioners of business history in those years described a sense of frustration that the orthodox theory of the firm proved to be of little use in analysing the historical business problems with which they were confronted in their research.[19] The legacy of the Center was to put the entrepreneur, the individual, back into the writing of business history and to do so in a manner that highlighted the value of interdisciplinary research. One of the Center's many distinguished alumni, Alfred D. Chandler Jr, who replaced Hidy in the chair Gras inaugurated, has helped to make business history an international venture and continued the process of unification.

The third event which helped reconcile economic and business history was the aforementioned two Conferences on the History of American Business, one in 1958 and the second in 1961, arranged by Ralph Hidy and hosted by the Harvard Business School. The title was carefully chosen to 'indicate that the Harvard group wanted to encourage discussion of more than company histories'.[20] There is much in Louis Galambos's recollections that is of present concern:

> While these gatherings did not launch business history on a new course, they did help everyone in the field recognize what were the central problems. It was important that business historians consider these difficulties, for other branches of economic history and theory were beginning to explore from new points of view the subject matter which once had been the sole property of business history.[21]

Business history was considered to be a branch of economic history, but the nexus between economic history and theory that contributed to formation of the 'new economic history' was viewed as an external threat. Arthur Johnson, reporting on the 1958 conference, had a somewhat different perspective:

> The conferees were generally agreed that business history is a discipline distinct from economic history but that the two overlap. Again, as Abbott Payson Usher pointed out, it is a matter of focus and, to some extent, of the source materials used. Chairman Hidy added that one of the major distinctions between the two disciplines is the difference between emphasis on trend analysis and emphasis on the dynamics of decision-making.[22]

It was just at this time that the 'new economic history' began to delve more into microeconomic matters and, as noted, among the first to do so were Conrad and Meyer. Conrad was present at the 1958 conference and his comments led Johnson to report that economic theorists and business historians were becoming increasingly aware of their interdependence. This should have been especially obvious when, in summary, Johnson reported that the 'distinctive and essential feature [of business history] is its emphasis on the businessman and his decisions'.[23] As algorithms for business decisions became increasingly abstract and quantifiable, as computers made it possible to juggle large sets of data and to simulate the likely effects of alternative business decisions, the tools of the economist became increasingly useful to the business historian.

## III

One of the most promising developments in this vein has been the joint product of Alfred Chandler and Oliver Williamson on the usefulness of transactions cost analysis in understanding vertical integration.[24] Yet even as questions and techniques moved business history back toward the mainstream of economic history, business historians wriggled to maintain their sense of identity. In his role as banquet speaker at the second Canadian Business History Conference, Christopher Armstrong urged his colleagues to be friendly with economists, even though their limitations were well known. In his new book on the British steel industry in the interwar years, Steven Tolliday begins by commenting,

> It has proved difficult to widen the interpretative focus and relate the company to the wider economy, and historians have confined themselves to reiterating their conviction that entrepreneurship and corporate organization are major and systematic determinants of economic performance without being able to develop compelling explanatory models. In part this is a result of the theoretical legacy that historians have generally drawn on, which, insofar as it goes beyond a simple empiricism, centers on hypotheses derived from neoclassical and Keynesian theories. Yet both of these theoretical traditions are notoriously weak on the issue of the firm.[25]

Tolliday goes on to discuss how Oliver Williamson's approach is a variant of neoclassical theory with all its inherent weaknesses. Lastly, in her Presidential address to the Business History Conference, Mira Wilkins called for recognition of Business History as a separate discipline. She too had begun to teach business history with much the same outline as economic history, but noted that her business history course has evolved over the years to something quite distinct. She did not indicate whether she also made changes in her economic history course.[26]

Having come apart, it has been difficult to re-attach business history to the main body of economic history. The difficulty is more political than intellectual. The Business History Conference, the Cliometrics Society, and the Economic History Association are all healthy, viable institutions. Economic history has come to mean 'cliometrics' in the eyes of most historians and many cliometricians, yet that is illegitimate. Both cliometrics and business history are 'specialized sectional studies' of economic history, one differentiated by method, the other by data sources. Both have become broader and more open since successfully differentiating their subdisciplines, but a gap remains. There is a common ground on which few have trod.[27] Consider, therefore, the conclusion of T. S. Ashton's inaugural lecture given at the London School of Economics in 1946:

The study of what by yet another misfortune of terminology has come to be called business history should be pursued alongside the interpretation of the past with the aid of the apparatus of economic thought. For it is in the business unit that economic forces can be seen in operation, as it were in the front line. Business history may serve as a reminder that demand and supply, the various elasticities and multipliers, the determinants and stabilisers, are all generalizations, useful indeed, but causal factors at one remove; and that it is the wills and choices and acts of men and women that are the ultimate data for economists and historians alike.[28]

Unfortunately, many within each camp blissfully cling to the belief that economic history and business history represent different product markets. This is the major remaining impediment blocking a return to the close ties between the two, a return to the optimism that characterized the early 1920s.

### Acknowledgement
I gratefully acknowledge the contributions of Leslie Hannah, Jonathan Hughes, Ian Parker, Samuel Williamson and Harold Williamson.

### Notes
1. The origins of economic history (and business history) in the United States are discussed in Arthur H. Cole 1968, 'Economic history in the United States: formative years of a discipline', *Journal of Economic History*, pp. 556–89; N. S. B. Gras 1920, 'The present condition of economic history', *Quarterly Journal of Economics*, pp. 209–24, and 1927–8, 'The rise and development of economic history', *Economic History Review* I, pp. 12–34; and Herbert Heaton 1941, 'The early history of the Economic History Association', *Journal of Economic History* (*Tasks of Economic History*), December 1941, pp. 107–9. See also William Parker 1980, 'The historiography of American economic history', in Glenn Porter (ed.), *Encyclopedia of American History*, New York.
2. G. N. Clark, 'The Study of Economic History', an inaugural lecture delivered at the University of Oxford on 21 January 1932, reprinted in N. B. Harte (ed.) 1971, *The Study of Economic History: Collected Inaugural Lectures 1893–1970*, Frank Cass, London, p. 77.
3. Clark notes that 'Adam Smith is still by common consent the greatest of economic historians' (ibid., p. 73).
4. Ibid., p. 77.
5. This appears in a report written to President Lowell quoted in Fritz Redlich 1962, 'Approaches to business history', *Business History Review*, Spring, pp. 61–2.
6. Ibid., p. 62.
7. Quoted in Harold F. Williamson 1975, 'The Business History Conference and business history: some reflections', *Proceedings of the Business History Conference*, 2nd series, no. 3, ed. Herman Krooss, Bloomington, IN: Division of Research, School of Business, Indiana University, p. 3. See also 'Charter of the Business History Society, Incorporated', *Bulletin of the Business Historical Society, Inc.* 1, June 1926.
8. Quoted in Redlich, op. cit., p. 62.
9. R. Richard Wohl 1954, 'The significance of business history', *Business History Review*, Summer, p. 129.
10. This was discovered and reported in Redlich, op. cit., pp. 63–4. Gras's version of this episode was published in *The Development of Business History up to 1950:*

*Selections from the Unpublished Works of Norman Scott Bryan Gras*, compiled and ed. Ethel C. Gras, Ann Arbor, Mich., 1962.

11. Quoted in Herbert Heaton 1965, 'Twenty-five years of the Economic History Association: a reflective evaluation', *The Journal of Economic History*, December, p. 472. The Agricultural History Society was created in 1919 and still thrives, while the Industrial History Society was stillborn.

12. Wohl, op. cit., p. 130. In support of this proposition, Wohl cites Gras 1934, 'Business history', *Economic History Review*, p. 384, and 1939, *Business and Capitalism*, New York, pp. vii-viii, 28.

13. N. S. B. Gras 1950, 'Past, present and future of the Business Historical Society', *Bulletin of the Business Historical Society*, p. 10.

14. N. S. B. Gras 1947, *Are You Writing a Business History?*, Business Historical Society, Boston, p. 10, quoted in Williamson, op. cit., p. 4.

15. Williamson, op. cit., p. 6.

16. Ibid., p. 7.

17. See, for example, Arthur H. Cole 1945, 'Business history and economic history', *Journal of Economic History (Tasks of Economic History)*, December, pp. 45–53; and 1946 'An approach to the study of entrepreneurship', *Journal of Economic History (Tasks of Economic History)*, December, pp. 1–15.

18. The work of the Center broadened the concept of the entrepreneur well beyond that envisaged by Schumpeter, who was himself affiliated with the Center. This broadened conception may have made any focused abstraction an impossibility. Like the Business History Conference, which spent a considerable amount of time initially trying to define what it was about, the Center found it was intellectually more profitable simply to 'get on with it'. For one participant's perspective on the Center, see Alfred D. Chandler, Jr 1984, 'Comparative business history', in D. C. Coleman and Peter Mathias (eds), *Enterprise and History: Essays in Honour of Charles Wilson*, Cambridge University Press, New York, pp. 3–26.

19. None the less, one student of the Center attributes its closing as the defeat of Parsonian sociology by cliometrics, in spite of the fact that one of the first pieces in the 'new economic history', Conrad and Meyer's work on the profitability of slavery was not published until that year and, given its data sources, can be considered to be largely within the field of business history. See Steven A. Sass 1976, 'Entrepreneurial historians and history: an exploration in the organization of intellect', *Business and Economic History*, 2nd series, no. 5, pp. 151–4.

20. Arthur M. Johnson 1959, 'Conference on the history of American business', *Business History Review*, Summer, p. 205.

21. Louis Galambos 1967, *American Business History*, American Historical Association, Washington, pp. 19–20.

22. Johnson, op. cit., p. 207.

23. Ibid., pp. 207–10.

24. See, in particular, the papers by Chandler and Williamson 1982, both in *Business and Economic History*, 2nd series, vol. 11, pp. 105–34. Another place where this connection is made explicit is Williamson 1981, 'The modern corporation: origins, evolution, attributes', *The Journal of Economic Literature*, December, pp. 1537–68.

25. Steven Tolliday 1987, *Business, Banking, and Politics: The Case of British Steel, 1918–1939* Harvard University Press, Cambridge, Mass., p. 11.

26. Mira Wilkins 1988, 'Business History as a Discipline', *Business and Economic History*, second series, no. 17, pp. 1–9.

27. As noted, Alfred Chandler and others have encouraged business historians to stretch beyond their Grasian corporate biographies and to tackle broader issues. One place where this broad thematic approach has taken root is the Business History Unit of the London School of Economics initially under the leadership of Leslie Hannah. The LSE included economic history as one of its major concerns from its founding in 1895. Steven Tolliday's dissertation research on the British

steel industry was under the direction of Professor Hannah prior to his move to
LSE.

28.   T. S. Ashton, 'The Relation of Economic History to Economic Theory', an inaug-
ural lecture delivered at the LSE in 1946, reprinted in N. B. Harte (ed.) 1971,
*The Study of Economic History: Collected Inaugural Lectures, 1893–1970*, Frank
Cass, London, p. 179. A second opinion can be found in Herman E. Krooss 1958,
'Economic history and the New Business History', *Journal of Economic History*,
December, pp. 467–80.

# Author Index

Adelman, Irma, 58
Angresano, James, 157, 162
Armstrong, Christopher, 189
Ashley, William, 179
Ashton, T.S., 189
Aspromourgos, T., 1
Augello, M.M., 11

Barber, W., 11
Barone, 126, 127
Baumgardt, D., 14
Bax, E. Belfort, 68
Beattie, James, 34–5
Beeton, Mr., 65
Bell, Charles, 30
Benham, F.C., 136
Bentham, Jeremy, 10–26
Bernstein, E., 82, 83, 95
Bertrand, Joseph, 126, 128
Beveridge, William, 179
Bland, Hubert, 68
Blaug, Mark, 58
Blomfield, Charles, 30, 31, 32, 33
Böhm Bawerk, E. von, 70
Bortkiewicz, L. von, 93
Breit, William, 161
Brown, W.J., 107
Buchanan, J.M., 160
Buckland, William, 30
Bukharin, N.I., 88, 89, 90, 94
Burrow, J., 11

Cairnes, J.E., 168, 169, 171–2, 173
Campbell, J.R., 113–14, 115
Cantillon, Richard, 1–2, 13, 117–18, 122
Caves, Richard, 171
Chadwick, Edwin, 30, 31, 32, 37
Chalmers, Thomas, *see* theology of economics *in subject index*
Champion, H.H., 68
Chandler, A.D., 188, 189
Clark, G.N., 183

Clark, J.B., 147–54
Coats, A.W., 11
Cole, Arthur, H., 177, 179, 184, 185–7
Collini, S., 11, 64
Collison Black, R.D., 66, 67
Condillac, 13
Conrad, 188
Cook, J., 149
Craver, Erline, 179
Cunningham, 65

Danielson, Nikolai, 85, 89
Darwin, Charles, 40–41, 43, 45–8
Donham, W., 183–84
Dorfman, J., 147
Duménil, G., 8
Dumont, E., 18, 21–2
Dupuit, Jules, 118–21, 122
Dutt, Palme, 104, 107

Edgerton, F.H., 30
Edgeworth, F.Y., 65
Ekelund, R.B., 119
Ely, R.I., 149
Erreygers, G., 7
Ethier, Wilfred, 170

Feldman, G.A., 89
Fetter, F.A., 136
Fetter, F.W., 11
Foxwell, H.S., 65
Franz, Joseph, 186
Fraser, L.M., 136
Fripp, E.I., 65

Galambos, Louis, 188
Galiani, F., 13
Garegnani, P., 7
Gay, Edwin, 176, 179, 183–5
George, Henry, 64–5, 68, 150
Gerschenkron, Alexander, 180
Gladden, W., 149

*193*

# Subject Index

Printed and bound by CPI Group (UK) Ltd, Croydon, CR0 4YY

23/04/2025

14661002-0001